Popular Consent and Popular Control

POPULAR CONSENT

and

POPULAR CONTROL

Whig Political Theory in the Early State Constitutions

DONALD S. LUTZ

Louisiana State University Press / Baton Rouge and London

Designer: Albert Crochet
Typeface: VIP Sabon
Typesetter: G & S Typesetters, Inc.

Portions of the material reprinted herein with permission have appeared in slightly different form in the following:
"Bernard Bailyn, Gordon S. Wood, and Whig Political Theory," in *Political Science Reviewer*, VII (Fall, 1977), 111–14; "Popular Consent and Popular Control: 1776–1789," Chapter 3 in George Graham and Scarlett Graham (eds.), *Founding Principles of American Government: Two Hundred Years of Democracy on Trial* (Bloomington: Indiana University Press, 1977); "The Theory of Consent in Early State Constitutions," in *Publius: The Journal of Federalism*, IX (Fall, 1979), 5–37.

LIBRARY OF CONGRESS CATALOGING IN PUBLICATION DATA

Lutz, Donald S
  Popular consent and popular control.

  Bibliography: p.
  Includes index.
  1. Whig Party. 2. Political science—United States—History. 3. State governments.
4. Consensus (Social sciences) I. Title.
JK2331.L88   342'.73'029   79-17876
ISBN 0-8071-0596-1

To Charles S. Hyneman, friend and teacher

Contents

Tables and Maps

Tables

Maps

Acknowledgments

Every author must take full responsibility for what appears under his or her name. By the same token, it seems impossible to write a book without considerable help, and while the persons named below cannot share any of the blame for errors, they certainly should share in any praise. The Earhart Foundation of Ann Arbor, Michigan, provided support for a leave of absence from teaching duties, during which this manuscript was written. The simple yet effective manner in which the grant was administered produced a situation ideal for carrying forward such research. For the freedom that the foundation afforded me and for the continuing encouragement by Richard Ware, its president, I am extremely grateful.

Jeanne Kitchens typed the original draft, much improving its punctuation, and then finished her law degree. Cathy Stern offered to do an editing for grammar and style despite her own studies and the demands of her family. Chapters eight and nine were also improved by her generous research on the Federalists. At a crucial point in researching the manuscript, the American Enterprise Institute provided a grant that permitted me to attend a conference at the National Archives and speak firsthand with many of the historians relied upon in the text.

Throughout the six years spent working on this book, Linda Westervelt, my wife, provided the kind of encouragement and intellectual atmosphere for which any author would be extremely grateful. She has been both wife and friend. I am thankful to Marlene La Roe and De Witt Shelton for timely aid and support, and also to Austin, Genny, Suzanne, Peter, Patrick, and Andrew for keeping before me the reasons why a book such as this needed to be written.

Finally, I wish to thank the man who set me to this task long ago. Certainly, Charles S. Hyneman is one of the most persistent, imaginative, productive, and loving students of American politics ever to teach in our universities. His suggestions started me on this project, and his continued presence greatly improved my knowledge and understanding of American politics and history. This ongoing conversation with Charles Hyneman has been both illuminating and deeply satisfying from my point of view. There is, therefore, no person more appropriate to whom I could dedicate this volume.

Introduction

It has been frequently remarked, that it seems to have been reserved for the people of this country by their conduct and example, to decide the important question, whether societies of men are really capable or not, of establishing good government from reflection and choice, or whether they are forever destined to depend, for their political constitutions, on accident and force.

Alexander Hamilton
The Federalist 1

With these words, Hamilton laid bare the fundamental nature of the American political experiment. What is remarkable about this passage from the opening page of the Federalist papers is not that it moves so quickly and easily to the heart of the matter, for most Americans at that time probably did not need to be told again what they had heard many times before, but that it states the problem in terms that could be assented to by the various political factions then contending for power. Some Americans, fearing the resurgence of a monarchy or the rise of a privileged class, could agree that constitutions should not be written by men having power as a result of a birthright or a monopoly on military force. Other Americans, projecting their fear of the restless common man, could agree that constitutions should not be written by those injected into the political system through the power of an uninformed majority. Instead, dependence should be placed upon men of demonstrated ability, sobriety, and success.

To say that Hamilton's statement was a masterpiece of rhetoric does not diminish its theoretical importance, since he does enunciate a basic continuity in American political theory. Rather, it cautions the reader that the context in which the Federalist papers were written was more complex than the average American of today probably realizes—indeed, somewhat more complex than many students of American political theory realize. It has been barely two decades since the Federalist papers were "rediscovered" by political scientists and placed once again at the apex of American political thought. We understand today, perhaps more firmly than ever, that these supposed propaganda tracts not only constitute a sophisticated and coherent rationale for the American Constitution but collectively represent the most important and most sustained contribution made by American political thinkers to the history of political thought. As a result of their rediscovery, college students and other citizens can be taught that the theory underlying our Constitution is quite different from the political theory we often try to project backward from our own times.

Unfortunately, along with the renewed emphasis on the Federalist papers, other perspectives have developed, each based upon some assumption that is just as misleading as those assumptions dominant before we began to take these collected treatises by Madison, Hamilton, and Jay more seriously. One of those new assumptions is that little, if anything, theoretically important was written before 1776. Textbooks in American political thought often draw upon a few Puritan documents and some pamphlets and usually give the impression that these are piecemeal precursors to the Federalist papers. Other texts pursue earlier work in greater detail, under the assumption that its coherence lies in a gradual evolution toward the theory contained in *The Federalist*. Even when contradictory theories from earlier years are noted, political scientists still tend to assume that at least the work between the writing of the Declaration of Independence in 1776 and the adoption of the United States Constitution in 1789 evolved naturally. If there was ever much doubt, recent work by historians leaves little choice but to reject all three of these views. One purpose of this volume is to summarize and expand these findings, which curiously have had relatively little impact on the way in which political scientists report the history of American political thought.

Many average Americans, having little interest in or information about such matters, probably assume that our government was made from whole cloth during the Convention of 1787; in fact, the remarkable discussion during that meeting drew upon a rich experience in self-government. Historians in an earlier era were fond of pointing out that all our institutions had been tried previously at the state (or colony) level, and, strictly speaking, they were correct. However, the quarter-century before the adoption of our national Constitution witnessed a prolonged theoretical and polemical debate of astounding complexity and diversity. Coupled with the practical experience of living under many state constitutions, this debate produced by 1787 a political culture considerably evolved from that surrounding the writing of the Declaration of Independence. The thesis to be advanced is even stronger, namely, that the United States Constitution represents a significant departure from the American political tradition that had been dominant during the first two hundred years of our existence as a people. The tendency has been to emphasize continuities, as if the Declaration of Independence led logically to the Constitution of 1787. A careful examination of the state constitutions written in the period between these two documents will reveal that the discontinuities are more important. It is my intent to examine the ideas and institutions rejected as well as those adopted, not only to place the resulting Constitution in context, but also to determine the implications of those choices.

This will not be, strictly speaking, a history, although historians may be interested in what political theorists make of their work. Instead, the book's emphasis will be on analysis of beliefs, intentions, acts, and accomplishments more likely to be of interest to the political scientist or political theorist. More explicitly, the following pages contain an extended analysis of the political theory underlying the first state constitutions. This coherent theory centers on the concept of consent. To adequately understand the nature and origins of the theory, it is necessary to examine the development of colonial political institutions, ideas, and practices. The theory evolving from the colonial political experience made it natural to appropriate English Whig political ideas, and then to bend these ideas to meet American needs. This American Whig theory, firmly in place by the 1770s, was then challenged, politically defeated, and replaced by Federalists who appropriated, modified, built upon, and ultimately rejected many Whig political symbols to create the political theory still dominant in the United States.

The central conviction underlying this volume is that we need to reexamine our beginnings more carefully because the rich debate of that era has much to teach us about current political problems. It is my conclusion that even in adapting our political institutions to the circumstances of the late twentieth century, there is at least as much to be embraced as rejected, and that a deeper understanding of the foundations of our political society will lead, not to a wholesale dismissal of that legacy, but to an impatience with those who do not take the American experiment seriously.

Popular Consent and Popular Control

I

The Notion of Republican Government

Upon leaving the last session of the Constitutional Convention in the summer of 1787, Benjamin Franklin was reportedly asked by an unnamed woman what form of government the delegates had constructed. He is reported to have replied, "A republic, if you can keep it." This brief exchange, widely recognized by Americans, is part of the collection of dramatic phrases that summarize the meaning of the American Revolution. Invariably, the textbooks assume that the reader understands what Franklin and his colleagues meant by the term *republic*. A further assumption not only ignores the central political problem of the day—what *form* of republican government to erect—but also overlooks the significance of what America contributed to political theory and practice between 1776 and 1789.

During that relatively short period, Americans not only had to choose among several competing republican theories, they also elaborated theories far beyond anything derived from their European heritage. The institutions written into the American Constitution were heavily dependent upon colonial experience and practice, as well as upon the framers' experience of having written and lived under eighteen state constitutions between 1776 and 1786. But it is not widely known that as many institutions were rejected as were adopted and that political theory, to the extent a coherent theory underlay colonial institutions, was completely revamped. Indeed, the Whig theory of politics that predominated in 1776 was replaced first by a more radical Whig theory and then by Federalist theory, which, while retaining many of the same words, gave them new meanings derived from a completely different set of principles.[1]

What allowed our Founding Fathers to get along at all was a common adherence to government by consent. They were, however, divided in the answers they gave to the following four questions: (1) who is to give consent, (2) to whom is consent given, (3) what act or acts constitute giving consent, and (4) over what range of issues must consent be permanently withheld? Each definition of republic implied a different set of institutions, which in turn implied a different theory of consent with its own answers to these four questions. For example, an American Whig in 1776 was likely to believe that those who manifested their stake in the community by possession of property gave consent to a legislature over a wide range of issues through elections. A more radical Whig a few years later was likely to demand less restrictive suffrage requirements as defining those who give consent, to regard elections only as giving consent for his particular representative to hold office, to favor withholding certain issues from legislative control—such as framing a constitution, ratifying it, or amending it—and to insist on more direct consent from the people for specific pieces of legislation. The Federalists tended toward a third set of answers and, of course, there were many combinations and permutations. Even the Tories, who opposed the Revolution, had a consent doctrine; and occasionally, in listing republics, they would include mixed governments with hereditary elements and thus include even England. Every alternative except continued allegiance to the king would, at one time or another, be seriously defended by some Americans as the very essence of republican government. In a sense, then, Franklin's response quoted above is a classic case of a politician obscuring the issue. It merely called up the one thing all the delegates agreed upon, the necessity of republican government—government by consent—without answering the essential questions: what form of republic and, therefore, which theory of consent?

There was also considerable irony in Franklin's comment, in part

1. For an excellent, exhaustive discussion of these shifts, see Gordon S. Wood, *The Creation of the American Republic, 1776–1787* (Chapel Hill: University of North Carolina Press, 1969).

because only twelve years earlier the statement would have met with considerable confusion as well as controversy. As late as the end of 1775, the term *republic* had primarily negative connotations.[2] Worse, to be branded a republican in the 1750s was equivalent to being termed a socialist in the 1950s insofar as it implied being a radical, or someone outside the dominant political culture who was not to be trusted because of subversive tendencies. In November of 1775, John Adams still used *republic* in its pejorative sense, and not until January of 1776, barely five months before the writing of the Declaration of Independence, did he become the first major American thinker to use the term in a favorable sense, as a form of government to be sought.[3] It is significant that not one of the eighteen state constitutions adopted between 1776 and 1787 used the term and that the federal Constitution adopted in 1789 was the first major public document in American history to use the term *republic*. It appears only in Article IV, which guarantees states a republican form of government without giving any hints as to how republican government is to be identified.

Although in 1775 the colonies had local self-government or home rule, representative legislative assemblies elected on a more or less liberal franchise, second houses serving as senates, well-established judiciaries, governors (Connecticut and Rhode Island actually elected theirs), and limitations on those governors (who represented the crown), only a few individuals would have been willing to label these governments republican, and such individuals would have

2. See George M. Dutcher, "The Rise of Republican Government in the United States," *Political Science Quarterly*, LV (1940), 199–216, especially 204; Cecilia M. Kenyon, "Republicanism and Radicalism in the American Revolution: An Old-fashioned Interpretation," *William and Mary Quarterly*, 3rd ser., XIX (1962), 166; and W. Paul Adams, "Republicanism in Political Rhetoric Before 1776," *Political Science Quarterly*, LXXXV (September, 1970), 397–421.

3. George M. Dutcher outlines the process in some detail. In a memorandum to Richard Henry Lee dated November 15, 1775, John Adams still had not embraced the term, but his *Thoughts on Government* published in January, 1776, in response to Thomas Paine's *Common Sense* came down clearly in favor of republican government. Paine used the term in his pamphlet, but in a neutral sense, usually for descriptive purposes rather than as a part of his proposal. There were several positive uses of the term in the press about this time, the earliest being November 23, 1775, in the Essex *Gazette* (Salem, Mass.).

been considered rash indeed. To speak of establishing a republic was subversive to the established order since it meant, by definition, breaking with the monarchy.

Furthermore, there was a strong tendency to identify republican government with democracy.[4] Democracy continued to be defined by most people in the classic Greek sense. This entailed the notion of the entire populace gathering in one place to vote as a body on political matters. Aristotle had equated democracy with anarchy on the basis of the Greek experience, and American political leaders, being good students of the Enlightenment, continued to make the same connection. Thus, to favor a republic was, in some quarters, to imply support for anarchy. In England, those opposing the Whigs continually attempted to fasten the label *republican* on the Whigs so as to smear them with the unsavory implications. The Tories in America, supporters of continued allegiance to the English king, attempted to smear American Whigs in the same fashion.[5] As a result, the Whigs attempted to distinguish a republic from a democracy in an effort to find an alternative to continued ties with England that would be acceptable to Americans. In no sense was the American Revolution fought to create a democracy, although the Constitution does embody the democratic principle in at least one institution. Rather, it was fought to establish a republic, something other than a monarchy.

In a letter to John Adams on July 20, 1789, Roger Sherman cites the English dictionary definition of republic—"a commonwealth without a king."[6] By that time Americans had moved considerably beyond such a rudimentary notion, but at the onset of the Revolution, there were still only two basic forms of government to Englishmen and colonists alike: monarchies and republics. Samuel Johnson's dictionary, a prominent English work first published in 1775, defined republic as a "commonwealth; state in which power is

4. For a complete and careful discussion of the relationship of democracy to republic, see Robert W. Shoemaker, "'Democracy' and 'Republic' as Understood in Late Eighteenth-Century America," *American Speech*, XIV (May, 1960), 83–95.

5. See W. Paul Adams, "Republicanism in Political Rhetoric Before 1776," 402–403.

6. Charles Francis Adams (ed.), *The Works of John Adams* (10 vols.; Boston: n.p., 1850–56), IV, 437.

lodged in more than one."[7] This not only implied the absence of heredity as the basis of political power but it also implied several rulers. Under such a broad definition, everything from an oligarchy or aristocracy to a pure democracy could be termed a republic. Yet in the same book, commonwealth was defined as a "government in which the supreme power is lodged in the people; a republick." If republican government technically meant the absence of a monarch, considerable evidence exists that there was enough confusion among Americans on the matter that they frequently used *republic* to mean government by the people.[8] Given the tendency among some political theorists of the day to equate republic with democracy, this confusion is not difficult to understand. At the same time, "government by the people" did not necessarily denote a democracy.[9] Aside from the more radical elements in society, most Americans seemed to be thinking of a much less drastic alternative, something similar to business as usual under a parliament, without the king. General agreement that republican government meant rule by the people still left open the crucial question of who was to be included among "the people," that is, how many were to be included among the many, and in what sense were they to rule?

In addition to the rule of the people, the generally accepted notion of republican government contained three other ideas: rule of law, political virtue, and representation.[10] These concepts did not render republican government any less fuzzy, but each should be discussed in greater detail before looking explicitly at the prominent alternative definitions of republic around which the political debate of the era centered.

The Rule of Law

John Adams, the most articulate and sophisticated Whig theorist in the New World, was most prominent in arguing that republics

7. Gerald Stourzh, *Alexander Hamilton and the Idea of Republican Government* (Palo Alto, Calif.: Stanford University Press, 1970), 47.

8. W. Paul Adams, "Republicanism in Political Rhetoric Before 1776," 404–21.

9. Shoemaker, "'Democracy' and 'Republic' as Understood in Late Eighteenth-Century America," 87.

10. Stourzh, *Hamilton and Republican Government*, 44–45; and Wood, *Creation of the American Republic*, 46–75.

were, by definition, limited by the rule of law. Especially in his *Defense of the Constitutions of Government in the United States of America* did he labor to show that all men being equal under the law was the essence of republican government, or, as he put it, a republic is "a government of laws, and not of men."[11] Certainly it is central to our understanding today that republican government is not arbitrary but is distinguished by laws that stand above special interests and are applied consistently in the same manner, regardless of who is in control of the government at the moment. Of course, any government—aristocratic, oligarchic, democratic—could become a republic under this vague, minimal definition. An important doctrine, it is insufficient by itself for defining republican government.

The problem is too complex and important, however, to dismiss this easily. As Gerald Stourzh points out, "The Founders saw three different entities competing for the title of sovereign: the legislature, the community, and natural law. Sir Ernest Barker has aptly observed that the Americans chose a fourth—the sovereign constitution."[12] If the more traditional Whigs believed in legislative supremacy and the more radical Whigs preferred majority rule by the people at large, both groups still recognized that government should not be arbitrary. Prohibitions against bills of attainder and *ex post facto* laws reflected this concern, and to a certain extent bills of rights were assumed to be anchored in natural law. But there is no getting around the fact that almost all early state constitutions permitted the legislature to abrogate rights if it was deemed necessary, and legislatures frequently did so. Placing sovereignty in the constitutions appeared to solve the problem but, in fact, only papered it over. In effect, government, or the legislature, was limited by constitutional provisions; but the constitutions were derived from the people with no intermediaries, so that sovereignty in practice resided in the people. Presumably, then, the people could alter the constitutions in any way they wished, and what was to prevent a majority from being arbitrary? Nevertheless, it is notable that as those writing state constitutions gradually made bills of rights less

11. C. F. Adams (ed.), *Works of John Adams*, IV, 106.
12. Stourzh, *Hamilton and Republican Government*, 59.

tentative and more binding in their limits on legislatures, the writing, ratifying, and amending of constitutions was taken out of the hands of the legislatures and placed in the hands of the people. However, despite stronger and longer bills of rights, state legislatures became demonstrably more arbitrary in their legislation, and this tendency toward arbitrariness was prominent in Federalist minds when they sat down to frame the federal Constitution. It may be important, therefore, that in the federal Constitution it was made difficult, if not impossible in practical terms, to amend the document without participation of the legislature; and both ratification and amendment were removed enough from direct control by the people to require an extraordinary majority on their part to enforce their will.[13]

In sum, to speak of a "government of laws, and not of men" as defining republican government implies that some general principles of reason and justice remain true and valid, regardless of popular approval or disapproval, and that in certain respects republican government is not the rule of the people. On the other hand, it is difficult to find these true and valid principles, since in practice the Constitution or any of the state constitutions are subject to amendment by the people, if not by the legislature. Of course, it can be argued that the people act in a special way when involved with constitutional matters, in contrast, for example, with the way they act as an electorate. But it would appear that defining republican government as the rule of law ends up raising the same questions as those raised by the definition based on a plurality of rulers: who is to be included among "the people," and in what sense are they to rule?

Despite these difficulties, it should not be concluded that few people believed in the concept of rule of law. Then, as now, belief may cloud the perception of logical inconsistency. That rule of law

13. Article V of the Constitution provides several avenues for amendment, only one of which avoids the legislature. In that case, two-thirds of the state legislatures call for a national convention to amend the Constitution. Aside from the involvement of the state legislatures, Congress technically still has a role. It must call the convention, though it has no choice but to do so, and then decide whether it will require three-fourths of the state legislatures or three-fourths of the states in convention for ratification. This last point is no small matter. Only once has the national convention method been tried, and the effort fell two states short of calling the national convention.

might not always be compatible with majority rule did not prevent its being so widely praised that it became, and remains, an essential part of the American perspective on politics. The possible contradiction with majority rule was not immediately apparent. Although majority rule was represented institutionally from the first state constitutions, rule of law only gradually came to be represented in constitutional provisions, and even in the federal Constitution it is represented largely by the absence of discriminatory provisions such as religious tests. Rule of law remained more a commonly held value than an institutionally based political principle. The courts became its champion, and to a certain extent we have used the Supreme Court to graft *post hoc* heavier and heavier burdens of meaning on the Constitution, based on our devotion to the principle. The state legislatures, in becoming increasingly susceptible to majority rule, produced more and more legislation contrary to the sense of fair play embodied in the notion of the rule of law. This departure from the esteemed principle led the Federalists to a deeper appreciation of the possible contradiction between majority rule and the rule of law than the Whigs ever had. They did not, however, produce a coherent theoretical solution.

Republican Virtue

Anyone who has limited his or her reading about the revolutionary era to the Declaration of Independence would be surprised to learn that from the pulpit, in the press, in pamphlets and private correspondence, Americans were as likely to argue for independence from England on grounds of preserving American virtue as they were on grounds of freedom from tyranny. In 1776, virtue had more than one meaning, and the predominant meaning would shift significantly over the next thirteen years. Since the idea of virtue was intimately connected with republican government throughout, a closer look at this shift in meaning goes a long way toward illustrating the evolution of republican democracy.

There was, of course, the traditional Christian understanding of virtue as encompassing brotherly love, humility, and piety. Many of the clergy were prominent in agitating for independence, and there is little doubt that this is what they had in mind. To understand how religion and politics came to be intertwined, it must be remembered that large numbers of immigrants to the New World were members of dissenting and fundamentalist sects, fleeing religious persecution under the Church of England. As the English attempted to reinstitute economic control over the colonies in the middle 1700s, they also strengthened the place and role of the Anglican church in American affairs; at least this is how it was perceived by many Americans. Since the king was head of the English church, the colonists naturally opposed him as well as the English church, which they regarded as being full of covert "popery" and corrupt doctrine. Although religious fervor had considerably diminished in the colonies by 1776, it remained enough of a force to serve as a potent source of opposition to continued British rule.

Of perhaps greater importance in 1776, and certainly in the years to come, was another view of virtue, one gleaned from the classics and handed down to the colonists in altered form through the writings of Machiavelli, Hume, Montesquieu, Mably, Rousseau, Harrington, and Sydney. In this sense, virtue was a "passion for the public good." The altered sense was a blend of the desire to erect a public-spirited commonwealth along the classical model of republican government and the modern psychological view that human nature was dominated by passion rather than by reason.[14] With the addition of the modern element, it was no longer sufficient to rely upon the process of education to produce virtue, as Plato and Aristotle had. Instead, "a public-spirited, free government, was possible only if an equality of fortunes, based on general frugality, turned the private and selfish passions for enrichment and aggrandizement into zeal for the public good. In other words, virtue became a function of external institutional contrivances rather than of an intrinsically perfectible human nature."[15] Most Americans were convinced that too much wealth, especially if concentrated in a few hands, tended to corrupt both individuals and government. They viewed England as the prototype of such a society, characterized by luxury, venality, effete cowardice, and a love of refinement and

14. My discussion in this section relies heavily upon Stourzh, *Hamilton and Republican Government*, especially Chap. 2; and Wood, *Creation of the American Republic*, Chap. 2.
15. Sourzh, *Hamilton and Republican Government*, 64–65.

distinction. On the contrary, they viewed Americans as embodying the sturdy traits of the traditional English yeomen—frugality, industriousness, temperance, simplicity, openness, and virility. If excessive wealth and inequality were the cause of English corruption, and a moderate wealth more or less equally distributed in America was the source of virtue, then the lesson was straightforward: preserve American institutions and the social conditions supporting them from English corruption. The longer the connection with the home country was maintained, the more America would be corrupted by English institutions, especially since England was beginning to bring the colonies under much closer control.[16] The enlightened rationalism of the Whigs and the evangelical Calvinism of the clergy were not at odds but rather reinforced each other in pointing to the necessity for a break with the crown.[17] That each was based on a different view of human nature and argued from a different sense of virtue made little difference in 1776.

The connection between a noncommercial society and virtue as the core of republicanism would continue to be made, most notably by Thomas Jefferson. His *Notes on the State of Virginia* celebrated the virtues of the American farmer and proposed that we rely on England for manufactured goods in return for our farm products. In this manner, we could retain our pristine virtues intact. The Federalists, on the other hand, came mainly from commercially oriented towns and cities and were committed to further development.[18] Alex-

16. H. Trevor Colbourn, *The Lamp of Experience* (Chapel Hill: University of North Carolina Press, 1965), 50–51, 168–69, 186–87; Wood, *Creation of the American Republic*, 28–36, 65–70; and Bernard Bailyn, *The Ideological Origins of the American Revolution* (Cambridge, Mass.: Belknap Press, 1967), 86.

17. The blending of Calvinist theology and Whig doctrine was striking. In a sense, this was only to be expected, since Americans, as a result of their religious organization and environmental conditions, had been following Whig political practices long before Whiggism became a coherent theory in England. For an excellent example of blended Calvinist and Whig ideas, see Phillips Payson's election sermon given during the 1780 Massachusetts election. It is reprinted in John Wingate Thornton (ed.), *The Pulpit of the American Revolution* (Boston: Gould and Lincoln, 1876), 329. Of similar interest is John Dickenson's "Proclamation for the Encouragement of Piety and Virtue," one of his proclamations as president of Pennsylvania during 1782. It is reprinted in George Edward Reed (ed.), *Papers of the Governors: 1759–85*, in *Pennsylvania Archives*, Vol. III (Harrisburg: State of Pennsylvania, 1900), 868–71.

18. Van Beck Hall, *Politics Without Parties, 1780–1791* (Pittsburgh, Pa.: University of Pittsburgh Press, 1972), 295; and Jackson Turner Main, *Political Parties Before the Constitution* (Chapel Hill: University of North Carolina Press, 1973), especially Chap. XIII.

ander Hamilton unabashedly desired America to become another England commercially and did everything in his power to aid the process. This, in itself, indicates the extent of the change as Federalist political theory gradually replaced Whig thought.

At the core of Whig theory was the assumption of a homogeneous people. Whigs did not deny that interests would vary from person to person or place to place, but maintained that on essential matters there was a community of interest. Furthermore, this community of interest was not the sum of individual interests, or some compromise of various demands; it was rather almost an entity in itself, somewhat along the lines of Rousseau's General Will. While the people at large might sometimes be mistaken as to what the community interest was, they would, given time, recognize these mistakes and correct them.

The Whig vision of republican government would gradually be supplanted by the Federalist vision. The Federalists, rather than use the community of interest as the measure of virtue, would instead use the self-interest of the individual as the yardstick of the public good. They assumed that self-interest lay at the core of human nature, and that out of the interaction of private passions would arise demands that worked for the common good. In effect, the Whig view of virtue was inverted by the Federalists. If self-interest was the basis of vice for Whigs, it was the basis of virtue for Federalists. Where Whigs saw community, Federalists saw faction. What is interesting is that both could make the intimate connection between virtue and republican government.

In its derivation, republic (*res publica*) means, literally, "public matter" or "public affair." A republic was, therefore, a government aimed at the public good rather than the good of one man. The Whigs and Federalists did not disagree on the end; they disagreed on how best to achieve the end of the common good. The radical Whigs believed equality would produce republican virtue. This, in turn, would create and preserve the community of interest. The Federalists believed the interaction of private interests would produce government for the common good. In both cases, government was to be based on common consent. The radical Whigs felt common consent was best realized by allowing the people a maximum voice in the government. The Federalists were not as sanguine about equality or votes separated from property. They tended to see virtue as being concentrated among the more affluent, and Hamilton baldly stated at one point that the advantage of character belonged to the wealthy.[19] If virtue was an essential aspect of republican government, once again we are led to the same questions raised by the other two general definitions of a republic: who is to be included among the people, and in what sense are they to rule?

Representation

If the word *republic* usually called to mind rule of the people, the rule of law, and public virtue, it also called to mind representation. Again, precisely what picture of representation it called to mind varied considerably from person to person and time to time, but by the time of the writing of the Declaration of Independence there was little argument that republican government called for *some* form of representation.

Traditional Whigs, while agreeing with the more radical Whigs that a certain level of equality was essential for free government, nevertheless recognized formal divisions in society related to function. They took their cues from the English Whigs who were fond of referring to "mixed government" as most conducive to freedom. The concept of a mixed government went back to Aristotle and consisted of blending the three governmental types in one constitution, these being the democratic principle, the aristocratic principle, and the monarchic principle.[20] In England, the House of Commons, the House of Lords, and the king represented each of these principles, respectively. After the Revolution, the president or governor represented the monarchic role in America, at least in theory. It is important to understand that the Whigs did not think in terms of representing individuals, interests, or factions. The representatives would be disinterested men elected for their superior abilities and experience, not as spokesmen for certain interests. They were to spend their time working for the common good, the interests of the

19. Stourzh, *Hamilton and Republican Government*, 74.
20. Although Aristotle first developed the concept, the colonists were more likely to encounter it in their reading of Cicero and the Romans.

people at large. In this respect, then, elected officials were not representatives in the present sense of the word. A senator was a senator and not a representative, a governor was a governor, and a legislator was a legislator. They were supposed to be so unconcerned with special interest that public campaigning for election was considered, at best, unseemly. Furthermore, since the community was assumed to be homogeneous, it made little difference what person was elected to office, as long as he had a demonstrated ability to deal with complex issues, especially those involving finances, and a reputation for honesty and moderation. Gordon S. Wood relates the story that the first time James Madison ran for office in 1777, he attempted to preserve this vision of representation by doing away with the personal soliciting and treating of voters. Madison lost to a former tavern keeper, and his disillusion with traditional Whig assumptions was typical of many Whigs.[21]

The more radical Whigs took equality more seriously, and while retaining the assumption of a homogeneous population with a community of interests, they replaced the theory of mixed government with a system characterized by legislative supremacy. The legislature became increasingly egalitarian and in a few years was extremely responsive to the various interests within the community. Despite the intentions behind radical Whig politics, the operation of the institutions they designed quickly put the lie to their assumption of a homogeneous society. Although it has never been examined very carefully, it is entirely possible that the experience with radical Whig state legislatures may have demoralized the Whigs considerably and rendered their opposition to Federalist proposals both half-hearted and confused.

Madison and Hamilton minced no words when they described what the Federalists had written into the Constitution. Especially in *The Federalist* 10, Madison laid out the proposition that society was no longer viewed as homogeneous but as composed of many conflicting interests. Representatives were now intended to be just that—representative—and what they represented was not the disinterested good of the entire community, but specific interests with-

21. Wood, *Creation of the American Republic*, 122.

in society. The theory of representation had come a long way in only fifteen years.

Theory had come a long way, but not everyone had kept up with it. The year 1789 still found many old Whigs on the political scene, John Adams among them, and even more Whigs of the radical variety. There were other theoretical variations as well, and they all tended to be lumped together as "Antifederalist," despite the rather rich diversity of opinion this title encompassed.[22] The idea of republican government was still vague and amorphous enough to retain the allegiance of virtually the entire range of theory from old Whig to Federalist.[23] If Americans were held together during the war by a common enemy and the common goal of independence, they were held together after the war, at least in part, by a common vocabulary and a common set of political symbols that tended to minimize their apparent differences. Compared to the range of political theory found in Europe, their differences did not then and do not now look that profound; but that is not to say the distinctions were unimportant. Political battles were fought, and won or lost, that fundamentally altered American political theory. If the Whigs had won, our political system today might be indistinguishable from England's parliamentary system, or perhaps might operate in a fashion completely foreign to either England's system or what we have developed.

Republican government, then, was generally understood to include rule by the people, the rule of law, political virtue, and representation. In each case, there was considerable diversity in the meaning attached to the idea, and a development in the dominant meaning between 1776 and 1789. None of these general ideas pro-

22. It is difficult to convey the richness of the debate during the era. This discussion has of necessity been limited to the three most prominent political theories. For a partial entry into the diversity of the time, see Cecilia M. Kenyon's *The Anti-Federalists* (New York: Bobbs-Merrill, 1966). A superb example of what I mean is the pamphlet reproduced by Edmund S. Morgan in his "The Political Establishment of the United States, 1784," *William and Mary Quarterly*, 3rd. Ser., XXIII (1966), 286–308.

23. Shoemaker argues in his article that *republic* did not refer to any particular form of government, but to a characteristic of the purpose of government. Although the term was quite broadly defined, it did exclude forms such as monarchy and hereditary aristocracy. Shoemaker correctly implies that republican government was understood more in terms of an approach to politics than as a specific set of institutions, at least at first.

vided an obvious answer to two crucial questions raised by republican government: who is to be included among the people, and in what sense are the people to rule? Many definitions of republican government advanced during the period, some more specific than others, attempted to come to grips with these crucial questions. Each assumed these general ideas but pressed further to link republican government more explicitly with a theory of consent. It is to a consideration of these more explicit definitions that we now turn.

Definitions of Republican Government

After the Declaration of Independence, the Whigs defined republican government as that form of government they had brought with them from colonial status. The problem, of course, was that the thirteen republics varied a great deal in their institutions. Furthermore, there were forces present in almost all the states, pushing for stronger institutions of consent to broaden popular control. These forces arose partly because the rhetoric used to support the split from England was being turned against those in power in the new states, and partly because large numbers of average citizens were being politicized by their participation in revolutionary politics and military campaigns. Also, the usual economic dislocation that war brings created dissatisfaction and a greater interest in political matters. The stage was set for a struggle to define republican government institutionally.

It is possible to find hundreds of definitions of republican government in the literature of the period; but John Adams struggled longer and harder with the definition than anyone, and he had the habit of being precise with his words, so we shall begin with him in laying out the essential positions. "What is your definition of a republic? Mine is this: *A government whose sovereignty is vested in more than one person.* Governments are divided into despotisms, monarchies, and republics" (John Adams, in a letter to Roger Sherman, July 17, 1789).[24] Here, as mentioned earlier, is the prominent English dictionary definition of that era. Note that Adams carefully

24. C. F. Adams (ed.), *Works of John Adams*, IV, 428.

distinguished monarchies from despotisms, indicating that he still had the Whig admiration for English government and the concomitant belief that it was possible to have free government under a monarchy. Of even greater interest was his careful inclusion of the word *sovereignty*. The word has a long history during which it underwent many subtle alterations. It is not relevant to our purposes to review that entire history, but it is worth placing Adams' use of the word in context. Sovereignty generally referred to the supreme and independent power or authority in government. In England, until the seventeenth century, it was generally held that the king was sovereign, having been given that power by God. This formed the basis for what was known as the divine right theory. The civil war in England, followed by the Glorious Revolution in 1688, resulted in Parliament gaining an essential share in sovereignty, and divine right was overthrown. Because sovereignty was, by definition, not divisible, the English Whigs developed the legal fiction that sovereignty resided in "the king in parliament." This left the king as the symbol of ultimate authority but gave actual power to Parliament acting in his name. Because property, as well as people, was represented in Parliament, it was deemed inappropriate to speak of sovereignty residing in the people, and anyway, this would have seemed somewhat illogical to Whigs, for it would mean a hopeless division of sovereignty. This helps explain Adams' peculiar wording, which noted that sovereignty did not reside simply in the king, but avoided anything that might imply that it resided in the people.

Many American Whigs had, by 1776, come to recognize that the people could not be ignored. Furthermore, since the Whigs assumed a homogeneous community, to include the people would not imply a division in the supreme power. In another letter, Adams provided a definition more precisely reflecting the position held by American Whigs in 1776. "Whenever I use the word *republic* with approbation, I mean a government in which the people have collectively, or by representation, an essential share in sovereignty" (John Adams, in a letter to Samuel Adams, October 18, 1790).[25] Note that the people are viewed as a collectivity, in keeping with the Whig as-

25. *Ibid.*, 415.

sumption of a community. To say that the community can share in sovereignty through representation is to use representation in the Whig sense of electing men to dispassionately seek and serve the interest of the entire community instead of that portion of the electorate that respectively elected them. These men would not be representatives in the present sense of the word, but legislators performing a function in the name of all the people. Also, speaking of the people as a collectivity preserved the logic of sovereignty residing in a specific body.

The second definition does not differ from the broader first definition in one important respect—Adams' refusal to place sovereignty explicitly in the people. Their share represents only the democratic principle in a mixed government, which includes the aristocratic and monarchical principles as well. Samuel Adams chided John Adams on just this point in his letter of response. "Is not the *whole* sovereignty, my friend, essentially in the people? . . . Is it not the uncontrollable, essential right of the people to amend and alter, or annul their constitution and frame a new one . . . [have] annual or biennial elections . . . and by empowering their representatives to impeach the greatest officers of the state before the Senate" (Samuel Adams, in a letter to John Adams, November 20, 1790).[26] These are not mere quibblings over words. If the people at large only share in sovereignty, as John Adams has it, then the actions of government are only partially subject to the consent of the people; whereas if sovereignty resides entirely in the people, then we have complete popular control where, at least in theory, no governmental action can take place without the consent of the citizens. John Adams was trying to preserve some power for the few who own wealth in the form of property. Thus he was using the traditional Whig notion of balancing the interests of the few and the interests of the many by requiring the explicit consent of both groups. Samuel Adams, a more radical Whig of the sort that temporarily became dominant during the war years, was arguing for a more egalitarian notion of consent, as well as a more direct form whereby governmental action is so tied to popular consent that representatives essentially mir-

26. *Ibid.*, 421.

ror the general will. The institutions mentioned by Samuel Adams were not picked out of the air. They were precisely the institutional changes for which the radical Whigs argued in 1776 and 1777, and the state constitutions began to include these provisions and thereby to reflect the victory of radical Whig republican theory over that of the more traditional Whigs.

An even more radical definition current at the time carried the Samuel Adams definition through to its logical conclusions. While advocated by relatively few people in the late 1770s, it nonetheless exerted a powerful influence in some states, despite its impracticality. It defined republican government as "a government by its citizens in mass, acting directly, according to rules established by the majority" (Thomas Jefferson, in a letter to John Taylor, May 28, 1816).[27]

With this definition, republican government becomes indistinguishable from democratic government. Jefferson himself did not adhere to such a radical formulation; yet there were tendencies during the 1780s to push consent theories toward this direct, radical form. The trend was forceful enough to legitimize the term *democracy*, even if it did not legitimize truly democratic institutions. By 1787, even Alexander Hamilton had worked his thinking through to the point at which he could refer to the proposed federal Constitution as a "representative democracy." This term had become a common one for describing the Constitution by 1789, but not because it approximated the situation outlined in Jefferson's definition. Instead, there had been a subtle shift in meaning, just as there had been an obvious change in the popularity of the word *democracy*.

Hamilton is credited with being among the first to use the phrase, as early as 1777.[28] His notes for his speech to the New York ratifying convention ten years later clearly outline the subtle shift in meaning that had occurred in Hamilton's mind, as well as in the minds of many of the Federalists.

27. Thomas Jefferson, *Writings of Thomas Jefferson* (64 vols., Washington, D.C.: n.p., 1907), XV, 19.
28. Stourzh, *Hamilton and Republican Government*, 49.

Again great confusion about the words. Democracy. Aristocracy. Monarchy

I.   Democracy defined by some (,) Rousseau &c

        A government exercised by the collective body of the People

        2 Delegation of their power has been made the criterion of Aristocracy (This is both Hobbes' and Rousseau's definition of aristocracy.)

II.   Aristocracy has been used to designate government

       1. Where an independent few possessed sovereignty.

       2. Where the representatives of the people possessed it.

III.   Monarchy, where sovereignty in the hands of a single man.

Democracy in my sense, where the whole power of the government [is] in the people

1.   Whether exercised by themselves, or

2.   By their representatives chosen by them mediately or immediately and legally accountable to them

Aristocracy where whole sovereignty is permanently in the hand of a few for life or hereditary

Monarchy where the whole sovereignty is in the hands of one man for life or hereditary.

Mixed government [is] when these three unite.[29]

Clearly, then, under Hamilton's reconstruction there is only one possible combination for describing the Constitution, and that is a representative democracy in which representatives would be chosen by the people "mediately or immediately and legally accountable to them." Under earlier definitions, representative government would have been termed an aristocracy, but Hamilton and others had come to associate aristocracy with the rule of the few, either through inheritance or for life, and thus designated elective sovereignty as something distinct from aristocracy. Still, to call it representative democracy would have been considered self-contradictory to the likes of Hobbes, Locke, and Rousseau, for the simple reason that, in their minds, whoever had the power of legislation was the ruler, the sovereign. A representative democracy by definition divides sovereignty, placing part in the people and part in their representatives, which amounted to no sovereign at all.

29. *Ibid.*, 48–49.

If Hamilton's definition would have sounded strange to those from an earlier tradition, it should also appear strange to us for reasons that are usually overlooked.[30] It does not seem odd to us for the people to elect representatives to pass laws yet retain ultimate sovereignty themselves, but Hamilton is willing to use the term *democracy* for a system in which the people do not directly elect their representatives, who are thus not electorally responsible to the people but only legally responsible. For example, this means that the people could elect something equivalent to an electoral college, which would elect the members to Congress, or perhaps use a random selection process among the candidates. The representatives would be subject to removal only through impeachment during, say, a 20-year term. Since the offices are not hereditary or for life, it would not be an aristocracy, but a mediately elected "representative democracy." That Hamilton did, indeed, desire something other than what we normally consider a representative democracy is indicated by his major speech at the Constitutional Convention, in which he argued for a government in which the lower house would be elected triennially, the Senate for life (on good behavior), and the executive also for life. This is more properly termed a "mixed regime" under both Hamilton's definition and the Whig tradition, but then he went on to say that it is also a form of republican government as long as "all the Magistrates are appointed, and vacancies are filled, by the people, *or a process of election originating with the people*" (emphasis added).[31] A mixed government of this form thus becomes, through his own definitions, a representative democracy and a republic. Today when we hear frequent argument that the electoral college is undemocratic, just as earlier in our history we heard that election of senators by state legislatures was undemocratic, it should sound strange to hear that one of our more prominent Founding Fa-

30. Curiously, neither Stourzh nor any other commentator I have come across has noted the implications of Hamilton's shift in definition as here noted, though Stourzh does point out that Hamilton's position was not as "modern" as it would appear from a superficial reading.

31. Max Farrand (ed.), *The Records of the Federal Convention of 1787* (4 vols., Rev. ed.; New Haven, Conn.: Yale University Press, 1937), I, 290.

thers considered such indirect election both representative and democratic.

Hamilton's view of politics was in some respects unique among his contemporaries, but not in this respect. Just as the Whigs in 1776 initially defined republican government as simply "what we have," so, too, Federalists after 1787 defined republican government in terms of what had been written into the proposed Constitution. The Federalists, therefore, often defined a republic by detailing what were then familiar and favored institutions. Such definitions were often long and detailed, lacking theoretical coherence, as the following example illustrates. "What I mean by it (republican government) was, a government under the authority of the people, consisting of legislative, executive, and judiciary powers; the legislative powers vested in an assembly consisting of one or more branches, who, together with the executive, are appointed by the people and dependent on them for continuance, by periodical elections, agreeably to an established constitution; and what especially denominates it a *republic* is its dependence on the *public* or *people at large*, without any hereditary powers" (Roger Sherman, in a letter to John Adams, July 20, 1789).[32] As with Hamilton, the key is the absence of hereditary powers. There is no mention of direct elections or frequent elections, but rather "periodical elections" under the authority of the people. The "dependence on the public" may be direct or indirect. One more definition, written by the Federalist generally conceded to have been most influential in constructing the meaning of the federal Constitution, if not the document itself—Madison—was not considered controversial by Federalists. Republican government, it said, "derives all its powers directly or *indirectly* from the great body of the people, and is administered by persons holding their offices for a limited period, *or during good behavior*. . . . It is essential to such government that it be derived from the great body of the society, not from an inconsiderable portion, or a favored class of it" (James Madison in *The Federalist* 39 [emphasis added]).[33] Despite an emphasis on the people at large

32. C. F. Adams (ed.), *Works of John Adams*, IV, 437.
33. Jacob E. Cooke (ed.), *The Federalist* (Cleveland: Meridian, 1961), 251.

and a seeming similarity to the radical Whig definition attributed to Samuel Adams, there were subtle but important shifts in the Federalist formulation that resulted in a backing away from the directness of the radical Whig notion of republican government. The Federalists, while they placed sovereignty completely in the people, nevertheless would come to insist that institutions be so designed that consent was given much more indirectly. Such an approach results in representatives who were elected by the many, yet who were relatively free from direct influence by the people and not as subject to pressures to mirror popular demands. For example, the popularly elected House was checked by several other institutions that, while still resting on popular consent, were progressively less directly tied to that consent. At the same time, the Federalists were not merely moving back to the more conservative consent theory of the traditional Whigs like John Adams. The Federalists were not balancing the many with the few. Rather, they were facing squarely the reality that America was a heterogeneous people subject to countless factions, and were attempting to prevent the rights of any minority from being trampled (excluding, of course, blacks and Indians). For example, the Federalists did not press for disenfranchising Catholics and Jews, as did the traditional Whigs, because they felt no need to preserve the homogeneous community that the Whigs assumed. The difference in scale between towns and counties, which were the primary political units when the Whigs predominated, and a nation of millions with large cities, precluded this hope to any careful thinker in 1789.

To what extent, if any, the doctrine of consent enshrined by the Federalists in the Constitution was an attempt to remove national government from popular control will be the topic of the last chapter. Before that question can be answered fruitfully, there must be an examination in greater depth of the connection between republican government and consent theory, and a careful analysis of how consent-based institutions developed between 1776 and 1787.

2

Republican Government and Consent

The Genesis of Consent in America

For at least the past three centuries, any discussion of what we now term democratic theory or popular control of government necessarily has presumed some kind of consent by the people. The relationship between consent and popular control of government is so obvious and so intimate that it has unfortunately gone largely unexamined. Unlike research into the nature and origin of other important political concepts such as justice, majority rule, sovereignty, or representation, any investigation of consent in the extant literature reveals an embarrassingly small listing of works, a distressingly low level of analysis in those works, and a frustrating lack of consensus as to what the word might mean.[1] *Consent* does not often appear in modern political discourse, yet it remains the key assumption in all theories of popular control of government.

Americans were not loathe to use the word in the seventeenth and eighteenth centuries. It is difficult to find a political document, tract, treatise, article, letter, or sermon that does not use the term. Then, as now, most people assumed they understood what the term meant and were not very analytical in its use. Many bitter political debates and struggles revolved around different usages, often without the participants realizing the differential theoretical base for the institutions they supported. One major difference between now and the first two hundred years of our political history is that then Ameri-

---

1. Two notable exceptions to the charge of poor analysis are J. P. Palmenatz, *Consent, Freedom and Political Obligation* (London: Oxford University Press, 1968); and P. H. Partridge, *Consent and Consensus* (New York: Praeger, 1971). Part of the following discussion will be based on their work.

cans were busy evolving a doctrine of consent through the differentiation and elaboration of institutions. If the word was more popular then, it was because it had become an essential ingredient in their evolving view of political reality, regardless of how it was defined or understood.

From the very beginning, the people settling on American shores had developed and used institutions based on consent. The letters patent to Sir Humphrey Gilbert from Queen Elizabeth in 1578 declared that all Englishmen emigrating under the terms of the patent "shall and may have, and enjoy all the privileges of free denizens, and within our allegiance: any law custom or usage to the contrary notwithstanding." One of these privileges was the right to local self-government. Sir Walter Raleigh's charter in 1584, as well as the charters to the Virginia Company of Plymouth and the Virginia Company of London (1606), contained the same provisions. The colonists used these words to justify the erection of local political institutions based on popular control. In 1619, the Virginia Company summoned the first representative assembly in America, and the burgesses were elected by virtually universal manhood suffrage. In the Mayflower Compact of 1620, the Pilgrims laid the groundwork for a political system that was just as liberal and also assumed consent on the part of those who qualified as members of the community. The Fundamental Orders of Connecticut (1628) enshrined consent by the people as the foundation of political authority. The Massachusetts Body of Liberties (1641) set down popular rights in black and white and the pattern was set.[2]

That the first settlers were given considerable control over their political lives was no accident. English North America was settled,

2. It would be a mistake to assume that universal manhood suffrage was the rule in use. In every case, there was a principle to determine who could and who could not vote. Invariably, it amounted to demonstrating a stake in the community and thus in the commercial enterprise, through ownership of property. Usually it also meant demonstration of membership in the religious community, especially in New England, where colonies were often populated by religious sects emigrating as a group. In the beginning, since everyone who arrived was a member of the appropriate church or company, the principle in use amounted to universal manhood suffrage. However, because the various colonies were gradually populated by more and more people who could qualify under neither principle, the percentage of the population eligible to vote slowly and consistently declined until the beginning of the eighteenth century. To say that the colonies were governed by consent and run democratically is not to imply that all persons were citizens. For a while, some New

not by people sent by the king, but by people organized through private effort into companies for private gain. Stockholders wanted a return on their investments; colonists wanted their own land and religious freedom; and the king wished another source of revenue and settlement of the land that he claimed but could not control until it was inhabited by his subjects. The charters were contracts outlining the responsibilities of each party. Once the charter was approved, the company was largely on its own, as long as it fulfilled its part of the contract—usually to return a certain percentage of the profits. Those who came over in the ships were generally recognized as being engaged in an enterprise of some personal risk, and often they were stockholders risking their money as well. Under such conditions, it would have been foolish to expect anyone to emigrate if he had little or no control over matters in which he had invested his livelihood, indeed his life. Furthermore, the entire idea behind colonization was to establish the principle of incentive. If the colonists owned their land, they would be much more productive; but at the same time, in England, ownership of property carried with it the right of suffrage.[3] Thus, if the colonists were to be productive, they must also be given the right to local self-control. It was an arrangement with benefits for all parties, and English law and practice conspired to make government by consent one of the benefits for colonists.

Consent for operation of the colonies was often two-tiered, the charters providing for both a governing body in the colony and one in England. The board or council in England was supposed to review all legislation passed by the colonial body, but the time required for messages to travel twice across the Atlantic Ocean meant

England towns had so few people who could qualify under the suffrage principles in use that they amounted to religious oligarchies. Nevertheless, the principle of popular consent was preserved, and with the decline in religious fervor and the increasing per capita wealth of colonists, which was widespread due to the easily available land further inland, popular consent was applied to a broadening electorate in the 1700s. By 1770, the percentage of the adult male population eligible to vote in the northern colonies was approximately what it is today.

3. In England, this had been the case since at least 1430, when a statute was passed restricting the right to vote for members of Parliament to those who owned land with a rental value of forty shillings a year. See Chilton Williamson, *American Suffrage from Property to Democracy, 1760–1860* (Princeton, N.J.: Princeton University Press, 1960), 7. Unlike the situation in America, relatively few in England had sufficient property to qualify.

that the council had great difficulty keeping up with matters and in-
tervened only occasionally. Even then, there were problems of enforcement. Consequently, local government in the colonies often
approximated self-government. In effect, these colonial charters became the first written constitutions and were one fount from which
American political theory and practice would develop.[4] Because
joint stock companies were organized to give members a vote in
their operation, the positions of responsibility were elective. In the
colonies this meant that company officers amounted to elected political officers. Popular government in America has its roots, at least
partially, in the consent stockholders and colonists gave company
officers to conduct business.

The charters were somewhat deficient as true constitutions. Written by clerks who were paid by the line, they ramble on tediously
for many pages in long, convoluted sentences. From these highly
technical documents Americans developed the tradition of written
constitutions; but the charters themselves contained few specifics on
how the colonies were to be organized and run, beyond establishing a few general institutions to provide for the details of government. Some, such as in Pennsylvania, derived from the crown the
authority to construct a government, but others, such as the first
Connecticut constitution, were written by the colonists entirely on
their own with no interference from England. These native constitutions expanded upon the charters and initially differed little in their

4. Benjamin F. Wright makes this argument, saying that the honor of being first can be
bestowed on a number of documents, depending upon one's point of view. The 1606
Charter of Virginia contained a conformity clause whereby regulation of the colony was
to "be agreeable to the Laws, Statutes, Government, and Policy of this our Realm of England." The third Virginia Charter (1611–12) granted the additional power to police and
punish but still did not explicitly grant local self-government. Under this third charter,
however, the first representative assembly in America was called in 1618, although acts of
the legislature still had to be approved by the council in London. If the Massachusetts
Charter (1629) was used from the beginning as an instrument of government, it was the
1632 Maryland Charter that was first designed specifically for governmental purposes,
making it the first true provincial charter. The charters of Connecticut (1662) and Rhode
Island (1663) formalized systems of government already in use by the colonists to become
the first official native constitutions (i.e., written by the colonists in America), but the
Fundamental Orders of Connecticut (1639) was perhaps the first true native constitution,
though it lacked any ratification in England. See Benjamin F. Wright, Jr., "The Early History of Written Constitutions in America," Chap. XII, in *Essays in History and Political
Theory in Honor of Charles Howard McIlwain* (Cambridge, Mass.: Harvard University
Press, 1936), 344–71.

principles and institutions from charter provisions or English political practice, but gradually they formulated a unique American perspective on politics.

These indigenous instruments of government typically were passed by local legislatures as a total legislative package, but often lacked a formal title. It is little wonder that they are generally unknown. The documents written by the colonists are marked with an asterisk.

   1. Letters patent to Sir Humphrey Gilbert, 1578
   2. Sir Walter Raleigh's charter, 1584
   3. Charter of Acadia, 1603
   4. First Virginia Charter, 1606
   5. Second Virginia Charter, 1609
   6. Third Virginia Charter, 1611–12
  *7. Mayflower Compact, 1620
   8. New England Charter, 1620
   9. Ordinance for Virginia, 1621
  10. Charter, Dutch West India Company, 1621
  11. Grant of New Hampshire, 1629
  12. Massachusetts Charter, 1629
  13. Dutch Charter of Privileges to Patroons, 1629
  14. Charter of Plymouth to William Bradford, 1629
  15. Maryland Charter, 1632
 *16. Cambridge Agreement, 1632 (Massachusetts)
 *17. Dorchester Agreement, 1633 (Massachusetts)
 *18. Salem Agreement, 1634 (Massachusetts)
 *19. Watertown Agreement, 1634 (Massachusetts)
  20. Grant of New Hampshire, 1635
 *21. Pilgrim Code of Law, 1636 (Massachusetts)
 *22. Fundamental Orders of Connecticut, 1639
 *23. New Haven Fundamentals, 1639
  24. Grant of Maine, 1639
 *25. Government of Providence, 1639 (Rhode Island)
 *26. Government of Newport, 1639 (Rhode Island)
 *27. Government of Pocasset, 1639 (Portsmouth, Rhode Island)
 *28. Maryland Act, 1639
 *29. Agreement of Settlers at Exeter, 1639 (New Hampshire)

*30. Dover Combination, 1639 (New Hampshire)

*31. Bradford's Surrender of his patent of Plymouth to the freemen, 1640

*32. Agreement at Providence, 1640 (Rhode Island)

*33. Massachusetts Body of Liberties, 1641

*34. Piscataqua River Government, 1641 (New Hampshire)

*35. Government of Rhode Island, 1641

*36. New Haven Fundamentals, 1643 (revision of 1639)

37. Patent for Providence Plantations, 1643

*38. Acts and Orders of 1647 (agreement between Providence, Warwick, Portsmouth, and Newport in forming a common assembly)

*39. Wells, Gorgiana, and Piscataqua form independent governments, 1649 (Maine)

*40. Puritan Laws and Liberties, 1658

*41. Connecticut Charter, 1662

42. Charter of Carolina, 1663

*43. Rhode Island Charter, 1663

44. Grant to the Duke of York, 1664

*45. Concessions and Agreement (East Jersey), Nova Caesarea, 1664

46. Royal Grant to the Province of Maine, 1664

*47. Concessions of East Jersey, 1665

*48. Concessions and Agreements of the Lords Proprietors of the Province of Carolina, 1665

49. Charter of Carolina, 1665

50. Fundamental Constitutions of Carolina, 1669

*51. Declaration of the Lords Proprietors (Jersey), 1672

52. Grant to Sir George Carteret, 1674 (New Jersey)

53. Grant to the Duke of York, 1674

54. Royal Grant to the Province of Maine, 1674

55. Privileges granted by the Dutch to citizens of Delaware, 1673

*56. Charter of Fundamentals of West New Jersey, 1676

57. Charles II's grant of New England to the Duke of York, 1676

*58. Concessions of West Jersey, 1677

59. Commission for New Hampshire, 1680 (commission of John Cutt)
60. Duke of York's second grant to Penn and others, 1680
61. Pennsylvania Charter, 1681
*62. Fundamentals of West New Jersey, 1681
*63. Concessions to the Province of Pennsylvania, 1681
*64. Pennsylvania Frame of 1682
*65. Penn's Charter of Liberties, 1682
*66. New York Charter of Liberties and Privileges, 1683
*67. Pennsylvania Frame, 1683 (revision of 1682)
*68. Fundamental Constitutions, East New Jersey, 1683
69. Commission of Andros, 1688
70. Massachusetts Charter, 1691
*71. New York Charter and Privileges of the Majesty's Subjects, 1691
*72. Pennsylvania Frame, 1696 (revision of 1683)
73. Pennsylvania Charter of Privileges, 1701
74. Charter of Delaware, 1701
75. Explanatory Massachusetts Charter, 1725
76. Georgia Charter, 1732

Even this partial listing shows as many unofficial constitutions as there were officially approved ones. The colonists were not mere objects of legislation but active participants in designing their political culture. These often-forgotten documents contain several important milestones for republican government in America. For example, the Pilgrim Code of Law in 1636 used language that would be familiar and revolutionary over a century later: "We, the associates of New-Plymouth Coming hither as freeborn subjects of the State of England endowed with all and singular the privileges belonging to such being assembled; doe ordaine Constitute and enact that noe act imposition law or ordinance be made or imposed upon us at present, or to come but such as shall be imposed by Consent of the body of associates or their representatives legally assembled; which is according to the free liberties of the state of England."[5] The language and meaning was virtually identical to that used by

5. Harry M. Ward, *Statism in Plymouth Colony* (Port Washington, N.Y.: Kennikat Press, 1973), 17.

radical Whigs in England and America almost a century and a half later.

The New Haven Fundamentals of 1639 and 1643 are more specific and precise than the famous Fundamental Orders of Connecticut, and also are based upon, and confirm, the civil governments that had been in operation for several years. The Rhode Island Charter was specifically based on the Acts and Orders of 1647, which was the first successful federal system erected in America. This, in turn, was based on the governments of four towns that had been effectively operating on their own for at least a decade. The Acts and Orders of 1647, passed by the first assembly of the federation, was also the first code of law in America specifically based upon English principles of law instead of religious doctrine and practices.

The Puritan Laws and Liberties of 1658 was an abridgment and codification of laws that had been enacted by the colony to that point. It also included a definition of the "just rights and privileges of every freeman," which aided this document in becoming famous and influential throughout the colonies.

The New York Charter of Liberties and Privileges (1683), passed by the first General Assembly, outlined a constitution and a bill of rights in a form that would be quite familiar almost a century later. The General Assembly passed an even more elaborate and explicit bill of rights in the "Rights and Privileges of the Majesty's Subjects" (1691). This later document would be disallowed in England because of its "large and doubtful expressions," which is an understatement since it categorically prohibited the government from doing a number of specific things commonly granted to legislatures at that time. As Bernard Bailyn describes it, the document stated that "the individual was to be free from unlawful arrest and imprisonment, arbitrary taxation, martial law and the support of standing armies in time of peace, feudal dues, and restrictions on freehold tenure."[6] It also guaranteed trial by jury, due process of law in general, and full freedom of conscience and religion to Protestants. The breadth of rights contained in this document would not be seen

6. Bernard Bailyn, *The Ideological Origins of the American Revolution* (Cambridge, Mass.: Belknap Press, 1967), 195.

again until the state constitutions of the 1780s, and the statement of absolute prohibitions on government activity would not be seen again until the federal Constitution of 1787. Americans not only wrote their own constitutions as colonists, they engaged in astoundingly creative political thinking as well.

The crown and Parliament watched uneasily as these colonial legislatures became more and more independent. There was an attempt in the second half of the seventeenth century to curb their independence and enhance their commercial efficiency by making more of them crown colonies, but the Glorious Revolution in England overthrew the Stuarts and local government thrived again.[7] The colonists retained the power of paying the salaries of governors appointed by the crown, and with this lever, plus continued British preoccupation with continental affairs, the colonial legislatures gained the upper hand and preserved government based upon local consent. The attempt by the Parliament to reassert commercial and political control over the colonies in the 1750s, 1760s, and 1770s, through such legislation as the Navigation Acts, the Townshend duties, and the Stamp Act, set the stage for the Revolution. The colonists intended to retain control by local consent, which they had come to expect after more than a century of virtual self-government.

Between 1584 and 1789, there were at least thirty-six charters, forty-one documents of colonial origin equivalent to constitutions, eighteen state constitutions, and twenty-three plans for uniting the colonies or states.[8] Not counting the last category, at least ninety-

7. In 1688, the English went so far as to suspend the legislatures in all of New England, New York and the Jerseys. After 1689, this suspension was not palatable to the now-supreme Parliament, which wished to unite the colonies in the struggle against France to protect parliamentary government. It was also decided that governing the colonies without local legislatures would be, at best, inefficient. England had come to expect that most matters would be settled locally, and to construct a replacement bureaucracy, which might not produce similar results, would have been prohibitively expensive.

8. Another often-overlooked historical development was the recurring hope to unite the colonies under a general government. While probably not a complete list, these are the federation proposals of which I am aware.
1. New England Confederation of 1643
2. Acts and Orders of 1647
3. Commission of Council for Foreign Plantations, 1660
4. Royal Commission to Governor Andros to unite all of New England, New York, and the Jerseys, 1688
5. William Penn's Plan of Union, 1696

five important documents led up to the United States Constitution.
Popular government did not suddenly appear in 1787, or even in
1776, but was the result of a long historical evolution in political
institutions, based invariably upon some theory of consent. Consent is, therefore, the crucial concept for republican government in
America. But any examination of this connection requires a more
analytically coherent understanding of what the term *consent*
means.

The Meaning of Consent

Some argue that the concept of consent can be traced back to antiquity, and that during the Middle Ages consent described an essential part of the relationship between lord and vassal. For our purposes, it is perhaps more fruitful to begin with the judicious Richard
Hooker, for the simple reason that he first enunciated a fundamental ambiguity in the concept with which we still live. In the passage
cited below, which was written in the 1590s but not published until
1662, well after Hooker's death, he speaks of two forms of consent:
"whatsoever hath been after in free and voluntary manner condescended unto, whether by express consent, whereof positive laws

---

6. Report of the Board of Trade on union of New York with other colonies, 1696
7. D'Avenant Plan, 1698
8. A Virginian's Plan, in "An Essay on the Government of the English Plantations on the Continent of America," 1701
9. Livingston Plan, 1701
10. Earl of Stair's Proposals, 1721
11. Plan of the Lords of Trade, 1721
12. Daniel Cox's Plan, in "A Description of the English province of Carolina," 1722
13. Kennedy Plan, 1751
14. Franklin Plan, 1754
15. Richard Peter's Plan, 1754
16. Hutchinson's Plan, 1754
17. Plan of the Lords of Trade, 1754
18. Dr. Samuel Johnson's Plan, 1760
19. Galloway Plan, 1774
20. Franklin's Articles of Confederation, 1775
21. The Articles of Confederation, 1778
22. Drayton's Articles of Confederation, 1778
23. Webster's Sketches of American Policy, 1785
24. Randolph's Plan, 1787
25. Pinckney's Plan, 1787
26. The United States Constitution, 1787

My source for much of this list is Sydney George Fisher, *The Evolution of the Constitution of the United States* (Philadelphia: J. B. Lippincott, 1897), 9.

are witnesses, or else by silent allowance famously notified through custom reaching beyond the memory of man."[9] The first form, "express consent," implies a free, conscious, and deliberate decision. The second, "silent allowance," indicates acquiescence, which may not always be free, conscious, or deliberate. Hooker recognized that only occasionally are our actions the result of express consent. Most human activity conforms to the pathways set by earlier action, whether by ourselves or others—what we term custom or tradition.

It is worth contrasting John Locke and Hooker on this point since Locke's tacit consent might, at first glance, appear similar to Hooker's silent allowance, implying that Locke's open consent is the same as Hooker's express consent. As Locke was an important source of ideas during the era under study, any difference will prove instructive for later discussion. Locke recognized that even if one generation does sign a contract establishing a society and government, this can in no way bind future generations. He had to contend with the obvious fact that if there had been an historical contract, it was so distant in time as to be "beyond the memory of man." To solve the problem, he argued that when a man reaches adulthood, he can either stay where he is and thus give tacit consent to the ongoing society and government, or he can migrate to another place and thus express dissent. The only other possibility is to rebel; but, as Locke pointed out, the majority is the greater force and will invariably win, so that to rebel is basically futile.[10] On the other hand, if one is in the majority, there is by definition no need to rebel, since society and government will follow one's will as it follows the will of the majority. The only practicable alternatives, then, are migration or submission, and submission amounts to giving tacit consent. Perhaps migration was easier or less costly in Locke's England of 1669, but the only two avenues of dissent he offers are both quite forbidding. Furthermore, by American standards of the 1780s, tacit consent ends up being no consent at all.

9. Richard Hooker, *The Laws of Ecclesiastical Polity*, Book VIII of *The Works of Mr. Richard Hooker in Eight Books* (3 vols.; London; n.p., 1821), III, 242.

10. John Locke, *The Second Treatise of Government* (Indianapolis: Bobbs-Merrill Company, 1952), 55.

The problem runs deeper than this. Americans in the 1770s and 1780s were to wrestle with four levels of consent: societal consent, governmental consent, agency consent, and programmatic consent. Locke deals explicitly with only the first two, whereas the Americans developed institutions for all four. In so doing, they made important contributions toward a complete theory of consent.

Societal consent entails approval of an entire way of life, an entire social system. When men establish a society, they are in effect consenting to a culture, a set of social mores, a set of rules for carrying on social intercourse. Locke argued that there are two contracts. The first establishes a society and requires unanimity, for no individual is bound to a society to which he has not explicitly consented as an individual.[11]

Locke's second contract establishes a government through the action of a majority.[12] At this level, men agree to a set of procedural rules and institutions for collective decision making. Such is governmental consent. Once having given societal consent, says Locke, men are then bound by the majority when it comes to governmental consent. It is important to realize that, at this level, Locke did not see consent as resulting from individual action per se. Contrary to the common notion that men cannot be bound by decisions of a government to which they have not *personally* consented, Locke argued that governmental consent comes from the majority, not the individual. Consenting to live in the society has bound the individual to the will of the majority in future political action, and that is why migration—withdrawing individual consent from *society*—is the only real alternative. It must be emphasized that the Americans during the period under study generally understood consent as residing in the majority, though there was another tradition that tried to put certain matters beyond the power of the majority. Even though the rise of the Federalists brought a strong assumption of individualism into American political culture, they, as well as the American tradition before them, emphasized the majority rather than individuals as the source of consent.

Since the nineteenth-century, Americans have made individualism

11. *Ibid.*
12. *Ibid.*

a part of their core ideology. Therefore it is important that we recognize the relative weakness of this value during our entire history up until then. The attribution of individual rights to the Constitution is largely a *post hoc* one, as our judicial and political theory has developed over the last 170 years.[13] In part, it has created confusion in our theory of consent since, in practical terms, the requirement that every individual consent to a government or law is an impossibility. Certainly it was not part of the generally understood meaning of consent during the 1770s and 1780s. The manner and extent to which so-called individual rights were alienable at that time will be discussed more fully in Chapter 3 herein. The matter is important enough, however, to cite two typical constitutional provisions concerning the hallowed right to property.

> Art. II: That private property ought to be subservient to public uses, when necessity requires it; nevertheless, whenever any particular man's property is taken for the use of the public, the owner ought to receive an equivalent in money. (1777, Vermont)

> Art. X: Each individual of the society has a right to be protected by it in the enjoyment of his life, liberty and property, *according to the standing laws* ... no part of the property of an individual can, with justice, be taken from him, or applied to public uses, without his own consent, *or that of the representative body of the people.* In fine, the people of this commonwealth are not controllable by any other laws than those to which their constitutional representative body have given consent. And whenever the public exigencies require that the property of any individual should be appropriated to public uses, he shall receive a reasonable compensation therefore. (emphasis added; 1780, Massachusetts)

Such provisions are found in a majority of the first eighteen constitutions, regardless of how liberal or conservative they are in other aspects. As John Locke would have it, Americans apparently delivered themselves individually through the first contract to be bound by the majority on the second.

In a real sense, the nature of the second agreement, which estab-

---

13. For an incisive critique of the attribution of individual natural rights to the 1770s, see Willmoore Kendall and George W. Carey, *The Basic Symbols of the American Political Tradition* (Baton Rouge: Louisiana State University Press, 1970).

lishes government, is closely allied with the first, because the kind of political system erected will tend to reflect social and cultural presuppositions. It is probably for this reason that Locke shied away from openly advocating a particular form of government. The majority could establish any form it wished. While his readers in seventeenth-century England might naturally have imagined some type of monarchy with a powerful Parliament, another people with a different set of suppositions might have preferred other institutional arrangements without impairing Locke's theory.

Agency consent refers to the initial approval for those who will be the primary actors in the decision-making institutions established by governmental consent—the elected or appointed agents.[14] It involves the making of collective decisions by a specialized group of people rather than by the entire populace directly. Locke can be read to mean that the second contract simultaneously designates the government and the governing agents, so that when we speak of a government falling, it refers both to turning the agents out of office and to reordering the institutions of government simultaneously. Such a tortured interpretation creates more problems than it solves, and it is certain that neither the English, once they had true parliamentary government after the Glorious Revolution of 1688, nor the Americans ever practiced such an interpretation.

Programmatic consent refers to permission for specific pieces of legislation. Locke is almost completely silent here, although a straightforward inference can be drawn to the effect that until government breaks the contract by threatening our lives or our property, we will acquiesce to all its actions. By failing either to emigrate or to rebel when a bill is passed, we are giving tacit consent to the legislation. Locke does not create a theory of consent so much as he establishes a theory of dissent. That is, he emphasizes the conditions under which dissent is permissible rather than indicates the conditions for giving positive programmatic consent.

14. It needs to be emphasized that agency consent is not a simple matter. As noted earlier, agency consent under the traditional Whig notion meant only consent for a representative to hold office and do his best for the community. This is contrary to our idea today, which, whether tenable or not, implies something more, consent for the agent to pursue certain policies as he outlines them during the election campaign.

Returning to Richard Hooker, it is now clear that his notion of consent is more positive and more complete. He speaks of express consent producing "positive laws." Consent, for Hooker, requires positive action instead of acquiescence, and it implies that every piece of legislation requires specific consent. Even "custom reaching beyond the memory of man" is "condescended unto" only in a free and voluntary manner. Furthermore, Hooker speaks of "silent allowance" as being appropriate solely for custom, which implies that only the equivalent of Locke's first contract establishing society can be so approved. Locke, however, permits tacit consent for *both* contracts—that establishing society as well as that establishing government. Locke does not seriously consider the possibility of a society dissolving, though individual members may occasionally leave it. Therefore, for both Locke and Hooker, the important matter is consent for government. Hooker's position might be termed the "direct sense" of consent, whereas Locke's might be termed the "indirect sense." Generally speaking, the direct sense argues that positive permission constitutes consent, whereas the indirect sense holds that acquiescence is sufficient. The direct sense also implies a direct interaction between the two agents, whereas in Locke's sense, consent can be given without the actors ever seeing each other.

Indirect Consent involves always acting in a manner that the doer knows, or is assumed to know, will not prevent another from acting. As noted before, this is really a theory of dissent, since simply staying out of the way constitutes consent; and the alternatives are to attempt to block another's action or to emigrate and hence prevent the other's action from affecting one. *Direct Consent* exists whenever the right of one man to act in a certain way is conditional upon another man's having expressed the wish that he act that way.[15] In this case, there is a direct link between the two actors in the form of explicit permission given before action can take place. One could probably come up with complicated definitions representing various degrees between these two definitions, as well as more extreme versions, but it will be sufficient to distinguish

15. John Plamenatz, *Consent, Freedom, and Political Obligation*, 4.

between a theory that tends to rely upon institutions of *dissent* amounting to indirect consent and a theory that tends to rely upon institutions requiring direct, positive permission.[16]

Consent and Definitions of Republic

To speak of popular sovereignty is to place ultimate authority in the people. There are a variety of ways in which sovereignty may be expressed. It may be immediate in the sense that the people make the laws themselves, or mediated through representatives who are subject to election and recall; it may be ultimate in the sense that the people have a negative or veto over legislation, or it may be something much less dramatic. In short, popular sovereignty covers a multitude of institutional possibilities. In each case, however, popular sovereignty assumes the existence of some form of popular consent, and it is for this reason that every definition of republican government implies a theory of consent.

Consider, for example, John Adams' definition of republican government, which is representative of traditional Whig political theory. "Whenever I use the word *republic* with approbation, I mean a government in which the people have collectively, or by representation, an essential share in sovereignty." Adams sees the people as sharing sovereignty. Sharing with whom? How can consent be derived if not from the people? The answer, of course, is property,

---

16. For an excellent summary of the extremely diverse definitions that have been advanced for consent, see P. H. Partridge, *Consent and Consensus*, especially 32–36. The distinction will be one of *tendency*. As Partridge establishes, all definitions of consent thus far advanced have inherent ambiguities. The two definitions advanced here are relatively close in the kinds of conforming behavior they describe, that is, vis-à-vis most other definitions advanced. On the other hand, each definition is quite broad, and the lack of precision produces problems if we attempt to press their meaning in too rigorous a fashion. For example, the definition labeled *direct consent* is too limited in some respects. If we were to attempt to live by its strictures, then agency consent through elections would permit nothing more than for a legislator to move into his office and walk on the floor of the legislative chamber. Before he could speak, he would need further consent from his constituents. The definition labeled *indirect consent*, conversely, is too broad. A custodian at a university could rightly conclude that, under this definition, his ability to lock a professor's classroom, coupled with his decision not to do so, constitutes his consenting to the professor's teaching a course. In short, neither definition is advanced as philosophically coherent in a rigorous sense, or definitionally precise. Rather, they are general statements denoting poles of action that are preferred by whoever advances a theory of consent. Thus, the best we can do is indicate the tendency of any definition to lean in one direction or the other, and make a judgment about the relative strengths of their directness.

but property in a special sense, because the people at large also own property in order to have the right to express or withhold consent. *Property*, in Whig thought, really referred to wealth, to people holding considerable property. *People*, on the other hand, referred to those holding relatively small portions of land, enough to run a household in comfort, but not enough to significantly affect commerce or initiate projects requiring a concentration of wealth.[17] Of course, the Whigs did not believe that the interests of the many conflicted with the interests of the wealthy few. If the investments of the wealthy prospered, then the economy was healthy and everyone in the community prospered—an early version of "what's good for General Motors is good for the country." In this definition of republican government, whether popular consent was direct or indirect, it was not completely sovereign. Popular consent also tended to be indirect and incomplete under traditional Whig institutions. This can be illustrated by considering Samuel Adams' definition (see p. 17 herein), which is representative of radical Whig theory.

The radical Whigs placed sovereignty completely in the people, and in doing so carried the traditional Whig assumption of a homogeneous community to its logical conclusion. If the community does, in fact, have a community of interests, then there is no need to protect property by giving men of wealth a special role in consent giving. What may not be immediately apparent is that the content or meaning of sovereignty has been expanded.

As mentioned earlier, the concept of sovereignty was attached to lawmaking. Whoever made the laws was sovereign. Sovereignty, thus understood, implied only programmatic consent. If the people shared sovereignty through representatives, then it meant direct consent for the governmental agents, but only indirect program-

17. The classic statement of this Whig view is to be found in the Essex Result (1778). Written by citizens of Essex County in objection to the proposed 1778 Massachusetts Constitution (which was turned down by the people), the document continually stresses equality when discussing the lower house. This emphasis on equality and majority rule is so strong that at first the reader might think he has run across a radical Whig document. However, in discussing the upper house, the Essex Result argues that it does and should represent the "majority of property." In this fashion, every bill passed has the consent of the majority of people (from the lower house) and a majority of property (or those holding it) from the upper house. The Essex Result can most easily be found in Oscar Handlin and Mary F. Handlin (eds.), *The Popular Sources of Political Authority* (Cambridge, Mass.: Harvard Univerity Press, 1966), 324–65.

matic consent. At best it also constituted only indirect societal and governmental consent because there was little popular control over constitution writing or shifts in public morality. The radical Whig definition of republican government, however, gave the people direct consent over constitutional changes, and therefore provided for direct societal and governmental consent. It also explicitly mentions direct agency consent for legislative, judicial, and executive agents, although in the latter two cases, it is only more or less direct. Not apparent from the definition is another assumption, and that is the manner in which programmatic consent is given. True, there were to be representatives, but they were to be brought under increasing pressures from the people to respond directly to their demands, rather than to debate dispassionately what was best for the entire community. The radical Whigs were to press for as direct a form of consent as was possible under a representative form of government and to apply the directness to all four types of consent. Contrary to Locke, who saw direct consent as being expressed only at those rare moments when government was either violently overthrown or peacefully dissolved, the radical Whigs viewed consent as an everyday process, one in which the people could and did intervene in every phase of government.[18] The idea of sovereignty entailed much more for them than it did from the simple lawmaking perspective of the traditional Whigs.[19]

Thomas Jefferson's definition ("a government by its citizens in mass, acting directly, according to rules established by the majority") does away with representatives and makes consent completely direct in every respect, so that agency consent becomes irrelevant. Never a serious proposal as far as institution building was concerned, it nevertheless served as an ideal against which to measure the degree of directness achieved through institutions based on Samuel Adams' definition.

Sherman's and Madison's two representative Federalist defini-

18. Bailyn, *Ideological Origins*, 172–73.
19. The radical Whigs were actually pursuing a formula older than that sought by what I term the traditional Whigs. See Caroline Robbins' superb book *The Eighteenth Century Commonwealthman* (Cambridge, Mass.: Harvard University Press, 1959). See especially 338–39 and 364–74.

tions of republican government (see p. 21, herein), showed a new shift in consent theory. They both retained the people as the ultimate source of power, but the word *sovereign* disappeared. Merely omitting the word connoted the removal of ultimate power to a distance —a rejection of the requirement of immediate, overwhelming control. It also eliminated the connotation of the people being involved in lawmaking. Many Federalists still spoke of popular sovereignty, but their tendency was to make the connection more tenuous rather than less complete in scope, as the traditional Whigs had been inclined to do. Madison explicitly allowed for indirect as well as direct consent. A clear example was his permitting indirect agency consent, thus making programmatic consent less direct. Sherman, on the other hand, merely listed the primary institutions constructed by the Federalists without characterizing them, although the Federalist papers clearly spelled out the manner in which the institutions Sherman mentions were based upon the principles Madison elucidates. In both cases, it is noteworthy that the key requirement was a minimal one. In Sherman's definition, only hereditary oligarchy, or aristocracy, was excluded, whereas Madison's definition ruled out nonhereditary oligarchy as well—a slight improvement. The people rule by consent, but less directly than in the radical Whig formulation.

To point out that Federalists lacked confidence in direct consent is not to condemn them. In *The Federalist* 1, Hamilton argues that the experiment in government they were conducting was the replacement of government by force and accident with government based on reflection and choice. Today we are inclined to view force as the tool of the few, but the Federalists had reason to conclude that force could also be the tool of the many. John Locke explicitly called the majority the "greater force" in society, and the Federalists may well have concluded that a self-guiding republic must be based on the majority but not on the force of the majority.

We have, then, three perspectives on republican government— traditional Whig, radical Whig, and Federalist—each with its corresponding view of consent. There were other perspectives as well, but these three, or slight variations of them, were most prominent; between 1776 and 1789, the dominant view in America shifted from the first to the second and finally to the third (Federalist) position. Because there were thousands of pamphlets, letters, sermons, and documents written during the period, an analysis of republican governments and theories of consent is simplified through the study of state constitutions. All thirteen states claimed to be republics, and each had written at least one constitution by 1789. Some wrote two or three constitutions, which provides an easy way to separate widely held ideas from those that were brilliant yet peripheral to ongoing politics. Each constitution "freezes" the balance of forces at that particular time and place, and in effect becomes a written snapshot of the dominant political theory. The shifts in political thought during the era are reflected in the provisions and institutions written into state constitutions. An in-depth analysis of the early state constitutions taken as a whole has not been attempted in many years, and the earlier attempts were narrow in approach and lacked the insights and data compiled in the resurgence of historical analysis since the early 1960s. Concentrating on the state constitutions is probably as good a tactic as any to avoid being selective, and it is particularly useful for bringing order to the myriad of ideas that Americans were generating at that time.

There will be no attempt to argue that those writing constitutions between 1776 and 1789 were consciously developing a theory of consent. Any student of the period recognizes the extent to which institutions and theories were responses to experiences and events, rather than logical imperatives. My approach will be to abstract trends and connections from the constitutions, using internal evidence as well as the writing surrounding these documents, to uncover the assumptions that underlie thinking during the period and to link these assumptions coherently.

The men who wrote constitutions in America between 1776 and 1789 made three significant contributions to consent theory. First, they developed institutions for all four levels of consent. Second, they moved from a relatively indirect kind of consent to a more direct one for every level. Third, they tried to develop coherence by making all four levels approximately equal in directness. They failed with respect to programmatic consent, partly because one key institution, the council of censors, failed to catch on, and also because the Federalists downgraded consent-giving institutions somewhat as a result of perceived political instability. The Federalists made consent less direct with respect to some institutions but not all, with the result that the Constitution does not embody a coherent doctrine of consent. Rather, it blends the Whig and Federalist perspectives. Nevertheless, this blend resulted in a form of consent much more active and direct than had been experienced before by English-speaking people.

> Consent was not in itself a very active concept [in English political theory]. In Harrington's Oceana, the common people were to be entitled at the best to be consulted and to render their affirmative or negative vote to propositions handed down from above; while Locke's version was little more than a concrete statement of a legal fiction. William Penn had intended to put the Harrington idea into practice in his province, but was surprised by the independence of his people. Colonists . . . showed a capacity for participating in local government; from their activity, the vague ideas about the meaning and expression of consent that could be read in the Old Whig and the more orthodox books, began to take on a slightly more positive meaning. The onset of the Revolution itself helped advance and define that meaning, to make of consent an act of participation rather than an act of submission.[20]

Thus, the Americans of that period worked their way through to a relatively coherent and sophisticated theory of consent, but failed to exploit completely or retain the implications of their elaboration. Even with this failure, their contributions still represent a high point in the history of consent theory.

The General Use of Consent In Early State Constitutions

Between January 1, 1776, and the adoption of the Constitution in 1789, the original thirteen states plus Vermont wrote and adopted a total of eighteen constitutions. Between the adoption of the Constitution and 1800, these same states wrote seven more constitutions and were joined by Kentucky in 1792 and Tennessee in 1796 with

20. J. R. Pole, *Political Representation in England and the Origins of the American Republic* (Berkeley: University of California Press, 1971), 524.

their maiden constitutions.[21] During the last quarter of the eighteenth century, then, America wrote and adopted a total of twenty-eight constitutions. Others were written, debated extensively, and then rejected. It was an extraordinary period of constitution writing. The first eighteen documents contain the essential developments leading from Whig to Federalist political theory, although a comparison with those written between 1789 and 1798 will prove instructive.

The first eighteen constitutions can be divided into two "waves" of constitution writing. The first wave took place within a year after the writing of the Declaration of Independence. With the war swirling around them, Americans had a pressing need for effective government to prosecute hostilities and little time to debate the niceties of political theory. Consequently, the first state constitutions were little different theoretically from their respective colonial charters, to which they bore a strong resemblance. The only major change was a universal gutting of the executive power, since the executive had been the representative of the crown under the charters. Indeed, Rhode Island and Connecticut essentially readopted their colonial charters from the 1660s, and Massachusetts did not bother going through the formalities, being content to live under the 1725 charter as if nothing had changed. The only exceptions to the general trend were Pennsylvania and Vermont. Vermont was not yet recognized as an independent entity and would not be until 1791. Lacking a colonial charter of their own and anxious to distinguish Vermont from neighboring states claiming various portions of what was to become part of the new state, Vermont constitution writers closely copied the Pennsylvania Constitution of 1776. The Pennsylvania Constitution will be examined much more closely herein, as it represents an important development in consent theory; but for now it is sufficient to note that it departed somewhat from colonial practice during the first wave, and that Vermont had time to engage in the kind of deliberate constitution making that would be characteristic of the second wave.

21. Because there are problems of comparability given the absence of a lengthy political history by 1789, I will largely ignore the Kentucky and Tennessee constitutions in this analysis.

The first constitution in the second wave was the New York Constitution of 1777.[22] New York was heavily occupied by the British forces early in the war, and one consequence was that those writing the state constitution were kept constantly on the move, meeting whenever and wherever they could. Ironically, this seems to have given them more time to think matters through, for their constitution was the first to exemplify a number of trends that were to become common during the second wave of constitution making. Most notably, they began the resurrection of the executive branch, putting it in harness with the legislature in a manner we find familiar today.

There was increased concern for popular control over the process of constitution making. The first half-dozen state constitutions had been written and ratified by the state legislatures; the 1776 Constitution of Delaware was the first one drafted by a convention elected expressly for that purpose. In New York, likewise, the state legislature felt that "the right of framing, creating or new modeling civil government, is, and ought to be in the people . . . That doubts have arisen, whether this Congress are invested with sufficient power and authority to frame and institute such new form of internal government and police." A body elected with such express authority framed the New York Constitution, and such practice became standard. It was not until the Massachusetts Constitution of 1780, however, that a document was written by a special convention *and* submitted to the people for ratification.

It is interesting to observe how frequently *consent* was used in the first eighteen constitutions. An initial count shows the word being used ninety-three times in these documents, for an average of 5.2 times per constitution. The frequency of the term varies, as does the context. Generally speaking, it becomes much more common during the second wave of constitution making, as is evident from Table 1. *Consent* is used fifty-seven times in the six constitutions of the second wave, for an average of 9.5 mentions per document,

22. While the 1777 New York and 1777 Vermont constitutions are the first for these two states, historians generally consider them the first in the second wave. *Cf.* Gordon S. Wood, *The Creation of the American Republic, 1776–1787* (Chapel Hill: University of North Carolina Press, 1969), 433.

whereas the first twelve constitutions mention the word only thirty-six times, for an average of 3.0 mentions per document. If frequency of use means anything, then framers during the second wave were much more concerned with the idea than those during the first wave. The use of the word falls off during the third wave of constitution writing in the 1790s when the Federalists brought some state constitutions more in line with their principles. The seven third wave constitutions use *consent* thirty-four times, for an average of 4.9 mentions per document. Again, if anything can be made of such numbers, it would appear that the Federalists displayed a more moderate attachment to the concept than the radical Whigs of the late 1770s and 1780s. These frequency comparisons are not presented because they themselves prove anything, but because they constitute part of the evidence, are suggestive, and nicely summarize what, in fact, did occur.

Frequently, those who wrote constitutions used the words *assent* and *concur* to describe a relationship similar to that described by *consent*. In a few instances, the context implies that they were being used as a stylistic alternative for *consent*, but in other contexts, something a little different is implied. Usually alternative words were used to describe the relationship between the two legislative houses or between the executive and the upper house. Almost never were they used to describe the relationship between citizens and government, or in bills of rights. The context of their usage is also typically one in which action has already occurred and some sort of ratification is required.

The term *consent*, for a while, came more and more to mean a positive form of control, as exemplified in the definition of direct consent. *Concur* and *assent* often seem to imply something closer to what we defined as indirect consent. Such a distinction in the use of words can never be proved and, in fact, can easily be challenged, since the state constitutions of that era often were as susceptible to multiple interpretations as our federal Constitution. Nevertheless, an examination of the use of these words reveals an interesting pattern. *Assent* was used about equally in the early, middle, and late documents, but *concur*, used only once or twice in the early constitutions, becomes prominent in the third wave of constitution making, in which it is used twenty-one times, versus five times for *assent*. Coupled with this pattern, the tendency of these two words to be used in describing relationships within and between governmental

Table 1
THE FREQUENCY OF *CONSENT* IN STATE CONSTITUTIONS

Constitution	No. of Times Consent *Used*	No. of Times Assent *or* Concur	Combined Usage
1. 1725 Mass.	1	3	4
2. 1776 N.H.	1	1	2
3. 1776 S.C.	5	1	6
4. 1776 Va.	5	1	6
5. 1776 N.J.	1	1	2
6. 1776 Md.	6	4	10
7. 1776 Del.	2	0	2
8. 1776 R.I.	2	0	2
9. 1776 Conn.	0	0	0
10. 1776 Pa.	6	2	8
11. 1776 N.C.	3	0	3
12. 1777 Ga.	4	0	4
Subtotals:	36	13	49
Averages:	3.0	1.1	4.1
13. 1777 N.Y.	9	5	14
14. 1777 Vt.	6	2	8
15. 1778 S.C.	10	4	14
16. 1780 Mass.	13	3	16
17. 1784 N.H.	12	4	16
18. 1786 Vt.	7	2	9
Subtotals:	57	20	77
Averages:	9.5	3.3	12.8
19. 1789 Ga.	0	2	2
20. 1790 S.C.	1	3	4
21. 1790 Pa.	5	2	7
22. 1792 Del.	7	8	15
23. 1792 N.H.	12	3	15
24. 1793 Vt.	4	3	7
25. 1798 Ga.	5	5	10
Subtotals:	34	26	60
Averages:	4.9	3.7	8.6
Overall Totals:	127	59	186
Averages:	5.0	2.4	7.4

institutions implies that such relationships became somewhat more important during the second wave than during the first, and almost as important as consent relationships in the third wave of constitution writing. In fact, the Federalists were very concerned with such things as checks and balances and the relationships between the two houses and between the legislature and the executive. The increase in use of *concur* especially reflects this preoccupation. Any student of the Federalist papers will remember the concern of the authors over unbridled majorities and their related concern for institutional complexity to impede factions from taking over government. The shift from the radical Whig view that public policy accurately reflected popular will to the Federalist emphasis on downgrading that relationship through the interposition of balances and mutually interdependent institutions is indirectly summarized in Table 1. It is worth pointing out that during the second wave, the use of the alternative words is found about as often in each constitution as in the more Federalist-influenced documents of the third wave. The major difference is the substantial decline in the use of *consent* itself during the third wave.

The increased frequency of the use of the word *consent* during the second wave represents not only greater interest in the concept but also a more diverse usage. In the first twelve constitutions, consent is often mentioned in the context of a people or king establishing the body politic. At best, this represents an appreciation of what was earlier termed "societal consent," and perhaps "governmental consent" as well. Later constitutions speak of consent being given by and through a variety of actors. There is also a greater diversity in terms of what constitutes giving consent, to whom it is given, and the range of issues covered. All of these topics will be examined in depth later, but the reader may refer to Table 2, in which a number of passages dealing with consent indicate the variety in form and content.

It must be emphasized that, although all the examples in Table 2

Table 2
EXAMPLES OF PASSAGES GIVING CONSENT

The following examples cover the entire range of alternatives found in the first twenty-five state constitutions with respect to who may give consent.

1. The people at large—1792, Delaware preamble
   "Political society is derived from the people, and established with their consent."
2. The legislature—1776, Maryland, Article XXVI
   "That standing armies are dangerous to liberty and ought not be raised or kept up, without the consent of the Legislature."
3. Both of the above—1784, New Hampshire, Article XXVIII
   "No subsidy, charge, tax, impost or duty shall be established . . . without the consent of the people or their representatives."
4. An individual citizen—1780, Massachusetts, Article XXVII
   "In time of peace, no soldier ought to be quartered in any house without the consent of the owner."
5. Individual or legislature—1784, New Hampshire, Article XII
   "But no part of a man's property shall be taken from him . . . without his own consent, or that of the legislative body of the people."
6. A house of the legislature—1798, Georgia, section 21
   "Neither house . . . shall, without the consent of the other, adjourn for more than three days."
7. The executive council—1780, Massachusetts, Section X
   "All judicial officers . . . shall be nominated and appointed by the governor, by and with the advice and consent of the council."
8. An individual legislator—1777, Georgia, Section XXVI
   "Every councilor, being present, shall have power of entering his protest against any measures in council he has not consented to."
9. Majority of people in a specific location—1780, Massachusetts, First Amendment
   "No such [local] government shall be erected . . . unless it be with the consent, and on the application of a majority of the inhabitants of such town."
10. A jury—1776, Virginia, Section 8, Bill of Rights
   "To a speedy trial by an impartial jury of twelve men of his vicinage, without whose unanimous consent he cannot be found guilty."

Frequency of Usage of *Consent* in Each Format*

Example	Frequency in first wave	Frequency in second wave	Frequency in third wave	Total usage
1	8	7	4	19
2	6	9	7	22
3	0	2	1	3
4	2	1	3	6
5	3	9	8	20
6	2	6	2	10
7	5	15	7	27
8	7	4	1	12
9	0	2	0	2
10	3	2	1	6

* Excludes use of *concur*, etc.

are found in the state constitutions, some are much more common than others. For instance, item 4, wherein an individual citizen may give or withhold consent, is a rarity. In the vast majority of cases before 1789, bills of rights used the format exemplified in items 2 or 5.[23] That is, by far the most common format permits rights to be withdrawn or modified by the legislature acting in the name of the majority. This will come as a surprise to most Americans who are used to the "inalienable rights" formulation, because it contrasts strongly with the inability of Congress to pass legislation contrary to the Bill of Rights. We must remember that the first state constitutions were Whig documents, whether traditional or radical, and thus they assumed the rights of the community to be generally superior to the rights of the individual. Or, as the classic Whig document, the Essex Result, puts it: "All men are born equally free. The rights they possess at their births are equal, and of the same kind. Some of those rights are alienable, and may be parted with for an equivalent. Others are inalienable and inherent, and of that importance, that no equivalent can be received in exchange."[24] The document goes on to state that the only rights that are inalienable are those for which we are accountable to our Creator, or rights of conscience. Since these cannot be given up, then a constitutional provision which permits the legislature, that is, the majority, to affect them is not an inalienable right. The first state constitutions often permitted the legislature to confiscate property, limit speech, require a religious test for office, negate trial by jury, and affect just about every other right we today consider inalienable. In short, the Whigs considered rights alienable "if the good of the whole requires it." What, then, were the inalienable rights? That is never made clear in any list, but the list, if it had existed, would have been exceedingly

23. The numbers themselves can be misleading. First, the number of cases is so small that comparisons between usages cannot be made except in a very general way. Furthermore, there are shifts in usage that this table cannot show. For example, after 1789, the total usage of items 2 and 5 is reduced; yet this still represents a significant number of rights that the legislature can alienate. In fact, usage 2 during the third wave, with only one exception, is no longer employed with respect to rights but in other contexts, so that the decline in alienable rights is greater than the numbers alone would indicate. There can be no doubt that usage 4, unalienable individual rights, is rare, being used only three times out of ninety-three usages in the first two waves.

24. Handlin and Handlin (eds.), *Popular Sources of Political Authority*, 330.

short by our standards.[25] Consent, then, although derived from individuals is not given by individuals.

> If a fundamental principle on which each individual enters into society is, that he shall be bound by no laws but those to which he has consented, he cannot be considered as consenting to any law enacted by a minority: for he parts with the power of controlling his natural rights, only when the good of the whole requires it; and of this there can be but one absolute judge in the State. If the minority can assume the right of judging, there may then be two judges; for however large the minority may be, there must be another body still larger, who have the same claim, if not a better, to the right of absolute determination.[26]

Consent is given by the majority. This view is clearly reflected in the predominance of formulations 2 and 5 over formulation 4 in the first eighteen constitutions.

Still, the list of rights in bills of rights was to become longer as 1789 approached, and additional rights would be removed from legislative control. There would also be a strengthening in the words of prohibition. This trend, among others, would reflect an erosion in the Whig theory of politics, and the gradual rise of the Federalist concern for restraining the majority, whether through institutions of delay or outright restrictions on its activity. Emphasis upon

25. It is clear from the constitutions that "rights of conscience" referred primarily to religious beliefs. At least twelve of them clearly identify rights of conscience with religion, and put the right to worship as one pleases beyond the control of the legislature. Of course, this freedom specifically is granted only to Protestants. Kendall and Carey argue that the right to representative self-government was part of the list (see *Basic Symbols of the American Political Tradition*, 138). The right to trial by jury could probably be added to the list, as it was usually protected with strong language that did not permit legislative interference. The right to trial by jury, however, like the right to worship freely, was somewhat restricted by our standards. For example, the Maryland Constitution of 1776 explicitly permits a man to give evidence against himself if the legislature so deems it (Art. XX). Anything beyond this short list of inalienable rights is, at best, controversial. Leonard W. Levy in his *Legacy of Suppression* (Cambridge, Mass.: Harvard University Press, 1960) demonstrates that not only was freedom of speech and press not part of any list before 1789, it was the intent of the founders of the republic, even after the Bill of Rights was written, that speaking ill of the government or its agents should be illegal. The right to property, mentioned in virtually every constitution, was also clearly alienable, for almost without exception every mention of the right includes the claim that the legislature may alienate property. For now it is sufficient that the reader understand that the list of inalienable rights between 1776 and 1789 was very short, and the content of those rights on the list was quite restricted vis-à-vis our present understanding and political practice.

26. Handlin and Handlin (eds.), *Popular Sources of Political Authority*, 331.

individual rights would come only with the decline of the radical Whigs.

Items 6, 7, and 8 in Table 2 are also quite common and exemplify the kinds of situations in which *concur* tended to replace *consent* in later constitutions, explaining the apparent decline in the third wave. Use of the word *consent* in this context indicates how broadly Americans had come to apply it, and demonstrates again that the concept was not tied to individuals but was associated with some kind of majority, whether in society or in the legislature.

The general use of *consent* in the early state constitutions indicates a variety in form and content. What is important is that all four levels of consent defined earlier, including agency consent and programmatic consent, are institutionalized in these documents. Only four or five constitutions come reasonably close to being comprehensive in themselves, and it is significant that all but one are found in the second wave of constitutions.

The specific passages in which *consent* is used constitute a major part of the evidence in the analysis to follow. In addition, there are institutions that are described without using the word but that are nonetheless relevant. For example, there is no use of the word in any discussion of elections, even though elections were generally considered to be consent-giving situations. Thus, whenever a constitutional provision establishes a relationship in which one actor's ability to act is dependent upon another actor's actions, it is a candidate for consideration as a consent-giving institution.

3

Societal and Governmental Consent

Culture and Politics

The distinction between societal consent and governmental consent is usually overlooked simply because it is difficult to detect. There is little problem distinguishing theoretically between agreement to establish a society and agreement to form a government for the regulation of that society. John Locke, for example, required unanimity for the first contract but allowed majority rule to suffice for the second, thereby demonstrating that the difference was no small one in its theoretical implications. In a certain sense, the distinction can be made observationally as well. Anthropologists have established that reasonably complex societies can exist without formal governmental institutions, giving a certain veracity to the theories of Locke and others.[1] The difficulty lies in determining when, if ever, we are consenting to social or cultural rules, as opposed to political ones. Confusion on this matter had its genesis in modern definitions of politics, which are so broad as to exclude very few activities. A brief digression is in order here to appreciate the distinction between societal and governmental consent.

An essential aspect of the classical view of politics was the distinction between the public realm and the realm of the household.[2] The public realm was the political arena where men debated and made decisions concerning the good life. The household did not

---

1. In the anthropological literature two particularly lucid works are Max Gluckman, *Custom and Conflict in Africa* (New York: Barnes and Noble, 1956); and Morton H. Fried, *The Evolution of Political Society* (New York: Random House, 1967).

2. See Hannah Arendt, *On the Human Condition* (Chicago: University of Chicago Press, 1958).

refer to the private realm, but to the nonpolitical, which included such things as economic matters, normal social intercourse, and family life. In brief, the public realm, and thus politics, was quite restricted in scope because all those activities associated with securing the necessities of life were outside the public realm. This aspect of classical politics was accepted until relatively recent times. In fact, its replacement by a broader view of politics is part of what characterizes modern political theory.

Students of politics today are inclined to define their subject matter without differentiating between the public and the household. For example, "the authoritative allocation of value," "power processes and relationships," "conflict processes," and "collective decision making" all share the characteristic of including many phenomena that are not directly related to government. R. D. Laing has written a book, *The Politics of the Family*, which illustrates how our broad definitions could be extended easily to encompass family relationships.[3] Most current definitions do not and cannot separate political matters from social or cultural ones.

A society is a group of human beings sharing a self-sufficient system of action that is capable of existing longer than the lifespan of an individual. Social rules are those concerned with survival of the group and result in structured patterns of interaction conducive toward that end. In the classical political view, social matters would be outside the political realm because they are concerned with mere survival, the necessities. Culture may be defined as the totality of conventional behavioral responses acquired primarily through symbolic learning.[4] As such, culture provides the "glue" for creating structured patterns of interaction, because symbols provide meaning to objects, acts, and events, and thereby create shared motivations.[5]

If societies can exist without formal political institutions, they cannot exist without a culture, a shared set of symbols providing meaning. In a certain sense, culture functions as the political system

3. R. D. Laing, *The Politics of the Family* (New York: Random House, 1969).
4. Definitions are based on ones by Fried, *Evolution of Political Society*, 8, 7.
5. For a thorough discussion see Leslie A. White with Beth Dillingham, *The Concept of Culture* (Minneapolis; Burgess, 1973).

in traditional societies by providing ready-made answers to collective problems. Societies with formal political institutions—institutions specializing in collective decision making—cannot do without culture, either. The patterns of political interaction are given meaning by a set of symbols we call the "political culture," and highly developed political systems often rationalize their symbol system into more or less deductive theories which, when widely held, are usually termed "ideologies."[6]

One important aspect of a political culture is the scope of governmental activity it supports. There is a natural tendency for the political culture and the general culture to have many congruencies, but this does not necessarily lead to politics involving more than the relatively small set of symbols contained in the political culture. Some political cultures support government involvement in all symbolic matters. Such political systems are in effect totalitarian, since politics would regulate the total range of social activity in minute detail. It is perfectly possible for a political system to be run by a dictator who operates within a narrow range of matters as defined by the political culture, and thus not be totalitarian. By the same token it is possible for a popular government to be totalitarian if the political culture supports a wide scope of activity. In this respect, the difference between totalitarian and popular governments lies in the probability of arbitrariness. If a people (a majority of them) agrees to shift from applying the death penalty to a wide variety of offenses, including sodomy, horse theft, and blasphemy, to no death penalty at all, the probability that such a change in cultural mores is frivolous or will engender serious opposition because it is at odds with the fundamental beliefs of many people is far less than if the shift were imposed by a solitary ruler. If such changes require an extraordinary majority, the probability is reduced even further. Presumably, with popular consent, the shift in cultural mores has already taken place, so that the political decision is mostly a ratification of an accomplished fact.

6. There is precious little written on the relationship of politics to culture. One interesting exception is H. L. Nieburg, *Culture Storm: Politics and the Ritual Order* (New York: St. Martin's Press, 1973). Another, somewhat oblique approach is Murray Edelman, *Politics as Symbolic Action* (Chicago: Markham, 1972).

Recent scholarship has concluded that during the Middle Ages three cultures existed side by side throughout Europe: the peasant culture, the middle-class town culture, and the aristocratic or "high" culture.[7] While the peoples in these cultures were interdependent, the cultural borders were quite distinct and carefully maintained. Politics often involved the aristocracy's making decisions that directly affected only them. There was little or no interest in enforcing society-wide sociocultural rules. The advent of popular consent is associated with the rise of the middle class in power, numbers, and wealth. The attachment of the middle class to institutions of popular consent was instrumental in this class's being included in political decision making and eventually becoming politically dominant. Their attachment to political equality—applying laws in the same fashion to all members of society—was also essential if they were to break down the institutions of aristocratic privilege. The rise of the middle class brought popular consent, but it also introduced a wider definition of politics. This definition included collective decisions about sociocultural norms, for the struggle against aristocratic-based monarchies was as much a battle of middle-class culture against aristocratic culture as it was a matter of political dominance. In France, the shift from medieval institutions to modern ones was rapid, and the destruction of aristocratic privilege was almost equally sudden. In England, the process was characteristically slow and evolutionary; the gradual rise of popular consent was matched by an equally slow decline in aristocratic privilege. The current attempt in England to dismantle the elite subsystem of schools is an attack on what is perceived to be the last bastion of privilege.

America was overwhelmingly middle class from the beginning. Not only with respect to economic conditions, but also in attitudes, Americans consistently exhibited those political traits associated with the bourgeoisie, and among these traits was the inclination to legislate on cultural matters. If this tendency produced religious wars in Europe, the fact that America was overwhelmingly Protestant resulted in a less-bloody solution—community exclusiveness.

7. The discussion immediately following is based upon Robert T. Anderson, *Traditional Europe: A Study in Anthropology and History* (Belmont, Calif.: Wadsworth, 1971).

The relatively few non-Protestants were simply disenfranchised and thereby excluded from participating in the making and enforcing of sociocultural norms.[8]

This casts Americans' love for republican institutions in an interesting light. Their concern for public virtue naturally blended religious with political values. "A frequent recurrence to the fundamental principles of this constitution, and a constant adherence to justice, moderation, temperance, industry, frugality, and all the social virtues, are indispensably necessary to preserve the blessings of liberty and good government" (1792 New Hampshire Constitution, Art. XXXVIII; Thorpe, 2475).[9] This, typical of statements found in half a dozen of the early constitutions, echoes the Calvinistic middle-class values dominant in America. It also reflects the view Americans had of themselves as a people. Reconsidering the perception Americans had of English corruption vis-à-vis American virtue, it is apparent that their opposition to English institutions was based at least in part on a distaste for the aristocratic elements in English culture. The usual description of English mores found in American Whig pamphlets is based invariably upon the manners of the aristocracy rather than the sobriety and frugality of the rapidly growing English middle class. The split with England was justified partly on grounds of preserving American virtue, and this virtue was opposed to aristocratic political institutions and culture. Overlooking the fact that England was by then heavily governed by its Calvinistic middle class was convenient and necessary for successful propaganda.

To say that Americans blended politics with religion does not

---

8. John P. Roche effectively supports the contention that this approach worked in early American society because the openness and pluralism of that society permitted the various settlements to maintain their relatively homogeneous communities, while the various inhabitants could avoid those with whom there was disagreement over fundamentals. As he points out, there was no libertarian ideology operative to protect individual liberty. See John P. Roche, "American Liberty: An Examination of the 'Tradition' of Freedom," in M. R. Konvitz and C. Rossiter (eds.), *Aspects of Liberty* (Ithaca, N.Y.: Cornell University Press, 1958).

9. From this point on, all quotes from state constitutions will identify the constitution, section, and page number from Thorpe on which that particular passage is found. See Francis N. Thorpe (ed.), *The Federal and State Constitutions, Colonial Charters, and Other Organic Laws of the United States of America* (7 vols; Washington, D.C.: Government Printing Office, 1907).

imply that they were practicing totalitarian government. Instead, it implies that the political culture in 1776 supported governmental intervention in fundamental cultural matters. Rather than being characterized as totalitarian, Whig political theory is better described as supporting a relatively broad scope of governmental activity—broad relative to the narrower scope that would be supported by Federalist theory.[10] Basic socioeconomic values would be guaranteed, but these guarantees not only restricted governmental activity, they also established core societal values that could be enforced against those who did not hold them.

Bills of rights were the primary avenue for expressing basic cultural values. In reading the following, it will be helpful to keep in mind the potentially totalitarian nature of popular consent. The bills of rights in the first constitutions tended to prohibit certain pernicious practices used by the English monarchs, but did not put absolute prohibitions on these practices. Apparently the presumption was that, with the removal from crown rule, the danger was over, and listing these rights was more in the way of a celebration of cultural values. Approaching 1789, the list grew longer and the prohibitions stronger. There are indications that the Americans had begun to discover the tyrannical possibilities in majority rule, and concern shifted to limiting the operation of that majority through the legislature. The Federalists were to hit upon a more drastic solution than merely lengthening bills of rights. They were to limit government, *i.e.*, the majority, to a relatively narrow range of issues from the very beginning. They rejected altogether any involvement of government in cultural matters, and because this prohibition on political moralism was difficult if not impossible to enforce in Calvinist America, they would require extraordinary majorities when-

10. Here, as later in the text, *Federalist* describes a general position. However, those who called themselves Federalists varied a good deal in their respective political beliefs. The difference between James Madison and Alexander Hamilton on the matter of encouraging commercial development through involvement of the national government indicates how much simple use of *Federalist* hides. On the other hand, the point of this volume is to discuss what separated Whigs as a group from Federalists as a group. Generally speaking, the discussion in Hamilton, Madison, and Jay's *The Federalist* is drawn upon to characterize the Federalists as a group.

ever a matter of fundamental importance arose.[11] In this way, they would prevent anything more than mere ratification of cultural shifts that had already essentially occurred.

Societal Consent

Beginning with the Mayflower Compact, Americans had the habit of turning their major political documents into cultural statements as well, statements outlining the basic presuppositions of social and cultural activity in that particular society. For example, the Mayflower Compact reveals a religious people, devoted to "radical" Protestant theology, dedicated to deliberative social and political processes, and determined to measure human activity in terms of whether and how it contributes to the well-being of the entire community. Because these cultural presuppositions have obvious political consequences, and because students of politics often read only the major political documents, it is easy to pass them off as political assumptions. In fact, the Mayflower Compact establishes no particular government, nor do many other major documents generally celebrated as political statements, such as the Massachusetts Body of Liberties, Virginia Bill of Rights, and Declaration of Independence. In each case, we have an outline of the major sociocultural norms, not a design for government. Even the colonial documents explicitly designed to establish a form of government always began by laying down the basic sociocultural norms. The Rhode Island Charter of 1663 is quite typical in beginning by declaring its dedication to "sober, serious and religious intentions" as forming the basis for a "livlie experiment" in the erection of civil government.

The important fact is that religious beliefs had become political symbols, and political symbols had come to be as fundamental as religious beliefs. Representative government was as sacred as piety and temperance. Bills of rights did not hesitate to fasten *sacred* to

---

11. In the little-understood split among conservatives today, most of them hold an essentially Federalist position that emphasizes the individual and limited government in general, and specifically rejects governmental involvement in moral matters. Another group adheres to what is essentially a Whig formulation that places the community before the individual and believes in a moral order that can and should govern our actions. See Kenneth M. Dolbeare and Patricia Dolbeare, *American Ideologies* (Chicago: Markham, 1973).

trial by jury any more than they hesitated to encourage Sunday worship in the very next article.

Americans in the 1770s and 1780s were a highly politicized people. Since 1765, political matters had been constantly subjected to the closest analysis in the press, the pulpit, pamphlets, and taverns. One consequence was an orgy of self-analysis, as Americans—Whig and Tory alike—came to grips with the fundamental principles of their society, with their definition of themselves as a people. The bills of rights attached to the early state constitutions reflect this self-preoccupation. They make marvelous reading, for they blend ringing statements with homely observation and bring together, in various combinations, the English heritage drawn from Magna Carta with colonial social, cultural, and religious practices. As in earlier cultural statements, we find Americans devoted to radical Protestant theology, representative government, a community of virtue over private avarice, and the fundamental rights derived from English common law. We have a people defining themselves culturally; but we also have something else, which requires a short discussion of Whig political theory in order to fully appreciate these documents.

Central to traditional Whig thinking was the belief that the executive was the primary source of tyranny, with the legislature standing as protector between the executive (monarch) and the people. Since members of the legislature were returned to the people-at-large at the end of the session to experience their own laws, they were not really distinguished from the people. Equally important, traditional Whigs had an idea of limited government different from our idea today. Our view is Federalist in origin and holds that a written constitution limits government to the powers enumerated. Whig constitutions were written by the legislature and could, therefore, hardly limit the legislature. Whigs assumed that government had all power except for specific prohibitions contained in a bill of rights.[12] Having the legislature write the constitution makes sense when one remembers that the monarch was considered to be government, and bills of rights were designed as protections against his

12. See F. Richardson, "Early American Political Authority, 1733–1788" (Ph.D. dissertation, Brandeis University, 1973), 221–55.

power. The legislature provided legal content to the general prohibitions in its role as protector of the people. With independence, the source of tyranny was removed, making the function of bills of rights somewhat ambiguous.

Government, under the traditional Whig view, was balanced between the executive and the legislature. Independence undercut the legitimacy and the authority of the crown-related executives, with the result that the legislature was left holding all governmental power. The authority of Parliament was also undercut, but the state legislatures had their own legitimacy, if not authority in the strict sense. The new, radical legislatures worked hard to develop their own basis for authority, but in the meantime they were forced to rely upon the brute fact that they held power. The solution was to base the authority of the legislature on a written constitution flowing directly from popular sovereignty. One often-ignored implication of this solution is that if authority (the right to rule) is based upon popular sovereignty (the ultimate power) instead of upon the tradition of natural law, then there is no limit on the potential scope of government. It is in this sense that popular sovereignty can potentially support totalitarian government, in this case, totalitarian legislatures. Thus, rights come to be turned against the legislature out of necessity.

Technically, bills of rights were prior to and above legislative laws simply because they had their origin in colonial practice as well as in English common law. At the same time, bills of rights were traditionally associated with documents establishing instruments of government. The legislatures usually added them to the constitutions, but in doing so, legislatures were put in the position of granting or withholding rights, depending upon what was appended to the constitution. On the other hand, it was not clear that bills of rights were really a part of the constitutions. They invariably contained general admonitions with no specific legal content, and the language used in them lacked the positive, binding force of that used in the constitution proper. Article XXXVIII from the 1792 New Hampshire Constitution (on p. 57, herein) is a typical example. A blatant statement of fundamental sociocultural values, it nevertheless establishes no specific political process or institution and implies no specific legislation. A few more examples, from the 1776 Virginia Constitution, illustrate the consistency in detail to be found in state bills of rights.

> Sec. 15. That no free government, or the blessings of liberty, can be preserved to any people, but by a firm adherence to justice, moderation, temperance, frugality, and virtue, and by frequent recurrence to fundamental principles.
>
> Sec. 16. That religion, or the duty that we owe to our Creator, and the manner of discharging it, can be directed only by reason and conviction, not by force or violence; and therefore all men are equally entitled to the free exercise of religion, according to the dictates of conscience; and that is the mutual duty of all to practice Christian forbearance, love, and charity towards each other. (Thorpe, 3814)

As such, bills of rights did not so much prohibit use of legislative power as impede legislative will. A written bill of rights, by publicly stating fundamental sociocultural presuppositions, dramatized for citizen and legislator alike that some things ought not be tampered with lightly. Citizens were provided a vague yardstick against which to measure legislative law; and legislators, because they were invariably required to take an oath upholding the constitution, theoretically were forced to wrestle with the meaning of statements like those above when designing legislation.

Because the legislatures wrote the first wave of constitutions and could amend them, one could hardly be sanguine about the effectiveness of bills of rights. The next step was to place the most important portion beyond amendment, a step taken by New Jersey in 1776. It required that everyone elected to office take an oath not to repeal four sections of the constitution—two sections on annual elections and trial by jury, and two dealing with religion and the exercise of conscience (Sec. XXIII; Thorpe, 2598). Note that the prohibitions do not result directly from constitutional statements but from the force of an oath that is required. The constitution imposed a requirement for officeholding but did not directly prohibit or limit legislative activity on its own authority. As if to emphasize, or perhaps through an oversight, Article XXII in the same document prohibits the legislature from passing laws "as are repugnant to the rights and privileges contained in this Charter; and that the inestimable right of trial by jury shall remain confirmed as a part of the law of this Colony without repeal forever" (Thorpe, 2598). The 1776 Delaware Constitution contains a similar provision in Article 25 and then repeats it in Article 30. There are similar provisions in other constitutions, but preceding a discussion of them, a possible source of confusion must be clarified—the relationship of bills of rights to the crucial distinction Americans were to make between fundamental law and legislative law.

James Otis is given credit for first seriously advancing the idea in America that the legislative power could be limited by a constitution. This was in 1761. He did not, however, draw the conclusion that if this is true, it can only be because a constitution is more fundamental than the laws resulting from the institutions the constitution establishes. He, along with most Whigs, continued to believe that moral rights and obligations were not differentiated, as they would be today, from legal rights and obligations. Moral rights, as well as legal rights, naturally radiated from laws enacted by the legislature rather than laws limiting the legislature. Bernard Bailyn provides evidence that by 1776, Americans generally had changed their ideas on the matter and had come to regard a constitution as a fundamental law.[13] That is a reasonable conclusion to draw from reading the prominent pamphlets of the time, but the first state constitutions contain evidence which supports a contrary conclusion.

At first glance they support Bailyn. In addition to the above two prohibitions on altering portions of a bill of rights, the 1777 Georgia Constitution admonishes that laws not be "repugnant to the true intent and meaning of any rule or regulation contained in this constitution" (Art. VII; Thorpe, 780), and there are similar statements in the 1780 Massachusetts (Art. IV; Thorpe, 1894), 1784 New Hampshire (Pt. II; Thorpe, 2458), 1792 New Hampshire (Sec. V; Thorpe, 2476), and 1798 Georgia (Sec. 22; Thorpe, 794) constitutions. There is no doubt that these provisions reflect a desire to place constitutions on a different basis than legislative law, but as long as the legislatures could write and amend constitutions, these statements amounted only to admonitions for the legislature to be consistent in its lawmaking.

13. Bernard Bailyn, *The Ideological Origins of the American Revolution* (Cambridge, Mass.: Belknap Press, 1967), 175–84.

The constitutions did take the next logical step and prohibit legislative amendment. Pennsylvania, in 1776, adopted a constitution with this statement concluding Section 4: "But they [the legislature] shall have no power to add to, alter, abolish, or infringe any part of this constitution." Vermont, which copied the Pennsylvania Constitution, had the same provision in its Section 9. Significantly, both constitutions provided for a means of amendment other than through legislative action. An independent body, the council of censors, was to meet every seven years and recommend amendments if it was thought necessary, and then a special convention to consider possible amendments would be called. If one overlooks the fact that Vermont was not yet a state, that leaves only two of the first fourteen states which effectively made the distinction in their 1776 constitutions. Even so, the documents themselves were framed by legislatures or extralegal bodies acting as legislatures. The shift from constitutions being written by legislatures to constitutions being written by specially elected conventions and ratified by the people was a slow one. That this was not the manner of adoption in 1776 or 1777 is contrary to Bailyn's conclusion that the distinction was generally understood by then.

Two other provisions found in first wave documents further demonstrate the groping for the distinction between constitutions as fundamental law and as legislative law. They provide the first of three pieces of evidence that bills of rights were distinguished from the body of constitutions. Part of the ambiguity in their role was whether, and to what extent, they were part of any fundamental law. Although today we generally consider bills of rights as an essential part of the fundamental law, to the extent this was not the case in 1776, Bailyn's conclusion is brought further into question.

Consider Section XLIV of the 1776 North Carolina document. "That the Declaration of Rights is hereby declared to be part of the Constitution of this State, and ought never to be violated on any pretence whatsoever." The interesting aspect of this statement is not that it represents another example of an incipient distinction between a constitution and legislative law, but rather that the framers found it necessary to specifically include the declaration of rights in the constitution. This implies that unless they had included Section

XLIV, the declaration of rights would have been separate from the constitution as an instrument of government.

In the same year, Delaware ended its constitution with this provision. "Article 30. No article of the declaration of rights and fundamental rules of this State, agreed to by this convention, nor the first, second, fifth . . . twenty-sixth, and twenty-ninth articles of this constitution, ought ever to be violated on any pretence whatever. No other part of this constitution shall be altered, changed, or diminished without the consent of five parts in seven of the assembly, and seven members of the legislative council" (Thorpe, 568). Here, the declaration of rights appears more fundamental than the body of the constitution, because it is not subject to legislative law, whereas most of the body can be so altered. However, the declaration of rights specifically permits a simple majority in the legislature to alienate several rights, including the right to property. In any case, the word *constitution* does not include the list of rights, they were not attached to the constitution, and they are not reproduced in Thorpe as part of the constitution. A strange article indeed.

If these provisions are suggestive, the second piece of evidence is more substantial. A distinction between bills of rights and constitutions can be seen in the prescriptive nature of the former as opposed to the legally binding nature of the latter. The prescriptive nature of bills of rights is reflected in the first wave of constitution making and in much of the second wave by the use of the word *ought*.[14] For example, in the 1776 Pennsylvania Constitution, the bill of rights contains such phrases as: "freedom of the press *ought* not be restrained . . . standing armies *ought* not be kept up," and so on. The use of *ought* is standard in the early bills of rights, usually followed by the loophole permitting the legislature to alienate the right if it is deemed necessary for the common good. In all eighteen state constitutions, the word *shall* is used in the body of the document when discussing the formal instruments of government. The distinction is not without a difference as these are essentially still Whig documents, despite the prominence of more advanced ideas in pamphlets elsewhere. Only gradually do we see the prescriptive *ought, should,*

14. Charles S. Hyneman should be credited with first drawing my attention to this shift in language through private correspondence.

and *recommend* in bills of rights replaced by the stronger, legally binding *shall*, *will* and *do* (see Table 3). Not until the twentieth constitution, the 1790 South Carolina Constitution, do we find a separate bill of rights using only *shall* to the exclusion of the weaker *ought*, although four constitutions written prior to the federal Constitution make exclusive use of *shall* in rights mentioned in the body of the document. The third wave of constitutions, those written after the adoption of the United States Constitution in 1789, tend to adopt its format. Until this shift in language occurred, even if the constitutions *were* conceived as fundamental law, bills of rights did not effectively prohibit or limit legislative action.

A third piece of evidence that bills of rights were not generally incorporated into constitutions as declarations of fundamental law is the persistence with which constitutional framers permitted rights to be alienated by legislative action. If constitutions embodied fundamental law superior to legislative law, we would expect rights to be inalienable. Surveying all of the first three waves, encompassing the first twenty-five state constitutions, we find only two constitutions that do not permit legislative alienation of at least one important right. The 1776 New Jersey and the 1789 Georgia documents bury a few rights in the body and do not explicitly permit legislative encroachment on any. Otherwise, all other state constitutions until 1798 contain major rights that are alienable and therefore subject to legislative law. The 1776 Pennsylvania Constitution, usually considered the most liberal of them all, permitted confiscation of property, as did the 1780 Massachusetts, the 1784 New Hampshire, the 1790 Pennsylvania, the 1792 Delaware, and the 1793 Vermont documents, among others. The 1790 Pennsylvania, the 1792 Delaware, and the 1798 Georgia constitutions permitted suspension of the right of *habeas corpus*, as does the United States Constitution. At least six permitted alienation of the right to worship as one pleases, including the highly influential 1780 Massachusetts Constitution.

One should not conclude, however, that the distinction between fundamental law and legislative law was not made at all. The body of every single state constitution used the word *shall* in describing the institutions of government, and once the ratification and amend-

Table 3
USE OF *SHALL* AND *OUGHT* IN BILLS OF RIGHTS*

Constitution	Number of times ought *or* equivalent	Number of times shall *or* equivalent
1. 1725 Mass.	No bill of rights	No bill of rights
2. 1776 N.H.	No bill or rights	No bill of rights
3. 1776 S.C.	No bill of rights	No bill of rights
4. 1776 Va.	12	9
5. 1776 N.J.	0	5†
6. 1776 Md.	44	2
7. 1776 Del.	16‡	3
8. 1776 R.I.	No bill of rights	No bill of rights
9. 1776 Conn.	No bill of rights	No bill of rights
10. 1776 Pa.	11	14
11. 1776 N.C.	17	9
12. 1777 Ga.	0	5†
13. 1777 N.Y.	0	5†
14. 1777 Vt.	10	16
15. 1778 S.C.	0	6†
16. 1780 Mass.	11	19
17. 1784 N.H.	13	23
18. 1786 Vt.	12	18
19. 1789 Ga.	0	5†
20. 1790 S.C.	0	8
21. 1790 Pa.	0	31
22. 1792 Del.	1	21
23. 1792 N.H.	11	22
24. 1793 Vt.	11	11
25. 1798 Ga.	0	6†

*The figures below do not record the number of times the word or its equivalent appears, but rather the number of times a right is described using one or the other. Also, the numbers are approximate, as some interpretations are open to controversy.

†Indicates that rights are imbedded in the body of the document rather than in a separate bill of rights.

‡The Delaware declaration of rights was not written as part of the constitution proper but rather as a legislative bill attached to the constitution by Article 30 of the document. There is some question, therefore, whether the declaration of rights has constitutional status. Most authorities, such as Francis Thorpe, do not print the declaration as part of the constitution, in which case the 1776 Delaware Constitution can be said to have no bill of rights. Whether it is considered part of the constitution, it supports the general trend being reported here.

ment process was based directly on popular consent, at least the bodies or main portions of the state constitutions became higher law. However, not until the 1780 Massachusetts Constitution do we have the people giving popular consent through special constitutional conventions *and* popular ratification, and this was an isolated instance until well into the nineteenth century. Only when this combination occurred could we realistically speak of constitutions being treated as fundamental law. Furthermore, it was not until well after 1789 that bills of rights were, for the most part, considered beyond legislative alteration. The only clear exception was the 1790 Pennsylvania Constitution, which declares at the end of its bill of rights: "Sec. 26. To guard against transgressions of the high powers which we have delegated, we declare, that everything in this article is excepted out of the general powers of government, and shall forever remain inviolate" (Thorpe, 3101). Clearly, Americans were reaching toward the fundamental distinction, but the juxtaposition of sections supporting the distinction with those embodying legislative omnipotence is striking. At their core, the first three waves of state constitutions remained primarily Whig documents.

One can watch the radical Whigs learning from their experience. Bills of rights become longer, more detailed, and stronger in their prohibitions, producing a slow trend toward the Federalist concept of limited government.[15] However, no state chose to go the entire way suggested by the Federalists. This would have been to enumerate the powers available to government so explicitly, and to establish a system with so many safeguards and checks, that the decision-making process would become very deliberative as well as very limited in scope, with the result that a bill of rights would be unnecessary. The federal Constitution of 1787 was framed in this manner. Emphasis was placed on enumerated powers of limited scope and a complex system of separated powers, with checks and balances to force the decision-making process to be highly deliberative. The state constitutions, starting with legislative supremacy in the early years, gradually strengthened the governor and courts. Procedural restraints were added to enhance the deliberative nature of decision making, but the lengthy, detailed bill of rights was retained as their major restraint on the majority.

The state constitutions evolved and extended a step in consent theory begun in the colonial charters by blending societal consent

15. This trend does not necessarily imply a shift to Federalist theory which was considerably different. Also, the limitations developed by the Whigs through bills of rights never approached the theoretical limits set by the Federalists.

with governmental consent. The ratification of a constitution not only established a form of government, but also affirmed the essential sociocultural base upon which the government rested. The federal Constitution originally did not differ from them in degree but in kind. Whereas the states continued to rely heavily on expanding bills of rights to adjust to cultural change, the federal Constitution largely removed these matters from legislative concern and placed so much confidence in the deliberative process arising from the interaction of the three branches of government that it assumed legislation would be commensurate with general sociocultural presuppositions. The states, however, continued to permit societal consent to be given through normal legislation, with the result that amendments were continually needed to restrict or clarify legislative action.

Only the radical shift in approach, limiting the Congress to specific enumerated powers, permitted Hamilton, in *The Federalist* 84, to argue that a bill of rights was unnecessary. Of course, the adoption of the national Bill of Rights reintroduced the earlier notion embodied in the state constitutions and produced a partially schizophrenic document with respect to societal consent. Madison, in his lukewarm campaign to have the Bill of Rights added to the Constitution, continually stressed that it was essentially redundant, given the effect of the body of the Constitution, and thus would do no harm.[16] Of course, he was correct as long as the federal government remained restricted in its powers. However, with the expansion of its powers through, among other things, the "necessary and proper" clause, it has come more and more to be involved in fundamental matters of sociocultural content. The schizophrenic face of the Constitution has thereby caused increasing trouble, as one side argues that the Bill of Rights and subsequent amendments do involve the federal government in such matters, while others argue that the

16. Willmoore Kendall and George Carey, *The Basic Symbols of the American Political Tradition* (Baton Rouge: Louisiana State University Press, 1970), 128–31. On pages 131–36, Kendall and Carey submit a carefully reasoned argument that the national Bill of Rights was considered by those who adopted it recommendatory rather than legally binding. If correct, their argument would strengthen the one being made here. Madison's argument in Congress on this matter is reprinted in Charles S. Hyneman and George Carey, *The Second Federalist* (New York: Appleton-Century-Crofts, 1967).

theory underlying the body of the document prohibits such involvement.

In this light, it is interesting to compare the development of state constitutions with that of the federal Constitution. The federal system did not reflect sociocultural change until after the Civil War. Since World War I, the cultural content has increased, but still relatively slowly. The 13th, 14th, 15th, 18th, 19th, 21st, and 26th amendments all reflect cultural shifts. The proposed Equal Rights Amendment, the stalled School Prayer Amendment, and a number of near-misses also reflect the old Whig penchant for making constitutions embody societal consent. Whereas this national trend has been relatively recent and thus far only somewhat successful, the state constitutions have piled amendment upon amendment, some amendments shifting governmental consent, but many others passed in adjustment to what is euphemistically called "the changing times." Consequently, state constitutions have been completely rewritten from time to time as they become unwieldy (only Massachusetts of the first fourteen states still operates under its original, the 1780 Constitution), whereas the federal Constitution has remained short.

The distinction between state and federal documents should not be pushed too far, however. With the strengthening of the executive that developed in the state constitutions written nearer 1789, and with the freeing of the judiciary from close legislative control, there was the basis for a Federalist approach. The later state constitutions also came to use the phrase "separation of powers" in the Federalist sense in just one of several trends that opened the way for Federalist political institutions, but still these tendencies did not lead to adoption of the Federalist approach to societal consent.

An interesting case was the apparent disappearance of certain cultural presuppositions as one moved toward 1798, specifically those relating to religion. In 1776, there were frequent references to "the great Governor of the universe," as well as fairly explicit religious restrictions for holding office or even voting. By the 1790s, these disappeared. What this represented, however, was not a decline in cultural content, but a shift in cultural values. Whereas most of the early constitutions reflected a strong bias toward certain beliefs related to the dissenting Protestant sects that originally settled America, by the late 1780s there was a growing impatience with anything but complete religious toleration. The rewriting of earlier constitutions permitted a reflection of this cultural shift. Otherwise, amendments would have been required.

Let us summarize the answers to the four basic questions with respect to societal consent. Who gives consent? Initially, since the legislatures wrote the constitutions, the people gave consent indirectly through their representatives. However, beginning with the 1780 Massachusetts constitution (the first one framed by a constitutional convention and ratified by the people), the people at large gave consent directly. The federal constitution departs from this by removing societal consent from legislative concern.

To whom is consent given? To no one. It is the unique characteristic of societal consent that when the people agree to certain cultural norms but give the government no power to alter them, they are in effect giving consent to themselves to retain control of the matter.

What constitutes giving consent? Consent initially was given by failing to prohibit. If something was not forbidden by the bill of rights or protected in an unamendable section, then presumably the government had been given consent to make legislation. As the state constitutions slowly moved toward more direct reliance on the people, societal consent was given at precisely the same time and in the same manner that governmental consent was given—through amendments.[17] Blending societal consent with governmental consent produced the obvious need for strengthening both. Because of this blending, Americans have come less and less to understand the distinction between the two. Amendments giving one or the other are jumbled together without distinction, even in the United States Constitution. This particular contribution to consent theory perhaps enhanced coherence, but it also led to future misapprehension.

17. It is noteworthy that for action on the 1780 Massachusetts Constitution persons were permitted to vote who could not regularly vote in elections. See Elisha P. Douglas, *Rebels and Democrats* (Chicago: Quadrangle Books, 1955), 170 and 189. This broader suffrage on constitutional matters had also been permitted on the defeated 1778 constitution, as well as in the election of delegates to constitutional conventions in other states, such as Georgia.

Governmental Consent

The first state constitutions were not viewed as embodying direct popular consent. One piece of evidence for this lies in the manner in which the first state constitutions were framed and adopted. In effect, the members of the legislature consented to their own agency in writing the document, and then gave governmental consent by adopting it themselves. Such a practice was entirely in keeping with the Whig political assumptions of the time. Since the legislature was not looked upon as government per se, but as the buffer between the people and the government (the crown), and was not distinguishable from the people as such, the majority of the legislature was viewed as automatically representing the interests of the homogeneous community at large. The people could not all gather together to frame a constitution any more than they could gather to write legislation, so the body designed to embody the will of the community, the legislature, was the obvious instrument for both tasks. There was little objection raised to this logic in 1776.

However, the frequent and often bitter factional disputes within the legislatures during the war soon undercut any such set of assumptions. Instead, the Americans found themselves increasingly divided on important political matters, only one of which was the animosity and suspicion between the wealthier, more cosmopolitan cities and towns along the coast, and the smaller, more local-oriented towns of the interior. The legislatures reflected these splits, but with varying accuracy. The outcome of bitter legislative debate was more likely to reflect the balance of forces within the legislature than the pattern of sentiment in the general population, since legislatures invariably overrepresented the older, coastal towns. With the absence of the crown, and the state executives reduced to being creatures of the legislatures, the legislatures *became* government, the potential source of tyranny, instead of a buffer against an arbitrary executive.

The response to the new perceptions was a logical and straightforward one. If the legislature could not be trusted any longer to automatically reflect the interests of the community, then the community must become more directly involved with matters of government, especially on the most important matters. Since representatives giving themselves consent to write fundamental documents establishing procedural rules and institutions for collective decision making seemed improper if not illogical, the move to constitutional conventions and popular ratification was a natural one.

This shift, though logical and dramatic in its implications, did not proceed historically in a straightforward manner. Like many developments in America at that time, the process was fitful, indirect, and often unconscious. There were so many competing ideas involving so many people that the development could hardly be viewed as being directed by some commonly held architectonic plan. Nevertheless, the end result was coherent theoretically: the people at large gave direct consent to agents who were chosen specifically to write a constitution and who then submitted the document to the people for direct approval. There is no question that this represents a shift from an indirect form of consent, whereby people elected legislators with no idea of what they would subsequently write into a constitution, indeed with no idea whether they would even write one, to a consistently direct form of consent. The development is a fundamental one for what Americans would come to regard as republican government.

Subjecting constitutions to the direct consent of the people makes sense from another point of view. Whereas some of the first state constitutions only outlined procedures and institutions for collective decision making, a few documents in the first wave also had elements of societal consent inserted. The 1776 Virginia Constitution placed the Declaration of Independence at the beginning as a preamble. The New Jersey Constitution of 1776 jumbled everything up so that, for example, two sections on religious freedom were inserted between the section on proper form for writing legislative bills and the section containing an admonition to maintain separation of powers. During the same year, Pennsylvania and North Carolina approximated the example of Virginia and placed a bill of rights at the beginning in a preamble, while Maryland and Georgia approximated the New Jersey approach by mixing them in the body of the document.

Strictly speaking, the framers did not have to pursue such a strategy. They could have left specification of rights to the legislature or to the courts. Reiterating rights and primary cultural attachments perhaps seemed natural under the circumstances of declaring, at least implicitly, the reasons for their break with England. There was also the American tradition of supplementing charters with frames of government that included bills of rights. The implications of such an approach, however, were considerable. By inserting fundamental sociocultural principles into their constitutions, the framers made the documents too important to be left simply to legislative discretion. With the import of their contents greatly expanded, the state constitutions fairly pleaded to be subject to popular scrutiny. Indeed, those portions of proposed constitutions containing sociocultural presuppositions tended to become the focus of the most bitter and extended public debates.

The amendment procedure became equally direct. The constitutions written during the first wave were notable for generally having no provision for amendment, and of the three constitutions mentioning amendment, Maryland's required only that a majority of two consecutive sessions of the legislature consent, Delaware's specified approximately two-thirds of the legislature, and only Georgia's required a special convention upon petition by a majority of counties. While the 1780 Massachusetts Constitution was the first to be written by a separate convention *and* ratified by the people, the 1784 Constitution of New Hampshire was the first document to *require* such a procedure for amendment.

Massachusetts and New Hampshire also required that amendments, as well as new constitutions, be ratified by two-thirds of the voters. The use of an extraordinary majority, while not always required, has become common in America and was used in the federal Constitution. Requiring an extraordinary majority is consistent with requiring a separate convention for constitutional changes in that it implies a clear distinction between constitutional matters and ordinary legislation. This distinction is a fundamental one for American political theory.[18] It results, at least in part, from an implicit recognition that constitutions had come to contain far more than

18. Bailyn, *Ideological Origins*, 175–98.

rules of legislative procedure. The distinction supported attempts to make governmental consent, and then societal consent, as direct as possible.

Placing governmental consent directly in the hands of the people was a logical solution to at least four problems, permitting us to identify at least four good reasons for its being accepted: 1) the tradition of local popular government had formed the core political experience for Americans for almost a century and a half; 2) during the Revolution, Americans became used to direct political participation through committees of safety and correspondence and what Gordon S. Wood terms government by the "people out of doors"; 3) prior to the Declaration of Independence, American political institutions had operated within the context of the authority of the crown, and the severance from that source of authority required a new context within which to carry on politics; and 4) an undeveloped yet persistent distinction between fundamental law and ordinary legislation underlay the rights developed as protection against the English monarchs, and this distinction had been the basis for justifying the break with England.

In Chapter 2, we discussed the long history of consent and consent-based institutions on American shores. Without question, the tradition of popular government was too strongly entrenched for postrevolutionary America to reject it. But this does not explain the strong pressures for placing governmental consent directly in the hands of the people. Allowing the legislature to write constitutions was acceptable under the notion of popular government current at the time. What must not be forgotten is that the core tradition in America was *local* popular government. Most politics in New England and the northern states centered on the town rather than the state legislature, and in the southern states, the county was the focus of government. It was at the local level that the people were most directly involved in decision making, and it was there that the vast majority of political decisions affecting them were made.

Returning to the list of seventeenth-century "constitutions" (see pp. 27–29, herein), these documents, though bearing the names of what are now states, were actually relevant to local government. The Virginia charters regulated settlements so tenuous that the first one,

Jamestown, disappeared without a trace, and for many years the associated settlements numbered only a few thousand people. Massachusetts for many years referred only to what is now the Boston area and did not include Plymouth, for example, which had its own town code of law. The Fundamental Orders of Connecticut likewise pertained only to a small portion of the present state, as evidenced by New Haven (which was a cluster of several towns) writing its own "fundamentals" the same year. Scattered up and down the coast were isolated pockets of settlement, each with its own local government, which only gradually began to establish commercial links along "roads" that until the eighteenth century were often little more than cow paths strung end to end.

When towns in a region did form political unions, it was invariably along the model set by Rhode Island in the Acts and Orders of 1647. Four towns—Providence, Warwick, Portsmouth, and Newport—formed a common legislature in which each town had equal representation. By 1776, all state legislatures were apportioned according to towns in the north, counties in the south, and sometimes a mixture. These apportionment units were not mere electoral districts established by convention, as they are today. Rather, each was an identifiable unit, whether town or county, with its unique characteristics, and was the primary focus of political and social attachment for its inhabitants. These local political units did not generally grow through expansion of their boundaries, although some expansion did take place. Instead, there was a proliferation of local units in keeping with the desire to maintain homogeneous communities. Admission of citizenship in a town was closely supervised by the town fathers. There are records of towns that required the brothers or sisters of inhabitants to leave if they had moved in with their kin without permission from local authorities. A housekeeper might live with a family for forty years, but when the family died, she had to move because she was not a legal inhabitant.[19] The exclusivity of such a political culture goes far toward explaining how Massachusetts went from a handful of towns in 1641 to over

19. For these and other examples, see Anne Bush Maclear, *Early New England Towns: A Comparative Study of Their Development* (New York: AMS Press, 1967), 132–36. This is a reprint of a volume originally published in 1908.

340 incorporated towns and plantations by 1776, many of them cramped town line to town line along the coast.

To speak of "the people" in late eighteenth-century America was not to speak of an undifferentiated mass, but, in fact, to speak of towns and counties, for that is how the people spoke. A universal problem in the colonies, and then in the states, was the underrepresentation of interior towns and counties. This interior-coastal split dominated American politics for many years and can even be seen as an essential part of the Federalist–Antifederalist split.[20] Each town jealously guarded its representation in the state legislature, and it is here that we find a major reason for constitutions being written and ratified by groups other than the state legislature.

If legislatures tended to overrepresent the older, coastal towns, then their writing state documents insured perpetuation of such overrepresentation. If, however, constitutions were written by special conventions elected by all of the towns, and then were subject to ratification by the towns, this problem presumably could be avoided.[21] Because the people at large acted most directly through their town meetings, town ratification also amounted to ratification by the people. In this fashion, localism and the tradition of local control materially advanced the move toward direct governmental consent.

The second reason for moving to direct governmental consent can be found in the increasing demand for popular control of government arising from revolutionary experiences.[22] Several years before the writing of the Declaration of Independence, the increasing tendency of state legislatures to operate contrary to the wishes of

20. Evidence for this can be found in Van Beck Hall, *Politics Without Parties: Massachusetts, 1780–1791* (Pittsburgh, Pa.: University of Pittsburgh Press, 1972); Jackson Turner Main, *Political Parties Before the Constitution* (Chapel Hill: University of North Carolina Press, 1973); and Jackson Turner Main, *The Upper House in Revolutionary America, 1763–1788* (Madison: University of Wisconsin Press, 1967).

21. Sometimes it produced the opposite situation. If representation were based simply on towns, then smaller towns in the west would end up being overrepresented vis-à-vis the larger towns in the east. This did, in fact, occur in several states, but the situation was soon corrected by making town representation proportional to the number of voters it had, which necessitated larger legislatures.

22. The discussion in this section is based heavily on Gordon S. Wood, *The Creation of the American Republic, 1776–1787* (Chapel Hill: University of North Carolina Press, 1969), 310–43.

the crown led some governors to dissolve their state bodies. Matters had reached a point at which members of the legislature, to thwart this tactic, resorted to establishing legislative committees that functioned when the legislature was not sitting. Towns and counties established committees of correspondence that became the local government. In this manner, a "shadow" government was erected, independent of formal institutions and reaching all the way to a national convention.

With the outbreak of war, these committees proliferated at all levels, many of them *ad hoc* organizations for intimidating citizens at the local level and maintaining "order." Large numbers of average citizens were in this way drawn into political matters, and political participation expanded dramatically beyond voting or holding office. Local committees, regional associations and conventions, and national congresses—all served to regulate American society in extraordinary detail. The economy was regulated by groups who not only were involved with taxation but also had a view toward eliminating monopolies and unfair practices, affecting prices, and setting policy. After 1776, riots became far less common, as the "mobs" had become organized, arranged in a hierarchy, legitimized, and specialized.

In modern social science terms, the level of political efficacy was dramatically raised for substantial numbers of ordinary citizens through a high level of political participation. This high level of political efficacy led to popular scrutiny of every aspect of government and of many other things not ordinarily considered a part of politics at the time. People so aroused as to demand control of trivialities were unlikely to permit themselves to be ignored when it came to something as important as writing, framing, and approving a state constitution. Coupled with strong local prejudices, this trend made the matter of governmental consent at the state level an important problem whose solution was straightforward and obvious.

If there were natural demands that arose from the developing political practices of the time, there were also important theoretical problems that needed solving. Aside from participating in politics "out of doors," many thoughtful Americans were also engaged in making sense of their political situation. One pressing matter was the gaping hole in political authority that resulted from the break with England. Direct governmental consent provided a theoretical solution as well as a practical one.

The distinction between power and authority is important in political theory but is often overlooked in normal discourse.[23] Power has been defined by an eminent political scientist as "the ability of A to make B do something B would not otherwise do."[24] Among several ways to accomplish this is the use of force, which produces political obedience out of fear. But it is also possible to induce obedience through persuasion, an approach associated with more democratic forms of power. Another form of power is derived from the feeling that a command ought to be obeyed because it is proper, proper because the source of command is legitimate and therefore has the right to make such a command. Power which is legitimate and rests on a basis other than force or persuasion is authority.

There are several ways to legitimate power to create authority, but we will concern ourselves with two prominent ones—tradition and popular consent. Traditional authority, as the name implies, is derived from the psychological force of power having been rationalized and legitimated by some highly respected lawgiver(s) in the past, who are represented in the present through an unbroken succession of offices or the like. This lawgiver could be a Draco or Solon, as with the Greeks; a King David or the supreme deity itself, as with the Jews; the historical founder of a country, as with Saint Stephen of Hungary; the sum total of all ancestors, as in Japan; or a set of mythological gods or superhumans. Authority confers a sense of permanence on a political system and creates the feeling that there are natural historical ties between the leaders and the led whereby the leaders ought to be obeyed. Popular authority creates the basis for obedience through a contract between rulers and ruled, whether the contract is real or implied. The people agree or consent to follow certain rules in return for certain promises on the part of the rulers. Popular authority does not necessarily require con-

23. The idea for this section comes from F. Richardson, "Early American Political Authority," especially Chap. one.
24. Robert Dahl, *Preface to Democratic Theory* (Chicago: University of Chicago Press, 1963).

tinuous popular control as long as the foundations are popular. Dictators have tried to legitimate their regimes by arguing that their authority flows from the overwhelming approval of the people, and strictly speaking, if this were true and the people had the realistic alternative of withdrawing approval, it would qualify as popular authority (John Locke, for one, essentially argues this position). Governments based on popular authority often, over time, blend it with traditional authority as well. Our own Constitution is a case in point, as the Founding Fathers have taken on a mantle similar to that worn by Solon or Saint Stephen.

Fred L. Richardson neatly summarizes the period from 1765 to 1789 as one in which Americans changed from 1) traditional authority to 2) a discredited authority to 3) popular power to 4) popular authority.[25] As late as 1765, Americans had a strong attachment to English political tradition. If they had always made a practice of avoiding or ignoring legislation made in England, it was probably more a matter of knowing such laws were generally not enforced than a matter of denying the right of the king and Parliament to make such laws. Beginning in 1765, the inhabitants of the thirteen colonies began referring to themselves more often as Americans than as Englishmen in their press, and by 1774, English authority was badly discredited.[26] When many colonists no longer accepted the right of Parliament to make laws governing them and thus denied that American political institutions took their legitimacy from British authority, Americans began erecting the network of committees and conventions, based upon popular power, to fill the void. As is always the case when authority breaks down, political order became more dependent upon force and the threat of force. It was a time of experimentation, as new institutions and new versions of old institutions were tried in an enormous outpouring of political creativity. The period was exciting, but it was also unstable, and clear heads recognized the need for a new basis for authority to restore permanence and reliability to political institutions. Many persons seriously discussed the creation of an American monarch

25. Richardson, "Early American Political Authority," 4.
26. For a fascinating discussion of these matters see Richard L. Merritt, *Symbols of American Community, 1735–1775* (New Haven, Conn.: Yale University Press, 1966).

on which to base authority, and no less a figure than Alexander Hamilton was among them.[27] The solution, as we all know, was to convert popular power to popular authority, and the specific instrumentality for this shift was the move to direct, popular governmental consent.

In choosing this solution to the problem of authority, Americans were adopting a theoretical formulation that had become quite prominent through the writings of men like Locke and Rousseau. At the same time, they were playing to a natural inclination within the public which was commensurate with the core American political tradition, especially as it had developed during the turmoil of the Revolution. Having the state constitutions written by conventions elected by the people for that purpose, and then submitting the proposed constitutions to the people for their direct approval, could insure a rapid shift from popular power to popular authority. If order was not completely restored in this fashion, legitimacy was.

Another theoretical problem, and a fourth reason that direct governmental consent was a logical development, had to do with the elaboration of the distinction between fundamental and legislative law. As discussed earlier in the chapter, the distinction was slow to be reflected in the wording of the bills of rights. With only a few exceptions (New Jersey, Georgia, New York, and their lists are minimal), rights were usually alienable by legislative action, and this continued to be the case right up to 1789. Also the shift from *ought* to *shall* was a slow one.

A number of constitutional practices were devised in the search for institutions embodying the distinction. Both the Delaware and New Jersey constitutions of 1777 declared certain articles immune from alteration. Delaware's further required five-sevenths of the assembly and seven members of the legislative council to consent to any amendment of those sections that could be amended. Maryland's (1776) required the approval of two successive legislatures for amendment, South Carolina's (1778) required ninety days' notice plus approval by both houses, and Georgia's (1777) could be altered only by a special convention, after the assembly was peti-

27. Gerald Stourzh, *Alexander Hamilton and the Idea of Republican Government* (Palo Alto, Calif.: Stanford University Press, 1970), 52.

tioned by a majority of voters in a majority of the counties. Pennsylvania (1776) and Vermont (1777) designed a council of censors, a body that was separate from the legislature and met every seven years, partly to review the need for amendments. At least ten other constitutional provisions were designed to place some portion of a constitution, in some manner, beyond legislative control. All of these constitutional wrinkles bespeak a desire on the part of the framers to distinguish between the constitutions and legislative law.[28]

If there were inclinations, no matter how strong, to institutionalize the distinction, they bore little fruit in 1776. W. F. Dodd makes the point that nine of the first twelve constitutions were drafted by legislative bodies especially empowered by their constituents to take such action, and in South Carolina and Virginia, expediency was urged as the reason why similar authorization was not sought. He argues further that the creation of independent conventions was risky because the revolutionary governing bodies had gained control largely through united and aggressive action and might not be able to control separate bodies.[29] This is a reasonable argument until you realize that in nine states, all subject to the dangers outlined by Dodd, the legislatures (or revolutionary state committees that in a few instances functioned as legislatures) were empowered by "risky" statewide polls, and this fact alone argues against his explanation of the absence of special conventions. It also raises the question of why the documents were not subject to statewide polls later. A better explanation is that American political thought had not yet worked out the implications of a written constitution. Voter approval for the legislature to frame a constitution is more properly programmatic consent than governmental consent.

Agitation for popular ratification was coextensive with and based upon the same arguments as that for special drafting conventions.

28. At least one state, South Carolina, gave no indication of drawing the distinction. Its 1778 constitution was framed by the General Assembly as an "act," and its preamble stated that "the following articles . . . be deemed and held the constitution . . . unless altered by the legislative authority thereof." The state supreme court shortly thereafter declared that both the constitution of 1776 and the constitution of 1778 were simple acts of the legislature, and could be repealed and amended at the legislature's pleasure.

29. W. F. Dodd, "The First State Constitutional Conventions," *American Political Science Review*, II (1908), 558.

Citizens of Mecklenburg County, North Carolina, sent instructions to their representatives at the provincial congress (1776) outlining the distinction between legislative law and matters approved by the people at large. The idea did not catch on in North Carolina but was intensively pursued in two New England states. The proposed Massachusetts constitution of 1778 was defeated at the polls, as was the proposed New Hampshire constitution of 1779, which required a three-fourths majority. The requirement was lowered to a two-thirds majority, but the people of New Hampshire rejected proposed documents in 1781 and 1782. The 1780 Massachusetts Constitution and the 1784 New Hampshire document became the only successful examples before 1787 to embody the distinction between legislative law and fundamental law. Indeed, only two constitutions between 1789 and 1800 were submitted for popular approval—Pennsylvania's in 1790 and New Hampshire's in 1792. None of the others, including the first Kentucky and Tennessee constitutions, were subjected to popular ratification. If one includes the United States Constitution, which was ratified by state conventions elected by the people, then only five of the twenty-eight constitutions adopted between 1776 and 1800 had popular approval. If Americans were groping toward the distinction between fundamental law and legislative law in 1776, they were still groping for the full implications of the distinction as late as 1800.

After 1780, however, state constitutions were invariably written by special conventions elected by the people.[30] In the absence of popular ratification, popular amendment, and ironclad prohibitions against legislative alienation of rights, special drafting conventions were, at best, an indirect form of governmental consent. The tactic was sufficient to distinguish constitutions from statutes, but it did not solve the problem of authority, since constitutions could not really be said to rest on either the authority of the people or the authority of a supreme legislature. Massachusetts, first, and then New Hampshire, discovered the formula that tied it all up into a

30. Only Delaware (1776) and North Carolina (1776) had used a specially elected convention prior to Massachusetts. It should also be noted that since 1930 several state constitutions have been written by unelected commissions, although the documents were then subjected to popular approval.

neat bundle. The formula was a consistent use of direct popular consent for instruments of government.

The Massachusetts Constitution of 1780, written largely by John Adams, was extremely influential and became the model for most state constitutions written, down to the present. Its use of an elected drafting convention separate from the legislature, plus popular ratification, moved governmental consent, and thus societal consent, from indirect to direct dependence upon the people. This pattern, from indirect to direct consent, was pursued in every phase of politics, and although it may have been a little slow developing with respect to governmental consent, there was no such problem when it came to giving consent for political agents.

4

Agency Consent

Popular consent for political agents has been an essential part of American government for over 350 years. There has been argument over who should be allowed to vote for representatives, what these representatives are supposed to represent, and how responsive the representatives should be to their constituents; but there has never been serious doubt that Americans prefer representative government to any other form. Before the public good was replaced by private interests in American political theory, and before constitutions were written by popularly elected conventions and ratified by the people, election of representatives was the primary consent-giving institution.

Merely assenting to a person's holding office with no further implications is a constricted view of consent and quite different from today's thinking, but it is consent nonetheless. The development of consent theory, from the simple Whig notion of electing representatives who dispassionately sought the common good to one in which representatives found their election tied to particular interests and their legislative actions held accountable by certain segments of society, contains the essential inner revolution that progressed parallel to the struggle for independence from England. It has become a commonplace among historians that the American Revolution was a double one. There was the obvious break with England, and most Americans probably believe that the bicentennial celebrates this fact alone. But there was also a social revolution, associated with the upheaval of war and given form by the justification for independence, that transformed thirteen colonies possessing institutions of consent into the first modern nation and the first nation governed by true popular consent erected on an egalitarian social theory. In some respects, the second revolution is the greater cause for celebration.

A long-standing debate among historians as to just how revolutionary this second revolution actually was has heated up again in recent years.[1] The general argument that consent moved from indirect to direct forms in the early state constitutions supports those emphasizing the significance of this social revolution. At the same time, the constitutional evidence also partially supports those who argue that the social revolution was boxed in by Federalist theory and institutions. In the course of this chapter and the next, we will consider more carefully the social upheavals that accompanied the general move toward direct consent.

If elections always give consent for political agents to hold office, they do not always do it directly. The electoral college is an instance in which direct consent is given to electors who choose a president, but only indirect consent is given to whomever the electors choose. This fact is masked today by the automatic nature of the electoral college, but occasional electors who cast their votes for someone other than the two major candidates serve as reminders that the president of the United States is, technically, elected indirectly. Even if we consider election of the president essentially direct, we are giving only indirect consent to the cabinet members and other political agents he appoints.

In another sense, too, consent may be indirect. Persons under the age of eighteen give their consent indirectly through their parents. This sense of indirect consent may be considered trivial until one remembers that throughout much of our history, most adults gave their consent indirectly through other adults. Until passage of the Nineteenth Amendment, women were held to give their consent in such a manner, and in the eighteenth century, a significant proportion of adult males were also spoken for by someone else. Under such circumstances, voters gave their direct consent and the indirect consent of others at the same time. The matter of agency consent

1. For a thorough and intelligent review of the controversy, see Jack P. Greene, "Changing Interpretations of Early American Politics," in R. A. Billington (ed.), *The Reinterpretation of Early American History* (San Marino, Calif.: Huntington Library, 1966), 151–84.

thus boils down to two important considerations: 1) what proportion of political agents are directly elected, as opposed to appointed or indirectly elected, and 2) what proportion of the adult population can give direct consent, that is, vote?

Direct Election of Agents

With respect to the lower houses, there was virtually no variation in the pattern. All of them were elected directly by the people, and all but two state constitutions written before 1798 provided for annual elections. It is difficult to imagine a more relentless commitment to direct agency consent. The design of the lower house would remain a constant throughout the era, whether dominated by traditional Whigs, radical Whigs, or Federalists. Change would come, not from a redesign of the institution, but from cumulative alterations in suffrage requirements, which would significantly change the type of legislator being elected.

It is to be expected that the institution embodying the democratic principle in Whig political theory should be so directly linked to the people. The upper house, however, was supposed to embody the aristocratic principle and more vigorously defend the property interests. This role was an essential one in the Whig theory of mixed government, balancing democratic principles with aristocratic and monarchic principles. A brief historical review is in order if one is to appreciate their altered status.

The upper house in colonial America was, almost without exception, appointed by the crown. Upper houses had developed from an expanded privy council designed initially to advise the governor, and while colonists had succeeded in gaining some influence over them, the councils still had strong inclinations to support the governor and defend the royal prerogative. They also tended to defend property and the colonial elite. This latter tendency was not viewed in the negative, as it was simply what the upper house was supposed to do. The problem, as far as the Whigs were concerned, was that the councils were not independent enough from the executive to fulfill their designated role effectively. The obvious solution, after the Declaration of Independence, was to convert them into full-fledged legislative bodies, separate from the executive, and make them elec-

Table 4
ELECTORS AND TERMS OF OFFICE

Constitution	Lower House Elected by	Term	Upper House Elected by	Term	Executive Elected by	Term
1. 1725 Mass.	people	1 yr.	people	1 yr.	people	1 yr.
2. 1776 N.H.	people	1	people	1	people‡	1
3. 1776 S.C.	people	2	people	2	legis.	2
4. 1776 Va.	people	1	people	4*	legis.	1
5. 1776 N.J.	people	1	people	1	legis.	1
6. 1776 Md.	people	1	electors†	5	legis.	1
7. 1776 Del.	people	1	people	3*	legis.	3
8. 1776 R.I.	people	1	people	1	people	1
9. 1776 Conn.	people	1	people	1	people	1
10. 1776 Pa.	people	1	no senate		legis.	1
11. 1776 N.C.	people	1	people	1	legis.	1
12. 1777 Ga.	people	1	no senate		legis.	1
13. 1777 N.Y.	people	1	people	4*	people	3
14. 1777 Vt.	people	1	people	1	people‡	1
15. 1778 S.C.	people	1	people	2	legis.	2
16. 1780 Mass.	people	1	people	1	people‡	1
17. 1784 N.H.	people	1	people	1	people‡	1
18. 1786 Vt.	people	1	people	1	people‡	1
19. 1789 Ga.	people	1	people	3	legis.	2
20. 1790 S.C.	people	2	people	4*	legis.	2
21. 1790 Pa.	people	1	people	4*	people	3
22. 1792 Del.	people	1	people	3	people	3
23. 1792 N.H.	people	1	people	1	people‡	1
24. 1793 Vt.	people	1	people	1	people‡	1
25. 1798 Ga.	people	1	people	1	legis.	2

* Staggered terms.
† Elected by electoral college, which was itself popularly elected.
‡ If no candidate received a majority, the legislature made the final decision by balloting.

tive. Unlike the colonial councils, which had some legislative and advisory functions, the state senates were given full legislative powers, although they could not usually initiate money bills. The two houses were equal powers in a truly bicameral legislature, a pattern that only the first Pennsylvania and Georgia constitutions failed to match, for they relied upon unicameral legislatures.

As the upper house was to embody the aristocratic principle and represent property, certain devices were used to enhance its fulfilling the designated role. Property requirements for those seeking a seat in the senate were typically twice as high as for those standing to the lower house (see Table 5). In about a third of the constitutions before 1789, the term of a senator's office was more than the one year invariably designated for the lower house (see Table 4). Instead of basing representation on the number of voters in a town or county, some states allotted each county an equal number of senators (North Carolina, South Carolina, Delaware, and New Jersey); two states (Massachusetts and New Hampshire) apportioned according to the amount of taxes paid.

These devices were not sufficient for their intended purpose. Their effect was seriously undercut by the almost universal practice of having the senates directly elected by popular vote. This practice was doubly counterproductive because the property requirements defining the suffrage for senate elections were invariably identical with those for house elections (see Table 6). Suffrage requirements were quite liberal, with the result that both houses were elected by the same broad electorate.

Although six constitutions in the first two waves had senate terms longer than one year, the remaining ten provided for annual elections. And six states did not base representation upon number of voters, though six did. High property requirements for holding the office of senator were expected to be most effective in assuring a distinction between those elected to the senates and those elected to the houses. These requirements were, in fact, not very high and excluded far fewer from the senate than was expected. In many cases, almost anyone with a freehold could qualify, and often when they could not, the matter was overlooked.[2]

Through more extreme measures a few states did manage to elect senates that were closer to expectations. Maryland, for example, the only state that did not use popular elections, used an electoral college, which placed the final decision in the hands of a small body of men more open to "aristocratic" influence. Massachusetts and New Hampshire required that a senator receive a majority of the votes cast for his position, and the few who managed this difficult hurdle selected the rest of the body themselves. Connecticut did not place

2. Jackson Turner Main, *The Upper House in Revolutionary America* (Madison: University of Wisconsin Press, 1967), 189.

Table 5
PROPERTY REQUIREMENTS FOR HOLDING OFFICE

Constitution	Lower House	Upper House	Executive
1. 1725 Mass.	£100 or £200*	£300 or £600	£1,000
2. 1776 N.H.	£100	£200	£500
3. 1776 S.C.	not in constitution†	£200 (£7,000 if nonresident)	£10,000
4. 1776 Va.	a freehold	a freehold	none specified
5. 1776 N.J.	£500	£1,000	none specified
6. 1776 Md.	£500	£1,000	£1,000
7. 1776 Del.	none specified	a freehold	none specified
8. 1776 R.I.	none specified	none specified	none specified
9. 1776 Conn.	none specified	none specified	none specified
10. 1776 Pa.	none specified§	(no upper house)	none specified
11. 1776 N.C.	100 acres	300 acres in fee	£1,000
12. 1777 Ga.	250 acres or £250	(no upper house)	none specified
13. 1777 N.Y.	none specified	£100	none specified
14. 1777 Vt.	no requirement	no requirement	no requirement
15. 1778 S.C.	clear of debt	£2,000 (£7,000 if nonresident)	£10,000
16. 1780 Mass.	£100	£300 or estate taxed at £60	£1,000
17. 1784 N.H.	£100	£200 estate	£500
18. 1786 Vt.	no requirement	no requirement	no requirement
19. 1789 Ga.	200 acres or £150	250 acres or £250	500 acres and £1,000 sterling
20. 1790 S.C.	500 acres‡ or £150	£300 clear of debt	£1,500 sterling clear of debt
21. 1790 Pa.	no requirement	no requirement	no requirement
22. 1792 Del.	a freehold	200 acres or £1,000	no requirement
23. 1792 N.H.	£100	£200	£500
24. 1793 Vt.	no requirement	no requirement	no requirement
25. 1798 Ga.	$250 clear or $500 taxable property	$500 or $1,000 taxable property	500 acres and $4,000

* In all cases the first figure on the left side of a column indicates the size of a freehold.
† The constitution refers to an election law for specification of sum.
‡ 500 acres plus ten negroes.
§ Although the constitution mentions no requirement, statutory law required that voters had paid taxes. In 1777 Vermont became the first state-sized political entity to completely separate officeholding from property, just as it separated suffrage from property.

Table 6
PROPERTY REQUIREMENTS FOR VOTING

Constitution	Lower House	Upper House	Executive
1. 1725 Mass.	£3 income* or £60 value	same as lower house	same as lower house
2. 1776 N.H.	poll tax	same as lower house	same as lower house
3. 1776 S.C.	50 acres or tax on same	same as lower house	elected by legislature
4. 1776 Va.	not specified in const.	same as lower house	elected by legislature
5. 1776 N.J.	£50	same as lower house	elected by legislature
6. 1776 Md.	50 acres	electoral college	elected by legislature
7. 1776 Del.	freehold	not specified in const.	elected by legislature
8. 1776 R.I.	not specified in const.	not specified in const.	not specified in const.
9. 1776 Conn.	not specified in const.	not specified in const.	not specified in const.
10. 1776 Pa.	freemen paying taxes	(no upper house)	elected by legislature
11. 1776 N.C.	freemen paying taxes	50 acres	elected by legislature
12. 1777 Ga.	£10 or 6 mo. residence	(no upper house)	elected by legislature
13. 1777 N.Y.	£20 or 40 shilling rent	£100	same as upper house
14. 1777 Vt.	no property requirement	same as lower house	same as lower house
15. 1778 S.C.	50 acres and paid taxes	same as lower house	elected by legislature
16. 1780 Mass.	£60	same as lower house	same as lower house
17. 1784 N.H.	poll tax	same as lower house	same as lower house
18. 1786 Vt.	freemen	same as lower house	same as lower house
19. 1789 Ga.	paid taxes	same as lower house	elected by legislature
20. 1790 S.C.	50 acres or 3 shil tax	same as lower house	elected by legislature
21. 1790 Pa.	no property requirement	same as lower house	same as lower house
22. 1792 Del.	no property requirement	same as lower house	same as lower house
23. 1792 N.H.	paid taxes	same as lower house	same as lower house
24. 1793 Vt.	freemen	same as lower house	same as lower house
25. 1798 Ga.	paid taxes	same as lower house	elected by legislature

* Refers to property that earns at least £3 per year in rent.

names on the ballot but required the voter to write in a name, which insured that only the well known, usually the incumbents, had a chance of winning. The overall result was that senates were somewhat more conservative than lower houses and protected property more carefully; but they failed to provide a consistent check on lower houses, as had been intended. They were, in fact, largely indistinguishable from the lower houses, and most senators, far from refining the democratic influence, responded as one would expect legislators elected for short terms by small property holders to respond.[3]

The failure of senates to consistently defend particular economic interests introduced considerable ambiguity into their role. As the Whig theory of mixed government was losing its hold on Americans, a key institution embodying that theory was decaying into just another branch of the legislature. Theory no longer accounted for behavior, primarily because social and political conditions had changed. The recent resurrection of a true bicameral legislature increasingly lacked justification, forcing a reevaluation of the role of the upper house. Whigs, as well as Federalists, puzzled over the matter until finally, during the Constitutional Convention of 1787, the availability of an upper house with no clear role was to provide the Federalists with a solution to an entirely new problem—how to represent the states in a national government. Ironically, radical Whig attachment to one theoretical proposition, direct popular control, had undermined attachment to another Whig principle, balanced or mixed government. Nevertheless, while the Federalists were to base the national Senate on indirect consent, state constitutions would continue to subject upper houses to relatively direct consent as a legacy of political thought from the era dominated by the radical Whigs.

Of equal interest was agency consent as directed toward the chief executive. During the first wave of constitution making, only four of the twelve states elected their executives directly, the rest giving indirect consent through the legislature (see Table 4). Because the executive was a rather inconsequential figure in the early constitu-

3. *Ibid.*, 189–90.

tions, his not being elected directly was perhaps no great problem. He was usually a creature of the legislature, as befit the Whig desire for legislative supremacy, but his powers had been so restricted that he could not play his intended role according to the theory of mixed government. This restriction is understandable in light of the hostility that governors had evoked during the colonial days, when they embodied and invoked the royal prerogatives that Americans had found so obnoxious. In stripping the executive of these royal trappings, the Whigs destroyed the basis for executive power—effectiveness and efficiency. A passage from the 1776 Virginia Constitution best summarizes the new office. "A Governor, or chief magistrate, shall be chosen annually by joint ballot of both Houses . . . who shall not continue in that office longer than three years successively, nor be eligible, until the expiration of four years after he shall have been out of that office . . . and he shall, with the advice of the Council of State, exercise the executive powers of government, according to the laws of this Commonwealth; and shall not, under any pretence, exercise any power to prerogative, by virtue of any law, statute or custom of England" (Thorpe, 3816). With the exceptions only of Delaware and South Carolina in the first wave of constitutions, the executive served a 1-year term. Coupled with election by the legislature and limits on the number of terms an individual governor could hold, annual election insured the dependency of the office, making the prohibition on prerogative needless and redundant.

As if to add insult to injury, the early constitutions generally provided for an executive council of advisers that was either elected by the legislature or drawn from legislative personnel. During the colonial era, governors had been advised by executive councils or privy councils that also functioned as upper legislative houses. After the Declaration of Independence, these councils were, in effect, split in two. From them came the upper houses, now independent of executive influence and appointment, which in turn produced true bicameral legislatures. Also derived from the colonial councils was a new type of executive or privy council that had no legislative function but was merely advisory. Placing the previously combined advisory and legislative functions into two different bodies looks neat on paper, but the post-Declaration executive council really served little purpose. None of the governors had a veto power or much power of any kind. It is difficult to imagine what matters might require the governors to seek advice, and because the councils were creatures of the legislatures, one would expect them to advise the governor to follow the legislature's lead. That executive councils rested upon indirect popular consent through legislative appointment was not a breach of the trend toward direct agency consent mainly because the councils were of little consequence.

With the 1777 New York Constitution, the first of the second wave, came the first attempt to return the governor to his intended role in a mixed government. New York was torn by a greater degree of popular disorder than any other state at the time. The natural Whig inclination for legislative supremacy was therefore offset by a fear of excessive democracy, and the consequent design for the executive reflected the tension between fear of executive tyranny and fear of majority tyranny. The primary institutional shift was the reintroduction of the executive veto, modified in form, through the ingenious council of revision. The council, composed of governor, chancellor, and supreme court judges, could be overridden by a two-thirds vote in both houses, but it nevertheless gave the governor an important political role to play. New York also designed a council of appointment that comprised the governor and four senators elected by the legislature. The power of appointment was thus lodged in neither the legislature nor the governor, but because the governor once more played a role, his office was, in effect, strengthened.

The 1780 Massachusetts Constitution, written by that grand old Whig John Adams, went the entire distance and gave the governor alone the veto. But, like that of the council of revision, his veto could be overridden by a two-thirds vote. In this highly influential document, we find a revival of the theory of mixed government.[4]

---

4. This was not, however, a revival as far as Massachusetts was concerned, since the 1725 Constitution, in effect until 1780, gave the executive veto powers. The 1780 Constitution emphasized the resurgence of the executive, in Article XIII of Section 1: "As the public good requires that the governor should not be under the undue influence of any of the members of the general court" (Thorpe, 1903).

Vermont followed suit and gave the executive veto power, the federal Constitution eventually copied the provision in detail, and executive veto based on the Massachusetts model became standard in state constitutions. Along with increased power went increased independence, as the governor's term of office became longer in five states than the 1-year terms for the legislatures. Although still second in power to the legislature, the executive was once again a powerful figure.

Increased power was linked with increased popular control in a logical and consistent manner. Whereas the executive had generally been elected by the legislature prior to the New York Constitution, only Georgia and South Carolina thereafter wrote constitutions that failed to have him elected through direct popular consent (see Table 4). Georgia and Pennsylvania joined South Carolina, Delaware, and New York in having executive terms longer than one year, but as late as 1798, five of the eight states electing the governor by direct popular consent still limited him to 1-year terms. Even the three state executives elected popularly to multiple-year terms were limited to three years. In state constitutions the tendency toward direct consent and short terms for the executive runs contrary to the indirect consent and unlimited 4-year term for the executive in the United States Constitution. In the latter case, increased power was not linked with increased popular consent; the only state trends embodied in the federal Constitution with respect to the executive were the enhanced powers of appointment and the strong veto power.

There had been no tradition of electing the judiciary in the colonies. Instead, judges had usually been appointed by the crown. Furthermore, there was no tradition of the judiciary being an independent branch of government. Both Whig theory and English practice made it part of the executive power—a practice dating back to the time when the king traveled from place to place in his realm, adjudicating differences among his subjects. The king would assemble his entourage and interested citizenry in the castle courtyard or in large castle rooms called court rooms, and he was thus said to be "holding court." The lord of a manor likewise held court for adjudicating small matters among his tenants. To handle the case load, the king would appoint certain lords as judges to travel circuits of courts to adjudicate serious matters in his name. The corpus of decisions gradually built up by judges became the basis for English common law, as a set of judical principles slowly became "common" bases for settlement throughout the kingdom.

Americans had chafed under crown-dominated courts in the colonies and were determined to remove the judiciary from executive control.[5] There being, as yet, no concept of three governmental powers, the early state constitutions placed the courts under the only other power available—the legislature. With the exceptions of Maryland, which still permitted judges to be appointed by the governor with the advice of his council, and Pennsylvania, which gave the executive a partial role, the first wave of constitutions sought to make the judiciary so dependent upon the legislature that judges would merely work out the legal details of applying legislative will. Judges were elected by the legislatures, dependent upon them for salary, subject to impeachment by them, and often limited in their tenure.[6] American legislatures also had the habit of interfering with the process of adjudication by amending court decisions with statutory law. This was in keeping with their belief in legislative supremacy and reflected, as well, a distrust of judicial discretion.

In the late 1770s almost every state constitution contained some provision for maintaining so-called separation of powers, but these provisions were aimed primarily at preventing governmental agents from holding multiple offices. Under the crown government, officials were sometimes given several posts so that the combined salaries would support the politically favored agents in sufficient style. This resulted in any number of abuses. Colonists would appeal a judicial ruling to the privy council, only to find the judge who made the ruling was also a member of the council. Proceedings would be undertaken against an official appointed by the crown, and the judge would turn out to be the person in question. There was also the pernicious practice of a governor buying legislative compliance

5. For a nice summary of colonial court structure, see George Dargo, *Roots of the Republic: A New Perspective on Early American Constitutionalism* (New York: Praeger, 1974), especially 46–48.

6. Gordon S. Wood, *The Creation of the American Republic* (Chapel Hill: University of North Carolina Press, 1969), 160–61.

by appointing members to well-paying executive positions. Separation of powers, therefore, was initially a means for preventing political corruption rather than a principle describing fundamental institutional relationships. In colonial times there was no need to differentiate political power, as the legislative clearly derived its power from the people, and the executive derived its power from the crown. Independence destroyed the basis for the distinction and, increasingly, all power was recognized as being derived from popular sovereignty. This being the case, there was no theoretical distinction between a popularly elected legislature and a popularly elected executive. Both derived their authority from the same source, both were based on direct consent, and thus, in a sense, both were representative of the people.[7] As all governmental agents shared in political power drawn from the same source, it became less and less comprehensible in the 1780s to speak of balancing sources of power in a mixed government. With this development, plus increased perception of the legislature as a possible source of tyranny, the upper house, the executive, and the judiciary came increasingly to be regarded as checks on legislative power.

These shifts in thinking led not only to a reinvigoration of the executive but also to a desire for the judiciary to be more independent of the legislature. Beginning with the reconstitution of the executive in the 1777 New York Constitution, there were simultaneous attempts to use the governor's appointive powers as a means of removing the judiciary from legislative dominance. Still subject to impeachment by the legislature, the judges would owe their place, at least in part, to executive action, and life tenure would be more common. These tendencies never reached complete fruition in state constitutions. It was left to the Federalists to draw out fully the implications of separation of powers in the United States Constitution. State constitutions after 1789 would pay lip service to the Federalist principle, but four of the seven constitutions written in the third wave would still make the judiciary a complete creature of the legislature.

There was no attempt to make the judiciary subject to direct

7. *Ibid.*, 445–63.

popular consent in the state constitutions, yet the application of direct consent to the executive, and the temporary removal of the judiciary from the executive, combined to create an important ambiguity. Despite the absence of direct consent through elections, the judiciary nevertheless came to be viewed as embodying the will of the people. Since all power came from the people, and the judiciary was increasingly felt to represent a distinguishable function of political power, the courts were as much the political agents of the people as the legislatures. Legislatures, no longer the sole repository of the will of the people, held limited authority to act on their behalf. Because legislators were not supposed to substitute their will for that of their constituents, the courts were one means of insuring that the legislature stayed within its delegated bounds. From here, it would be only a short step to argue that a court could declare acts of the legislature null and void. This was not because the court was superior to the legislature, but because all branches of government were inferior to the people. Whenever the legislature stood in opposition to the direct will of the people as stated in the constitution, the judiciary must follow the will of the people and enforce the constitution.

Some states would provide for direct election of lower courts, but the primary tactic was to make the judiciary independent of the legislature, thereby aiding its role as protector of the constitution. The judiciaries in New Jersey, Virginia, New York, Rhode Island and North Carolina cautiously began to impose restraints on the legislatures by the 1780s.[8] The stage was set for Hamilton's argument in favor of judicial review set forth in *The Federalist* 78. More important, emphasis upon direct, popular agency consent had slowly but unmistakably shifted many thoughtful Americans from seeking balanced social order in a mixed government to seeking separation of legislative, executive, and judicial functions in order to prevent popular agency consent for the legislature from being converted into government by legislative will.[9] This, in turn, required a

8. *Ibid.*, 454–63.
9. I use the term "thoughtful Americans" because it is impossible to determine how widespread certain shifts in ideas were during the era. The pamphlets and newspaper articles in particular display great care and sophistication on these matters, and there is little doubt that the Federalists had generally shifted to viewing government as comprising three

shift from the assumption that the legislature was the protector of the people, to the realization that the legislature was as potentially dangerous as the executive.

In summary, except for the judiciary, there was a consistent attachment to direct agency consent for both houses of the legislature, and a trend to make the executive directly responsible as well. Subjecting the upper house and the executive to direct consent through elections produced ambiguities that were ultimately instrumental in undercutting the Whig theory of politics. Theoretical and practical aspects of the institutions in operation set the stage for a new American perspective that would come to be described as Federalist. The federal Constitution utilized indirect consent for both the executive and upper house, and thereby ran contrary to the clear and consistent pattern found in state constitutions. In this respect, more than any other, the Federalists were open to the charge of attempting to remove government from popular control. As we shall see later, this charge is in some respects misplaced, although it contains an element of truth.

The People as Defined by the Suffrage

The matter of suffrage is complex and in some respects controversial. It was once fashionable to argue that suffrage restrictions in the 1700s excluded most people from the polls and resulted in government by the few.[10] If this were true, all discussion of direct agency consent would be essentially meaningless. As it turns out, the preponderance of evidence does not support the elitist interpretation.

---

functions rather than three social orders; but most average citizens were considerably slower in altering their thinking. Many historians manage to avoid the problem by assuming that the common people had no coherent political view and simply responded to elite proposals on the basis of short-term gain. An interesting and important attempt to demonstrate that the average citizen in America participated in a widely held political theory and kept up more or less with theoretical shifts can be found in Lawrence H. Leder, *Liberty and Authority: Early American Political Ideology, 1689–1763* (Chicago: Quadrangle Books, 1968).

10. This argument was usually associated with the position that the American Constitution was written by economic elites for their own benefit. Data collected by historians like Jackson Turner Main have largely undercut this argument, and the article by Jack Greene cited in Footnote 1 above summarizes the reasons why the conomic interpretation of the Revolution has been modified. Also, see E. James Ferguson, *The Power of the Purse* (Chapel Hill: University of North Carolina Press, 1961), especially 334–43.

This is not to say that the colonies and states were without elites and were instead ruled by the people at large. It is, rather, that those who held office did not restrict the suffrage to a small percentage of the people of similar background. Consequently, before the Revolution, political leaders, while coming from backgrounds that tended to set them apart from the common man, were required to depend upon deferential voters who were overwhelmingly not of the elite. After 1776, political leaders were far less elite in their background characteristics and had to respond to masses of nonelite voters who were no longer very deferential. Both before and after 1776, American politics is largely comprehensible in terms of factional disputes between competing elites and within ruling elites, but the elite factions were invariably tied, both in their beliefs and in their interests, to substantial portions of the electorate at large. Prior to independence, elite factions carried on their incessant struggles with relatively little interference from the electorate, which was inclined to be either indifferent or aquiescent. From about 1774 onward, elites faced an electorate that was little changed so far as breadth of suffrage was concerned, but was now much more active, interested, and demanding. If "elite rule" conjures up an image of a small band of men quietly and secretly manipulating public affairs to their own advantage, then the American states after 1776 were definitely not ruled by elites. If, on the other hand, it means the tendency for those holding political office to be more educated, somewhat more wealthy, and more inclined to have things in common with other politicians than with the people at large, then America was ruled by elites after 1776. A few colonies may have, from time to time, approximated the first image of elitism, but even then, the instruments for popular intervention were not so much missing as unused. The primary instrument, one never absent from American politics, was a broad suffrage.

Most colonies, in the early years of their history, set voting requirements that produced virtually universal manhood suffrage. The essential requirement was that the person have an "independent will." This precluded children, slaves, prisoners, and the mentally ill, as they were considered to be physically dependent upon others. It also excluded women and those men who were financially dependent upon others and, therefore, could not be trusted to vote their own will as opposed to the will of those upon whom they depended for livelihood. In many places, this included tenant farmers, employed artisans, and those who lacked their own land. Land or wealth, independently held, was the primary criterion for demonstrating an independent will, but anyone who had some stature in the community because of known character or because he performed a useful task that did not require property, could and often did become a voter. This Whig perspective did not differ from that in England. The primary difference was the much greater number of people of independent will in America than in England. Also, there was no true American aristocracy to enforce the criteria in detail.

During the last half of the seventeenth century, suffrage restrictions increasingly tended to confine the vote to Protestant males who had property and were free, white, twenty-one, and native born. Ironically, the New England colonies, which were settled by religious dissenters and were the first to use a broad suffrage, introduced religious tests and more stringent property qualifications in order to retain control of communities increasingly inhabited by landless immigrants of other faiths. Although the religious oligarchs wished to preserve the purity of their communities, the Stuart monarchs, who were restored in 1660, wished to enhance efficiency, honesty, and harmony in colonial government for commercial as well as political reasons. Most charters were rewritten to suit the crown, and suffrage restrictions, redesigned to increase stability, became typical. For a brief period, just prior to the Glorious Revolution in 1688, colonial legislatures were suspended altogether.

The legislatures were quickly restored, but the somewhat restricted suffrage was not ended with the demise of the Stuarts. William and Mary had no reason to extend suffrage, and the mercantile interests dominating Parliament had a stake in prosperous, well-run colonies. In addition, property requirements were commensurate with the Whig notion that persons demonstrating a stake in the community, as well as those displaying the virtue of self-sufficiency through ownership of land, could give consent through elections. They were also congruent with the Whig attachment to virtual representation whereby those not owning property were assumed to be spoken for by those who did. This, in turn, was supported by the assumption of a homogeneous society with a community of interests. In such a community, it made little difference who voted or ran for office, since no one's interest was distinguishable from that of the entire community.

Although there was some opposition to the restrictions, it was not widespread. After all, these were by and large the same suffrage requirements as were found in England. Since 1430, property with a yearly rental value worth forty shillings had been required of voters and thus tradition ratified the practice.[11] Opposition was also undercut by the availability of cheap land. Land was cheap because it was plentiful; often it was only necessary to move far enough inland, and farms could be bought with the labor required to work them, that is, by "squatting." Despite suffrage restrictions, surprisingly few colonists were disenfranchised. The reason is clear. America was overwhelmingly middle class with a broad distribution of wealth.[12] The income ratio between the wealthiest 10 percent and poorest 10 percent was probably as small in the 1750s as it has ever been among a substantial body of people.

While there was considerable variety in detail, by 1778 the typical requirement was a freehold with a value of about fifty pounds sterling. This was not an inconsiderable sum to accumulate; best estimates indicate that 50 pounds was sufficient to support a family of seven for a year at the subsistence level, 100 pounds could support the family in decency, and 150 pounds provided real comfort. A bachelor could be supported by a yearly income of 25 pounds. A new house of average size on an average lot ran around 100 pounds.[13]

Using tax and probate records, Jackson Turner Main estimates that between 75 and 80 percent of adult white males owned prop-

---

11. Chilton Williamson, *American Suffrage from Property to Democracy, 1760–1860* (Princeton, N.J.: Princeton University Press, 1968), 5.

12. An impressive array of data supports this conclusion. See Jackson Turner Main, *The Social Structure of Revolutionary America* (Princeton, N.J.: Princeton University Press, 1965). Also, see Richard Hofstadter, *America at 1750* (New York: Alfred A. Knopf, 1971), especially Chap. v.

13. Main, *Social Structures of Revolutionary America*, 276.

erty at the time. If his sampling is representative, a 50-pound free-hold requirement excluded only about 25 percent of the adult, white male population.[14]

Over 50 percent were small- to medium-sized farmers or artisans and belonged to the middle class (defined as 50 to 500 pounds yearly income). This middle class averaged 300 pounds in real estate and 100 pounds in personal estate. Additionally, there were 15 to 20 percent in the upper middle class (500 to 1,000 pounds) and around 10 percent in the upper income category (over 1,000 pounds in personal property and 1,000 pounds in land). These figures are for the entire country. Northern states had a more egalitarian distribution, especially along the frontier, while southern states had a higher percentage of very wealthy and very poor.[15]

The implications in these figures have been supported by registration and election figures. Chilton Williamson concludes that in the colonial period immediately preceding independence, the electorate varied between 50 and 75 percent of the adult male population. The figures varied from colony to colony, as well as within each colony. Some areas in the north regularly had an 80 percent to 90 percent turnout. It should not be concluded that only those with property voted, given the evidence that the property requirement was frequently overlooked in the case of well-known inhabitants. A man of good character was often allowed to vote in the community where he resided, regardless of the property he held. After all, the property test was primarily used as objective evidence that a citizen

14. Bernard Bailyn summarizes the data as indicating between 50 and 75 percent of the adult, white male population was entitled to vote. See Bernard Bailyn, *The Origins of American Politics* (New York: Alfred A. Knopf, 1969), 87.

15. There is some difficulty conveying to the reader the equivalent of one pound in today's currency. Some currencies in the 1770s were backed up in sterling, others were not. Different values were given to the pound in different states. Jackson Turner Main, in *The Upper House in Revolutionary America*, 95, suggests the following rough equivalency:

1775	1965
£5,000	$250,000
£2,000	$100,000
£ 500	$ 25,000

These figures are of necessity approximate, but he suggests a conversion factor of fifty, so that a 1775 pound equals approximately fifty 1965 dollars. If anything, the conversion factor is a bit high.

could exercise an independent will and possessed a stake in the community. The property criterion could be waived if other, more subjective information indicated the same independence.[16]

A presidential election in the 1950s, in which 85 percent of the adult population was eligible to register after taking residency requirements into account, 85 percent of those eligible actually registered (leaving about 72 percent of the total population able to vote), and 85 percent of these actually voted (or about 62 percent of the total population), would be very close to the standard turnout rate for the 1770s in state elections in the more northern colonies.

The colonial property requirement and turnout figures above are for state elections. With minor exceptions, suffrage requirements for the many town, county, and local elections were considerably less, and, as one might expect, the turnout for these elections was even higher. Especially in the larger towns and cities, voting rights were given to all freemen instead of only to those with a freehold. A freeman was one having "town privileges," which included the rights to live within the incorporated area, move about freely, do business, and vote in elections. During the 1600s, one became a freeman when the town fathers voted it. In some towns, it was required that a person have a freehold—a household on property one owned— before being considered for freemanship. This, of course, made a freehold easier to obtain than status as a freeman. As towns became larger and as some became cities, they included more and more artisans and merchants who had no need for or interest in the traditional freehold, but who clearly warranted being freemen. Freemanship came to be separated from a freehold and, especially in the larger towns and cities, was much easier to obtain than the freehold. It made more sense in urban areas to permit freemen to vote rather than only freeholders, and the relative ease with which this status was achieved made the criterion a broadly enfranchising one. In smaller towns and in county elections, on the other hand, the freehold requirement could often be overlooked by the sheriff for

16. The figure should not be considered typical for other states, but in 1769 about 40 percent of those who voted in New York did not possess land but voted on the basis of their freemanship. See Albert Edward McKinley, *The Suffrage Franchise in the Thirteen English Colonies in America* (New York: Burt Franklin, 1969), 218.

the simple reason that numbers were small enough for him to be familiar with who was and who was not possessed of an "independent will." Local government was the most important level of government in an American's life and generated considerably more interest than state or national matters. For these reasons, local elections more often had a higher turnout rate in the 1770s than they do today.[17] All of this was before the Declaration of Independence. The electorate was to become even broader and more active after 1776.

Between 1776 and 1789, there was a general easing of property requirements for suffrage. Only Vermont completely separated property from voting, but there was a trend to replace the freehold criterion with the much less stringent tax-paying qualification. It is difficult to assess the overall impact of such changes, but Pennsylvania, one of the six states to drop the freehold test, finally qualified an estimated 90 percent of its adult males. Vermont went further and in effect instituted universal adult male suffrage. In New Hampshire, Delaware, Georgia, and North Carolina, tax-paying suffrage requirements virtually guaranteed universal manhood suffrage.

At the same time, religious oaths were largely eliminated, viva voce voting was gradually replaced by the secret ballot, and polling places were moved and increased in number to sharply reduce the average distance a voter had to travel, an important consideration in those days. Most elections were rescheduled for November; previously they had often been held in May, which interfered with planting in many areas. The vast majority of Americans worked the land, and by November crops were safely harvested. Late autumn elections had another benefit, as well. Rain, as is still the case today, tended to lower turnout, especially since the dirt roads then prevalent turned to quagmires. Snow, however, increased turnout in the north, since nothing facilitated land movement more than a nice

17. For detailed discussion of election laws at all levels, see McKinley, *Suffrage Franchise* and Courtland F. Bishop, *History of Elections in the American Colonies* (New York: Burt Franklin, 1968). McKinley's book was originally published in 1905, and Bishop's in 1893. Characteristically, these older works are stronger than more recent books on legal details but are decidedly inferior to more current work in discussing the impact of these laws and practices on turnout.

white blanket over which to pull the 1-horse sleigh. More important, November brought harder ground, if not snow.

The additional factors of the war experience and democratic rhetoric tended to break down the prewar "politics of deference" and replace it with an ethic of citizen equality. Although there is a debate raging among historians as to just how far the point should be pushed, it is clear that prior to the Revolution there was considerable deference on the part of the average citizen when it came to elections.[18] Deference was reflected in two behavior patterns. The first was to expect the "better sort" to hold office, because they were assumed to have greater skill and knowledge in technical areas of finance and the law. The second was to continually reelect incumbents unless they had made grievous errors that were well known to the public. The first pattern certainly follows from the Whig view of politics, emphasizing a community of interest with elections serving primarily as filters for elevating the "more virtuous" men to the top. We do not, however, have opinion surveys from the period to determine how widespread these ideas were among the general population or how strongly they were held. It is possible that much of what we attribute to deference on the part of an average voter may, in fact, have resulted from indifference to political matters. The same holds true for the pattern of returning incumbents to office. In many respects, incumbents in America today are just as likely to be reelected as they were in the 1700s, and indifference to political matters resulting from a general satisfaction among the people, as well as stable public authority, are probably contributing factors in both instances. Regardless of the cause, during the first half of the eighteenth century in America, election behavior could best be described as resulting from acquiescence based on habit, conformity arising from socialization, or the following of tradition.

Beginning about 1765, with resistance to the Stamp Act, Americans were increasingly willing to support candidates with new faces

18. A nice summary of the "politics of deference" and how far the idea should be pushed can be found in John B. Kirby, "Early American Politics—The Search for Ideology: An Historiographical Analysis and Critique of the Concept of Deference," *Journal of Politics*, XXXII (November, 1970), 808–38. Kirby's article also represents another review of the literature summarized by Jack P. Greene, but taken from a different point of view.

Table 7
SELECTED SOCIOECONOMIC DATA ON STATE LEGISLATORS
Economic Status of Representatives*

| | N.H., N.Y., & N.J. | | Md., Va., & S.C. | | Mass.† | |
	Prewar (%)	Postwar (%)	Prewar (%)	Postwar (%)	Prewar (%)	Postwar (%)
Wealthy‡	36	12	52	28	17	8
Well-to-do	47	26	36	42	33	17
Moderate	17	62	12	30	40	55

Occupations of Representatives

| | N.H., N.Y., & N.J. | | Md., Va., & S.C. | | Mass. | |
	Prewar (%)	Postwar (%)	Prewar (%)	Postwar (%)	Prewar (%)	Postwar (%)
Merchants and lawyers	43	18	22.5	17	(Data not available)	
Farmers	23	55	12	26		
Other	34	27	65.5	57		

*Taken from Jackson Turner Main, "Government by the People: The American Revolution and the Democratization of the Legislatures," *William and Mary Quarterly*, 3rd. ser., XXIII (1966), 391–407. Both tables are based on data relating to about nine hundred representatives.

†Data from Massachusetts is calculated differently so that sum of figures is not 100 percent.

‡The reader should not conclude that "average" citizens were being elected. In the colonies as a whole, about 30 percent of the adult white males owned property worth 500 pounds or more. About two-thirds of these had property worth 500 to 2,000 pounds; their economic status here is called *moderate*. Those worth 2,000 to 5,000 pounds are called *well-to-do*, and those with property valued at more than 5,000 pounds are called *wealthy*. Representatives still came almost exclusively from this top 30 percent. While not poor, these men were not an elite. They were owners of medium-sized farms or were artisans, did not come from prominent old families, and had not gone to college. Using various estimates, someone owning 500 pounds' worth of property in 1766 would be roughly equivalent to someone owning property worth $50,000 to $60,000 in 1976. The sum of 2,000 pounds would translate into roughly $200,000 in 1976 terms.

and from lower social and economic strata. It is impossible to sort out the relative impact of these various developments on voting. A decline in deference, reduction in property requirements, more numerous ballot boxes, November elections—all had some effect. For one thing, turnout rates were already so high as to not leave much room for improvement; for another, broader suffrage requirements brought in people who had not generally voted in the past, and, as we know today, marginal voters tend to have a low turnout rate. There is the further fact that almost all states disenfranchised Loyalists or required oaths of them. These men were not likely to be in-

terested in voting for radical Whigs anyway, and as they constituted
at least 10 percent of the population and upwards of 30 percent of
the politically active class, the fact that turnout did not decline indicates considerable increase in turnout among non-Loyalists. In
some states, such as New York, there was no material increase in
the percentage of men eligible to vote. In Pennsylvania, though, it is
estimated that, outside of Philadelphia, the electorate expanded by
5 to 10 percent during the late 1770s and 1780s, and the turnout
rate increased proportionately. In the face of Tory disfranchisement,
if not disenchantment, the net change must be considered significant.

Even more dramatic is the effect on the type of men being elected
to office. Despite only slight reductions in property requirements
for those seeking office, there was a significant shift toward middle
class representatives (see Table 5 for property requirements and
Table 7 for evidence of the shift toward middle class representatives). In several states, the percentage of farmers in the legislature
was almost identical with their percentage in the general population, and here we are speaking not of large landowners, but of owners of moderate-sized farms close to what Jefferson held as the ideal.
A factor perhaps more important than the decline in average wealth
was the recruiting of the postwar generation of legislators from outside the social elite. Prominent old families continued to send a dis-
proportionate share of their sons into legislatures, but unlike the
prewar situation, this portion of society became a distinct minority
where it had once dominated.

The data in Table 7 pertain to the lower houses, but the upper
houses, supposed bastions of wealth and aristocracy, did not escape
the social revolution. There the wealthy from established families
provided only about one-fourth the membership. Fewer than one in
five senators was an educated man. As a result, contrary to Whig
theory, senators did not defend particular economic interests but became almost indistinguishable from members of the lower houses,
though they were somewhat more conservative. This reality forced
a reevaluation of the bicameral system and the reasons for having
one. The Federalists at the Constitutional Convention made the

Senate represent the states as units, versus the House representing numbers of people. This shift in justification represents one of the great compromises at the Convention and was an imaginative solution to one of the most serious political problems facing it. The need for a new justification for bicameralism and the nature of the problem solved by the compromise go far toward explaining the break with earlier constitutional practice.

The easing of property requirements for voting did more than indicate the demise of virtual representation. It also reflected the strong demands for voting equality. Partly because districting by towns and counties introduced inevitable disparities in the number of representatives from different areas, and partly because equality was increasingly emphasized in discussions of representation, the second and third wave constitutions often contained stringent apportionment and districting sections to equalize voting district populations. Pennsylvania (1776) had the first provision linking representation to equal numbers of citizens, but it was not enforced until seven years after the constitution went into effect because, initially, representation was to be based on counties. The 1777 New York Constitution was the first to provide both for districts with equal numbers of people and periodic redistricting to adjust for population shifts.[19] By the 1780s, this provision was a familiar though not universal one in state constitutions. For reasons that are unclear, a 7-year period instead of a 10-year period was usually designated for periodic redistricting. Section 2 of Article I in the United States Constitution has its origin in the provisions first found in the Pennsylvania and New York constitutions.

Although there was some sentiment at the Constitutional Convention to reinstate more rigid property qualifications, the Federalists wisely decided to leave suffrage requirements to the states and specified that suffrage requirements for electing congressmen should be the same as those specified for electing members to the lower houses in the respective states. Although several theoretical justifications were advanced in support of states setting the requirements,

19. The New York provision is in Article V (Thorpe, 2629), and Pennsylvania's is in Sections 17 and 18 (Thorpe, 3086).

arguments of political expediency and practicality were apparently decisive. There was no hope of reversing the trend to broader suffrage without setting the wrath of the many against the proposed Constitution. The United States Constitution thus confirmed and underwrote the eased suffrage requirements by leaving the matter to the states. In this respect, at least, the Federalists did not impede the development toward more direct agency consent and greater popular control of government.

5

Programmatic Consent

To what extent, if any, is it possible for the people at large to give direct consent for specific pieces of legislation? Strictly speaking, this is possible only if all the people could gather together somewhere and pass the legislation themselves, although the initiative and popular referendum approximate this. Direct democracy, as this would be, is ruled out by definition when a political system uses elected representatives for collective decision making. Thus, giving agency consent rules out the possibility of direct programmatic consent in a strict sense.

There are, however, degrees of indirectness. A basic trend between 1776 and 1789 was the attempt to make representatives mirror the wishes of the people in order to make programmatic consent as direct as possible in a representative system. A nice statement describing the mirror theory of representation can be found in the Essex Result, written by Theophilus Parsons and sent by citizens of Essex County as a critique of the proposed Massachusetts Constitution of 1778. "Representatives should have the same views, and interests with the people at large. They should think, feel, and act like them, and in fine, should be an exact miniature of their constituents. They should be (if we may use the expression) the whole body politic, with all its property, rights, and privileges, reduced to a smaller scale, every part being diminished in just proportion."[1] John Adams had said essentially the same thing in his *Thoughts on Government* published two years earlier. Impossible as it sounds, there was a serious and reasonably successful effort to create legis-

1. The Essex Result is reprinted in Oscar Handlin and Mary Handlin, *The Popular Sources of Political Authority* (Cambridge, Mass.: Harvard University Press, 1966), 341.

latures that would produce legislation indistinguishable from that which would be passed by the people if gathered in the same room. There were at least four mechanisms available at the time for furthering this end: (1) frequent elections, (2) a broadly defined suffrage, (3) reduced requirements for officeholding, and (4) petitions and instructions to the legislatures. As the first three have already been discussed at length in another context, they will be regarded only briefly to clarify their impact on programmatic consent.

Whig doctrine, presupposing a common community of interest, urged the election of men possessing demonstrated ability and virtue. The first wave of constitutions often stated baldly that "persons most noted for wisdom and virtue" were to be chosen. Once in office, these representatives were on their own to protect the best interests of the community and were essentially left alone until the next election. The more frequent the elections, the more control citizens would have over legislation. The idea was that dissatisfaction with specific items of legislation would be demonstrated by "voting the scoundrels out of office." Thus, in theory, representatives would remain tuned to popular sentiment to insure reelection. Empirical research on modern legislatures casts doubt on the validity of this theory, although conditions in the 1700s may have made it a more realistic possibility then.

However well frequent elections worked in this regard, only two of the first twenty-five constitutions gave more than a 1-year term of office to members of the lower house. The branch of the legislature designed to embody the democratic principle was kept close to the people. The upper house, which was not supposed to reflect the democratic principle, was frequently given 1-year terms as well. This fact, as much as a broadened suffrage, was responsible for the senates being largely indistinguishable from the lower houses. Both were subject to yearly scrutiny, and with memories still fresh, the voters could maintain better control. Also, legislatures in those days did not pass nearly as many pieces of legislation as they do today. Records show that a busy session might produce only seventy or eighty bills, and a few sessions resulted in no bills at all. Certainly voters had an easier time than they do now, keeping track of their respective legislator's behavior.

There was a constitutional precedent for the Federalist design of an indirectly elected Senate with staggered terms of greater than one year (Maryland), just as there was a precedent for the electoral college (the Maryland senate); but the precedent was the exception to general constitutional practice. The important trend in the first twenty-five state constitutions in this regard was that there was no serious departure from the early Whig practice of keeping both houses of the legislature close to the people through frequent elections. In this fashion, agency consent became a reasonable form of programmatic consent as well.

With respect to the second mechanism for enhancing popular programmatic consent, a broadly defined suffrage insured that all the community would cast its light upon the mirror. The presumption was that people would vote for "their own kind," and if all kinds voted, then representation within the legislature would be proportionate, producing a miniature of the entire society. The miniature would act in a manner indistinguishable from that of the entire society gathered together.

With regard to the Whig distinction between upper and lower houses, the ideal was for legislation affecting property to be approved or consented to by a majority of property (or, more properly, those owning a majority of the property), and for laws affecting persons to be approved by a majority of persons. Because most laws affected both, consent from both was required. Requiring more property of both those running for and those electing to the upper house was, thus, a logical step. The first state constitutions, however, went only halfway. Table 5 shows the steeper property requirements for those running, but Table 6 indicates a general lack of distinction in suffrage requirements between the two houses. Apparently it was felt that the former arrangement was sufficient, but as explained in Chapter 4, it was not, and the two houses became largely indistinguishable in their membership and legislative output.

The theoretical distinction did have one initially unnoticed side effect. Since property was supposedly protected by the senate, and the lower house was to represent persons, there was no reason to restrict suffrage for the lower house. Freed from concern that a majority of persons could undermine property rights, the framers of the early constitutions could define a liberal suffrage for the legislatures with few qualms. Their error was in using the same liberal suffrage to elect the senates; and once this practice was established, it was difficult (if not impossible) to restrict suffrage in the face of an active electorate. Once again, it can be seen how the Whig commitment to equality inadvertently undercut the Whig principle of mixed government. The broadly defined suffrage undermined representation of property in the upper house and aided the move toward a more direct popular programmatic consent.

The third possible mechanism, reduction in property requirements for candidates to office, did not materialize. There were no major trends away from a property requirement or toward higher sums over the years in question. The few states altering the sums did reduce them slightly, but more typical was Georgia, which required a 250-pound freehold in 1777, 1789, and again in 1798. Keeping it the same actually amounted to a reduction, given currency changes and increased per capita income over the twenty-one years.

Reducing property requirements for officeholding would have aided programmatic consent by permitting a broader cross section of the population to run for office. If legislatures became more representative of all citizens, presumably they would produce legislation closer to what was desired by the people. There was also the important fact that the towns in the interior were poorer, and generally speaking, had few wealthy people, if any. Therefore, the property requirement also had geographical implications. That property requirements were only slightly reduced and not eliminated does not so much reflect a negative attitude toward popular programmatic consent—although there was a substantial amount of negative sentiment—as it reflects the general irrelevancy of the requirement. Americans were electing men to both the upper and lower houses that looked a great deal like the electorate as defined by broad suffrage requirements. Property requirements for holding office did not impede the trend toward more direct programmatic consent.

Petitions and Instructions

Americans during the revolutionary era had frequent elections, a broad electorate, and legislatures that were reasonably representative of the general population despite property requirements for officeholding; but they did not let the matter rest there. In addition, numerous passages proclaimed the right of citizens to petition or instruct their representatives. For example, "The people have a right, in an orderly and peaceable manner, to assemble and consult upon the common good: *give instructions to their representatives*, and to request of the legislative body, by the way of addresses, petitions or remonstrances, redress of the wrongs done them, and of the grievances they suffer (Massachusetts Constitution, 1780, Section XIX; Thorpe, 1892; emphasis added). Maryland was the first, in 1776, to break with the Whig practice of electing "virtuous" men and leaving them on their own. Two sections in the declaration of rights at the beginning of its constitution left no doubt that in the future, the legislature would be expected to perform in a manner similar to that later outlined in the Essex Result.[2] Pennsylvania and North Carolina followed suit in the same year and couched the right to instruct in almost the same words as those cited above from the Massachusetts Constitution. This formulation would be found in a majority of the early constitutions.

These were not mere paper promises. The people did press their demands vigorously and often, whether their state constitutions urged them to or not. The tradition of petitioning was an old one in America, but 1776 brought an entirely new attitude, one that reversed the role of petitioner and petitioned. Perhaps the best way to illustrate the matter is to cite several typical petitions from both the prewar and postwar years. The first example is typical for prewar years both in its language and in its being addressed to the governor, rather than to the legislature.

> To his Excellency Benning Wentworth Esq. Captain General & Governour in Chief in and over his Majestyes Province of New Hampshire:
> The Humble Petition of us the subscribers for ourselves and our

2. Sections IV and XI, Thorpe, 1687.

associates being in number Fifty one Humbly Sheweth that your Petitioners are desirous of Setling a Township in some of the unappropri-
ated Lands in said province.

Wherefore your Petitioners Humbly Pray that your Excellency will
be pleased to grant . . . Subjected to such orders and restrictions as
Your Excellency in Your Great Wisdom Shall See Meete. And as in
Duty bound they will ever pray etc. [signed by fifty-one men].[3]

Compare this with the following post war document.

At a legal meeting of the Inhabitants of the Town of Fitz William,
held upon adjournment august 14th 1783; Voted, To give their Representative for the ensuing Year the following Instructions—

. . . .
We do therefore recommend it to you, Sir to use your influence to prevent any alteration being made in the above mentioned Eighth article
of the Confederation. . . . we therefore request you, Sir, to use your
influence to prevent this pay being given to the officers of our army, as
we cannot consent to it, or any thing that is so subversive of the Principles of american Revolution—Further, we must Depend upon your
Exertions, and if need be that you Strain every nerve, to prevent the
return of those persons called Tories.[4]

Many are short and precise, while others, like this last one, go
on in great detail, anticipating and instructing with respect to every
issue that is likely to arise in the coming session. Instructions to the
legislatures were not always so friendly. "Your reelection at this important crisis, is a fresh testimony of the affection of your Constituents and of our confidence in your abilities and integrity; but as
we judge you desirous to find yourselves supported in the faithful
discharge of the high trust resposed in you by our suffrages, we have
thought fit to give you the following Instructions while we depende
upon your best exertions to carry them out." This not-so-subtle
threat at withdrawal of future support is followed by some very
terse language. "We instruct you to revise all the laws now existing
respecting our paper currency, and to use your influence for the re-

3. [29] Petition for a Grant of the Township, 1750, in Isaac W. Hammond (ed.),
Documents Relating to Towns in New Hampshire (Concord, N.H.: Parsons B. Cogswell,
1882), XI, 22.
4. [4-53] Instructions to their Representatives, 1783, in Hammond (ed.), *Documents
Relating to Towns in New Hampshire*, XI, 675.

peal of any inconsistent with those principles. . . . Acting in the legislative department you will not be unmindful of the judicial; but studiously endeavor, to render the courts of law independent of every kind of undue influence. . . . We wish an enquiry into the State of the treasury as well as frequent adjustments of all public accounts."[5] Imagine, if you can, citizens today sending a letter with such language to their state legislator on a regular basis and seriously expecting him to comply. Yet, during the revolutionary era, instructions from the citizenry did carry considerable weight.

One example of legislative response will be cited, for it dramatically illustrates both the new relationship between citizen and representative and the problems it sometimes created for the legislator.

To the Electors of Anne Arundel County:

GENTLEMEN: We were honoured on Saturday afternoon with instructions from a considerable number of inhabitants of this county, on points of very great importance, relative to the formation of a new Government for this State. As your Delegates, we esteem ourselves bound by your instructions, though every so contrary to our opinions. We conceive several of your last instructions, if carried into execution, destructive of a free Government. We are reduced to this alternative: we must either endeavor to establish a Government without a proper security for liberty or property or surrender the trust we have received from you. We submit to you the propriety of reconsidering your instructions. We would with pleasure wait on you at the most convenient places in the County, to explain our reasons against the restrictions your are pleased to impose upon us; but we are prevented by our necessary attendance on the publick business. . . . We are, gentlemen, with sincere respect and esteem, your obedient servants,

CHARLES CARROLL
BRICE T. B. WORTHINGTON
SAMUEL CHASE

Annapolis, August 19, 1776.[6]

That Messrs. Carroll, Worthington, and Chase had cause for concern may be better understood when it is realized that the letter of

---

5. [9-125] Instructions to Representatives, 1780, in Hammond (ed.), *Documents Relating to Towns in New Hampshire*, XIII, 289.

6. Peter Force (ed.), *American Archives: Fifth Series, A Documentary History of the United States of America*, I, 1055.

instruction from the citizens of Anne Arundel County was signed by 885 freemen. More often, instructions came from smaller groups, frequently from local committees of correspondence or safety, but the revolutionary legislatures depended heavily upon their local political base at a time when they were not certain of majority support, and they were not inclined to ignore petitions, no matter how they were worded. Feverish citizen lobbying, coupled with the larger number of middle-class legislators elected after 1776, resulted in very responsive legislatures.

Indeed, they were at times too responsive for some. The Federalists professed horror at the legislative flip-flops resulting from rapidly shifting popular demands, and no one was more insistent on this point than James Madison. During the Constitutional Convention, he was one of several who berated the flaws in state constitutions.[7]

Federalist Response to Direct Programmatic Consent

In April of 1787, barely a month before the Constitutional Convention was scheduled to begin, Madison wrote a paper entitled "Vices of the Political System of the United States."[8] The list of vices is impressive and it apparently gives almost equal weight to the inadequacy of the Articles of Confederation and the failure of republican government in the States.

1. Failure of the states to comply with the constitutional requisitions.
2. Encroachments by the states on the federal authority.
3. Violations of the law of nations and of treaties.
4. Trespasses of the states on the rights of each other.
5. Want of concern in matters in which common interest requires it.
6. Want of guaranty to the states of their constitutions and laws against internal violence.
7. Want of sanction of the laws, and of coercion in the government of the confederacy.

7. Max Farrand (ed.), *The Records of the Federal Convention of 1787* (4 vols.; New Haven, Conn.: Yale University Press, 1966), I, 48, 133–34, 255, 424, 525, 533; II, 285.

8. Gaillard Hunt (ed.), *The Writings of James Madison* (New York: G. P. Putnam's Sons, 1901), II, 361–69.

8. Want of ratification by the people of the Articles of Confederation.
9. Multiplicity of laws in several states.
10. Mutability of the laws of the states.
11. Injustice of the laws of the states.

Read one way, Madison's paper seems primarily an indictment of the Articles of Confederation. Read another way, it is a comprehensive indictment of state governments. Except for numbers 7 and 8, he was condemning the activity of state legislatures: they had overstepped their powers and made separate treaties, violated treaties made by Congress with other nations, supported fraud against citizens of other states, and constantly repealed or superseded laws "before any trial can have been made of their merits." He was saying that the Articles were ineffective, but state government was vicious.

The first paragraph under number 11 is the most striking summary of the issue separating Whig from Federalist to be found in the literature. "If the multiplicity of laws prove a want of wisdom, their injustice betrays a defect still more alarming; more alarming not merely because it is a greater evil in itself; but because it brings more into question the fundamental principle of republican Government, that the majority who rule in such governments are the safest Guardians both of public Good and private rights."[9] Madison here laid bare the difference in assumptions underlying the radical Whig definition of republican government (on p. 17, herein) and the Federalist definition (on p. 21, herein). Because it was questionable whether the majority was the best guardian of public good and private right, direct popular consent was also brought into question, especially direct programmatic consent.

Madison went on to discuss the causes of republican injustices at great length, and while he put part of the blame on improperly motivated representatives, the core of the problem lay in the people themselves. When split into factions with differing interests, "all civilized societies" were vulnerable to majorities that were formed, out of a "common passion" which failed to take into account the

9. *Ibid.*, 366.

interests or rights of the minority. Previewing the famous argument in *The Federalist* 10, Madison concluded that the solution lay in a more extended republic, which would make majorities more difficult to form, and in institutions which would "extract from the mass of the society the purest and noblest characters" and modify sovereignty in such a fashion as would "render it sufficiently neutral between the different interests and factions, to control one part of the society from invading the rights of another." While Madison was not as strong as Hamilton in his belief that a certain segment of society had the lion's share of republican virtue, he did share with Hamilton the belief that the remedy for defective republican government at the state level lay not in reforming state governments but in making them subject to a more adequately constructed national government based on a somewhat different view of republicanism.

To what extent was Madison's characterization of republican vices an accurate one? He provided examples for most of the vices, and for those which he did not, we can fill in the blanks ourselves. Vice number 6, which appears to catalog a weakness of the confederation, is actually a charge against state government and reflects a fear prominent in Federalist minds. At least three major examples of internal violence were found during the 1780s. In 1784, the inhabitants of four western counties in North Carolina formed a separate state called Franklin. Only in the spring of 1787 was the issue resolved and North Carolina made integral again. Also in the spring of 1787, inhabitants of the Wyoming Valley in Pennsylvania sought to secede and establish a new state. The governor of Pennsylvania responded by ordering the state militia into readiness, which was how the matter stood as Madison wrote his essay. Most important, there had occurred in central and western Massachusetts an armed insurgency led by Daniel Shays, a Revolutionary War veteran and officeholder in Pelham. The insurgents tried to prevent action against debtors by intimidating and closing the courts, and not until February of 1787 was the rebellion suppressed through force of arms. Shays's Rebellion had a dramatic impact. The call for a constitutional convention in the autumn of 1786 had been heeded by only three states and ignored by the Continental Congress, but in February of 1787, Congress itself called for a convention, and this time nine states responded promptly. Events in Massachusetts and the continuing problem of paper money legislation combined to spur action on a new national constitution.[10]

The multiplicity, mutability, and injustice of state laws were connected phenomena, as far as Madison was concerned, but it was the injustice of state laws that concerned him most. That the number of laws passed by state legislatures dramatically increased is confirmed through an examination of state legislative records. The matter of what constitutes an unjust law, however, cannot be settled by counting, for it is subject to normative judgments. The Pennsylvania Council of Censors issued a report in 1784 that listed many legislative violations of the state constitution and bill of rights. These included disallowing claims established by the judiciary, remitting fines, setting aside jury verdicts, giving the property of one to another, securing defective titles, dissolving marriages, and releasing persons being held in execution of debt.[11] Edward S. Corwin has examined the laws of New Hampshire between 1784 and 1792 and reported that they are "replete with entries showing that throughout this period, the state legislature freely vacated judicial proceedings, annulled or modified judgment, cancelled executions, reopened controversies, authorized appeals, granted exemptions from the standing law, expounded the law for pending cases, and even determined the merits of disputes."[12] These practices were not confined to Pennsylvania and New Hampshire but typified the operation of legislative supremacy in most states.

Were these practices unjust? They could be considered unjust if one supposes that the legislature was acting arbitrarily in these instances rather than applying coherent and consistent principles. Significantly, Madison nowhere makes this argument. The Pennsylvania Council of Censors argued that these practices were unjust

10. Edward S. Corwin, "The Progress of Constitutional Theory Between the Declaration of Independence and the Meeting of the Philadelphia Convention," *American Historical Review*, XXX (1924–25), 533. Also, for an impressive analysis and summary of state and federal financial matters during the era, especially with respect to the paper money issue, see E. James Ferguson, *The Power of the Purse* (Chapel Hill: University of North Carolina Press, 1961), particularly 109–14, 221, 243, 250, 285–86, and 334–43.

11. Alpheus T. Mason and Gerald Garvey (eds.), *American Constitutional History: Essays by Edward S. Corwin* (New York: Harper & Row, 1964), 8.

12. Corwin, "Progress of Constitutional Theory," 514.

because they were contrary to the state constitution and bill of rights. In this sense, justice is defined with respect to the lawfulness of an act. Leaving aside for the moment whether the council of censors was correct in its assessment, it is important to note that Madison does not make this argument either.

To comprehend Madison's position more clearly, it is useful to recall that Whig political theory was, in fact, based upon legislative supremacy, and the radical Whigs did not differ from traditional Whigs in this respect. Furthermore, as Corwin points out, these legislative practices were not only commensurate with "the teaching of the highest of all legal authorities before Blackstone appeared on the scene," they also "corresponded exactly to the contemporary necessities."[13] Sir Edward Coke fused what we today distinguish as "legislative" and "judicial" powers, and the collapse of the royal judicial establishment with the outbreak of war virtually compelled the legislatures to intervene with special legislation to disallow fraudulent transactions, cure defective titles, authorize urgent sales of property, and so on. In Corwin's words, "Between legislation of this species and outright interference with the remedial law itself, there was often little to distinguish."[14]

Also, the as yet undeveloped doctrine of separation of powers amounted to little more than a prohibition on multiple officeholding, at least as far as the Whigs were concerned. The Federalists, however, had developed a theory of political power that made all branches of government representative of popular will and viewed separation of powers as much more than a prohibition of multiple officeholding. For them, the doctrine meant a clear division and balancing of governmental powers.[15] Madison's characterizations of certain legislative practices as "evils" and "unjust" thus ran counter to the political theory generally adhered to by the Whig framers of early state constitutions. He, along with other Federalists, was opposed to legislative supremacy as such, not only to specific manifes-

13. *Ibid.*, 515. Blackstone was himself a strong advocate of legislative omnipotence, and thus, in this regard, merely reinforced Coke's influence.

14. *Ibid.*, 516.

15. Gordon S. Wood, *The Creation of the American Republic, 1776–1787* (Chapel Hill: University of North Carolina Press, 1969), 150–59 and 548–53.

tations of legislative power. In *The Federalist* 81, Hamilton defended judicial review against the Whig charge that it would undercut
legislative supremacy on grounds that would be conclusive from the
standpoint of modern constitutional theory; but at that time, he
could cite only Montesquieu in his defense, as his position contra-
dicted the views and practices prevalent in the states in 1787.[16]

Why Madison, Hamilton, and other Federalists cast a jaundiced
eye on legislative supremacy is clear both from Madison's "Vices"
and *The Federalist* 10. In the former, he wrote: "A still more fatal
if not more frequent cause [for these evils] lies among the people
themselves. All civilized societies are divided into different interests
and factions, as they happen to be creditors or debtors—rich or
poor—husbandmen, merchants, or manufacturers—members of
different religious sects—followers of different political leaders—
inhabitants of different districts—owners of different kinds of property, etc."[17] In *The Federalist* 10, he is even more to the point. "But
the most common and durable source of factions, has been the
various and unequal distribution of property. Those who hold, and
those who are without property, have ever formed distinct interests
in society. Those who are creditors, and those who are debtors,
fall under a like discrimination. A landed interest, a manufacturing
interest, a mercantile interest, a monied interest, and many lesser
interests, grow up of necessity in civilized nations, and divide them
into different classes, actuated by different sentiments and views."[18]
In summary, the Federalists considered the enumerated legislative
practices as unjust because the relatively direct programmatic consent, embodied in supreme legislatures based upon representation of
numbers, was consistently being applied against certain economic
interests. Since these economic cleavages were at the heart of political faction, to favor one set of interests over another was fundamentally destabilizing. This is not to argue an economic interpretation of the United States Constitution. If we take the Federalists at
their word, their intent was to produce institutions that would favor
no set of interests, but would be "sufficiently neutral between the

16. Corwin, "Progress of Constitutional Theory," 517.
17. Hunt (ed.), *Writings of James Madison*, II, 366.
18. Jacob E. Cooke (ed.), *The Federalist* (Cleveland: World, 1967), 59.

different interests and factions" so as to "controul one part of society from invading the rights of another." It is understandable, given state legislative supremacy and the manner in which this supremacy was used, why the Federalists discovered "majority tyranny" and elevated it to a problem of major theoretical importance. At the same time, their characterization of these practices as unjust flowed from a political theory not yet held or understood by most Americans.

Whig Response to Federalist Criticism

To be sure, framers of state constitutions were themselves somewhat apprehensive. A few constitutions in the 1780s began to insist upon separation of powers in the Federalist sense as a means of reducing legislative incursions into executive and judicial areas. Furthermore, they specifically prohibited, in their bills of rights, some of the more extreme behavior. For example, Section XVII of the 1786 Vermont Constitution reflects earlier abuse when it states, "No person ought, in any case, or in any time, be declared guilty of treason or felony by the Legislature." Yet this same constitution retains the provision stating the right of the people to instruct the legislature, as do most of the Constitutions after it.

If state legislatures were so unjust, it needs to be asked why those writing constitutions, and those approving them, continued down the same institutional road. It may well be because most people were satisfied with their state governments, and if there were flaws, new constitutions would be written or adjustments would be made in the old ones.

This was a time in American history when political institutions were treated as experiments rather than sacrosanct gifts from the golden past. There was constant tinkering and debate. Was the legislature too powerful? Add a few more rights and strengthen the language. Make the executive more powerful and divide the legislature into two houses. The effect was usually ameliorative. Because Whig principles continued to dominate at the state level, the resurrected executive was kept almost as close to the people as the legislature. He was unable to develop the independence and power to effectively neutralize the legislature. The senates became indistinguishable from the lower houses because they, too, were subjected to direct consent by essentially the same electorate. The judiciary was made independent in some states, but it lacked a truly independent political base. Besides, it was invariably dependent upon the legislature for salary. Bills of rights became more effective as barriers against legislative will, but did not become nearly as effective as they are today. The ability of the legislature to alienate many important rights was never rescinded at the state level during the eighteenth century. Most people seemed perfectly happy for their state legislatures to be highly responsive to the people. That had been the aim of the radical Whigs, and they had been successful. During the 1790s, Americans continued to press their demands vigorously at the state legislative level.

This should not surprise us, because Americans were dedicated to local control. Most government took place at the level of the town or county, and state legislatures continued to be viewed as creatures sustained from below, in contrast to our current tendency to view towns and counties as creatures of the state. Direct programmatic consent was based not only on the theory of popular consent, but also on the reality of political power residing at the local level.

One measure of how satisfied the people were with their Whig state constitutions is the lack of speed with which they were replaced. Between 1776 and 1798, a period of twenty-two years, the first fourteen states wrote and adopted twenty-five constitutions. During the next twenty-two years, these states would write and adopt a total of one constitution. Even this understates the case, as many states did not replace their radical Whig documents until the Civil War. By 1865, the average Whig document had lasted at least sixty years before being replaced. If there was such widespread dissatisfaction with the state constitutions, why was there not a wave of new ones after 1789 patterned on Federalist institutions? Why did those writing state constitutions continue to use the 1780 Massachusetts document as their model, one written by John Adams, the Whig, instead of the federal Constitution, written by men like James Madison, the Federalist? It is beyond the scope of this effort to answer such questions definitively, but it is worth hazarding a few guesses.

Table 8
DURATION OF WHIG CONSTITUTIONS

State	Last constitution before 1798	Replaced in	Duration
1. Mass.	1780 .... Still in use today		199 years‖
2. N.H.	1792 .... after 1865		73+ years
3. S.C.	1790 .... 1865*		75 years
4. Va.	1776 1830		54 years
5. N.J.	1777 1821		44 years
6. Md.	1776 1851		75 years
7. Del.	1792 1831		39 years
8. R.I.	1776† 1842		66 years
9. Conn.	1776‡ 1816		40 years
10. Pa.	1790 1838		48 years
11. N.C.	1776 1865		89 years
12. Ga.	1798 1865		67 years
13. N.Y.	1777 1821		44 years
14. Vt.	1793 1830		37 years
		Average:	67.9 years§

*The southern states—South Carolina, North Carolina, and Georgia—were forced to change their pre-1798 constitutions at the end of the Civil War. Thus, these three changes did not result from dissatisfaction on the part of the citizens.

†The 1776 document was actually the 1663 charter readopted, therefore, its duration is more properly 179 years.

‡The 1776 document was the 1662 charter readopted, making its true duration 154 years.

§If we take into account the actual duration of the Massachusetts and New Hampshire Whig documents, and the true duration of the Rhode Island and Connecticut Whig documents, the average life span was at least 85.6 years. We say "at least" because the three southern states had their old constitutions changed against their collective wills, and thus the average Whig document would have had an even longer life span.

‖The 1780 Massachusetts Constitution is currently the oldest written constitution in the world.

First, dissatisfaction with state constitutions was not so wide-spread as some Federalists would have us believe. Second, citizens became much less aggressive in pressing their demands as the revolutionary era was replaced by "normal politics." This alone would have eliminated most of the excesses that so unnerved the Federalists. Third, formal institutions developed at the state level to hem in popular or arbitrary demands. One such institution might be legislative parties. Another might be the development of a settled body of law, interpreted and administered by a judicial and legal system staffed by lawyers. In this last respect, it is sometimes forgotten that the Revolution had eliminated most judges, who were crown appointments. It is known that the ranks of trained lawyers were also depleted. The figures in Table 7 show few lawyers in state legislatures shortly after 1776. The gradual replenishment of state bodies with lawyers could not but ease questionable legislative practices based on ignorance or the absence of legalistic minds.

Whatever the reason, in 1790 Whig institutions still reigned supreme in the states, while Federalist ones, based on a different political theory, were enshrined at the national level. How this paradox came about is partially explained by the old observation that the Federalists arrived with a plan and set the context of the debate at the Constitutional Convention. It is also explained by the fact that the broad institutional design for the United States Constitution looked familiar to most Americans, and the words used, though now given a new meaning, were the same as those used by Whigs.[19] Many Antifederalists were concerned by unusual institutional arrangements in the proposed federal Constitution, but they were not possessed of a common view. The term *Antifederalist* referred to a grab bag of traditional Whigs and radical Whigs of various hues. It was impossible for them to produce a coherent counterproposal, since they lacked a common political philosophy for a national constitution. The Whigs were, after all, localist in their orientation, suspicious of government distant from the people, and uninterested in or hostile toward many aspects of trade and economic development. Some were inclined toward aristocratic views, and many others were extreme democrats.

That the Federalists based their power on superior organization rather than on superior numbers is attested to by their brief 10-year reign in American national politics. Individual Federalists like James Madison would remain influential at the national level, but the coming of the nineteenth century would witness the continued vigor of radical Whig ideas. The gradual expansion of the electorate to universal manhood suffrage, direct election of the Senate, pressures for direct election of the executive—all these would be touted as the rise of democratic government, whereas it could have been said with equal truth that they hearkened back to the Whig thought

19. Wood, *Creation of the American Republic*, 567. No one has done as good a job as Wood in describing and explicating this important shift in the meaning of words during the period.

of the 1780s. Initiative, referendum, and recall would be called "populist" ideas, but they were in tune with radical Whig preference for institutions of direct consent in all phases of government.

There was one radical Whig institution that attempted to combine all four types of consent—societal, governmental, agency, and programmatic. It was also an intermediate step toward initiative, referendum, and recall. This institution was the council of censors. Initially written into the radical 1776 Pennsylvania Constitution and copied by Vermont, this institution has been in some respects misunderstood and badly mistreated by historians, who often consider it simply a poor idea, an aberration of little consequence. In fact, it was the logical next step in radical Whig thought, and it failed partly because of errors in design and partly, perhaps, because it was not felt to be needed. It would have gone a long way, with a little adjustment, toward solving the problems of legislative excess. Its purpose, and the circumstances surrounding its demise, are worthy of consideration.

6

The Council of Censors

The 1780 Massachusetts Constitution was the most important one written between 1776 and 1789 because it embodied the Whig theory of republican government, which came to dominate state level politics; the 1776 Pennsylvania Constitution was the second most important because it embodied the strongest alternative. The Massachusetts document represented radical Whiggism, moderated somewhat by the form of mixed government, if not the actual substance. Pennsylvania Whigs wrote the most radical constitution of the era, one lacking even a bow in the direction of mixed government. It had a unicameral legislature whose supremacy was barely challenged by an anemic executive. The legislature was, in addition, subjected to the consent of the people in the most complete fashion. One notable practice was the requirement that all approved bills be printed for the consideration of the people at large; such bills could become law only when passed a second time in the next session. Since elections were annual, every election provided the opportunity for the voters to instruct and quiz their prospective representatives on bills passed during the last session. The requirement, contained in Section 15 of the constitution, was clearly an impractical one, forcing the legislature to consider every bill a temporary law until the following session. Nevertheless, it was impressive testimony to the strength of the commitment to direct consent.

The extreme directness of programmatic consent reduced concern for legislative tyranny. The legislature presumably acted only with the support of the majority, making legislative supremacy no danger. A second house and a strong executive, in this light, served only to thwart majority will and had no place. Hence, they were excluded.

In addition to annual elections and the requirements of Section 15, the radical Pennsylvania Whigs provided for the broadest rights of suffrage to be found in the first wave of constitutions, and required that legislators be limited to four consecutive terms and then be returned "to mix in with the mass of the people and feel at leisure the effects of the laws which they made." To aid the flow of information upon which voters would depend in evaluating legislation and the behavior of their representatives, the doors of the assembly were to remain open, votes were to be published weekly, and the press was to have the right to examine its proceedings or the proceedings of any part of government. The legislature was to be supreme, but only because it was directly under the control of the supreme sovereign, the people.

Description of the Institution

Pennsylvania was exceptional in its relentless pursuit of direct programmatic consent, and one manifestation of this was a unique institution designed to be the ultimate safeguard against legislative abuse of power—the council of censors. Recognizing that even the people could be mistaken in the short run and that the consequences of legislation were not always apparent after only one year, the drafters of the 1776 constitution designed what amounted to a statewide grand jury that would systematically review every aspect of republican government. Presumably, since it was to meet only once every seven years, the council of censors would not attract professional politicians because it was not conducive to building a political base. It was expected that ordinary citizens, who were in one way or another dissatisfied, would run for the council and form a critical body drawn from the people at large. The provision follows:

> SECT. 47 In order that the freedom of the commonwealth may be preserved inviolate forever, there shall be chosen by ballot by the freemen in each city and county respectively, on the second Tuesday in October, in the year one thousand seven hundred and eighty three, and

on the second Tuesday in October, in every seventh year thereafter, two persons in each city and county of this state to be called the *Council of Censors*; who shall meet together on the second Monday of November next ensuing their election; the majority of whom shall be a quorum in every case, except as to calling a convention, in which two-thirds of the whole number elected shall agree; And whose duty it shall be to enquire whether the constitution has been preserved inviolate in every part; and whether the legislative and executive branches of government have performed their duty as guardians of the people, or assumed to themselves or exercised other or greater powers than they are entitled to by the constitution; they are also to enquire whether the public taxes have been justly laid and collected in all parts of this common wealth, in what manner the public monies have been disposed of, and whether the laws have been duly executed. For these purposes they shall have power to send for persons, papers and records; they shall have authority to pass public censures, to order impeachments, and to recommend to the legislature the repealing such laws as appear to them to have been enacted contrary to the principles of the Constitution. These powers they shall continue to have, for and during the space of one year from the day of their election and no longer; The said council of censors shall also have power to call a convention, to meet within two years after their sitting, if there appear to them an absolute necessity of amending any article of the constitution which may be defective, explaining such as may be thought not clearly expressed, and of adding such as are necessary for the preservation of the rights and happiness of the people: But the articles to be amended, and the amendments proposed to be added or abolished, shall be promulgated at least six months before the day appointed for the election of such convention, for the previous consideration of the people, that they may have an opportunity of instructing their delegates on the subject.

Even a cursory reading shows that the council of censors was expected to make all four types of consent more direct. It was to recommend the repeal of any law contrary to the constitution or which raised or disbursed money improperly—programmatic consent. It had power to pass public censures, order impeachments, and determine whether any governmental official had gone outside the constitutionally set limits—a review of agents and agency consent. It could judge whether the constitution had been kept inviolate in every part, but it could also propose amendments that were judged necessary "for the preservation of the rights and happiness of the people." Clearly, it could initiate changes supportive of shifts in societal and governmental consent. In one institution, we find all four types of consent brought together in a coherent statement of a theory of republican government.

The council was to be elected by all freemen, a very liberal suffrage, and was itself prevented from being tyrannical through severely limited powers. It could censure and recommend but, beyond alerting the people to political evils, was unable to prosecute or legislate. The one thing it could do was call a convention to consider proposed constitutional amendments. This action required a two-thirds majority of the council, which was commensurate with a distinction between constitutional law and statutory law. Contrary to what some have concluded, the institution of the council of censors furthered the distinction rather than retarded it, simply by enforcing the subservience of the legislature and all governmental activity to the fundamental law contained in the constitution.[1]

The council could only recommend, but an elected convention had to actually amend. Even though amendments were not to be popularly ratified, the provision for a 6-month period between promulgation of the proposed changes and the election of the convention permitted the instruction of delegates. This was, in some respects, a stronger form of consent than mere ratification, since each delegate's election would rest upon his supporting a position favored by a majority of his constituents. The radical Whig inclination toward instructing delegates may help explain the slowness with which they moved toward popular ratification for constitutions and amendments. No matter how jaundiced our view today toward the efficacy of instructing delegates and representatives, if one believed in the tactic as the radical Whigs apparently did, then it was a very direct form of consent.

Based on the Spartan *ephori* and roman censors of classical times, the idea for the council of censors can be found in the writing of

1. One of those arguing that the council of censors retarded the development of a distinction between fundamental law and statutory law is Allan Nevins, *The American States During and After the Revolution, 1775–1789* (New York: Augustus M. Kelley, 1969).

Machiavelli, Montesquieu, and Rousseau.[2] All three were widely read by Americans, and early in 1776 several pamphlets proposed either a council of censors or a body similar to it. The final paragraph of *Four Letters on Interesting Subjects* initiated the idea, and *The Genuine Principles of the Ancient Saxon, or English Constitution*, signed with the pseudonym Demophilus, developed it.[3] H. Trevor Colbourn suggests that Demophilus was really George Bryan, and Lewis H. Meader reports that historical documents credit James Cannon and George Bryan with putting the institution into the Pennsylvania Constitution.[4] Bryan and Cannon were members of that extremely radical group in Pennsylvania which rejected the theory of mixed government entirely. This group was a large majority of the convention that framed the Pennsylvania Constitution, since few conservatives took part in the July 8, 1776, election. They wrote the most radical document of the era and spent the next thirteen years trying to preserve it from change or replacement. They would come to be known in Pennsylvania as "constitutionalists," and those attempting to rewrite the 1776 document would be called "anticonstitutionalists" or "republicans."

The Council of Censors in Operation

There were immediate demonstrations against the new constitution. One in Philadelphia is said to have numbered 1,500 persons. Opposition focused on the unicameral legislature and the council of censors on the grounds that they were impractical and too democratic, although at least a dozen other provisions drew strong objection as well. The opposition, centered in Philadelphia, was so strong that the legislature resolved to poll the people as to the desirability of a new convention. The statewide negative response to this proposal was even stronger, and after petitions bearing 13,000 names were entered in favor of keeping the current constitution, the legislature

---

2. Lewis H. Meader, "The Council of Censors," *Pennsylvania Magazine of History and Biography*, XXII (1898), 265–300.

3. *Four Letters on Interesting Subjects* (Philadelphia: n.p., 1776); Demophilus [pseud.], *The Genuine Principles of the Ancient Saxon, or English Constitution* (Philadelphia: n.p., 1776).

4. H. Trevor Colbourn, *The Lamp of Experience* (Chapel Hill: University of North Carolina Press, 1965), 191; Meader, "The Council of Censors," 280.

rescinded its resolution by a vote of 47 to 7.[5] Between November of 1778 and November of 1783, no further attempts were made to alter the radical document, though criticism in the press continued.

The bitter divisions within Pennsylvania went back to the period before the Revolution and could not be expected to die easily. It caused no surprise that the same divisions reappeared within the council of censors itself when it convened for its first meeting in 1783. Each of the twelve counties sent two representatives, as did Philadelphia. From the first day, it was apparent that the council was closely divided, with the anticonstitutionalists having a slight majority.[6] Every vote but one was decided along party lines, usually by a 12–9 or 13–10 margin. The president came from the majority, as did the committee that recommended substantial constitutional amendment, including abolishment of the council. The majority, however, was considerably short of the two-thirds required for calling a convention, and this produced a stalemate. Acrimonious debate ensued in both the council and the press, and the council adjourned with the understanding that an informal poll of the people would be taken on the matter.

The battle intensified. Opponents of the Constitution argued that the council was unrepresentative because the less populated western counties had the same representation as the heavily settled counties

5. This figure is given by Meader, "The Council of Censors," 287. Allan Nevins gives the figure 16,000 out of an electorate of 50,000–60,000, and says many were procured or forged. Meader's figures are used because Nevins' scholarship suffers somewhat from partisanship.

6. Council of censors voting records and biographical sketches in the back of Jackson Turner Main's *Political Parties Before the Constitution* (Chapel Hill: University of North Carolina Press, 1973), 432–39, indicate that during the first session there were fourteen republicans and twelve constitutionalists, with one person's party undetermined. This last delegate, a man named Hunter, never attended any session and was listed as deceased at the beginning of the second session, being replaced by a constitutionalist. John Evans, a republican from Chester County, never showed up either, meaning that at best the republicans could muster a 13–12 majority. However, several delegates were usually missing on any given day, more often than not from the constitutional side. Because the constitutionalists, on the average, had to travel greater distances to attend, and perhaps because they sometimes felt their assured minority status made their individual vote useless, they often had holes in their ranks. In any case, the recorded votes during the first session of the council show a greater republican majority than the actual 13–12 split. Due to two elections between sessions, the constitutionalists gained a 14–13 majority for the second session. Once again, absenteeism within the miniority made the difference greater, with 14–9 being a common roll-call. In short, neither side ever had more than the barest majority.

to the east.[7] There is no way of ever knowing the distribution of sentiment with certainty, since modern poll-taking techniques were lacking. It is probable, however, that the majority across the state was with the constitutionalists.[8]

The social revolution that had taken place within the Revolutionary War was nowhere more in evidence than in Pennsylvania.[9] The revolt against England afforded a favorable opportunity for the Scotch-Irish and the numerous Germans to free themselves from the heavy rule of the English Quakers.[10] There was a fundamental split between the agricultural west and the mercantile east. Also, the westerners were mostly Scotch-Irish and Presbyterian, and the Scotch-Irish Presbyterians were prominent among the constitutionalists. But it should not be forgotten that Presbyterians and Scotch-Irish also formed a large part of the electorate in the east, that the Germans were concentrated in the east, and that large numbers of mechanics and laborers in and around Philadelphia had been given the franchise as a result of the 1776 Constitution. Their majority

7. On page 162 of the council of censors minutes, during the second session, the republican minority argued that if apportionment were by population instead of by county, they would have a 14–12 majority instead of being in the minority. Because this 14–12 majority is virtually what they had during the first session, apportionment by county was not far off the mark, or else the republicans had little idea what difference apportionment by county did make. Either way there seems little basis for their complaint.

8. The republicans themselves tended to identify their supporters as the right-thinking few, and those of the constitutionalists as the debtor majority. More decisive is the fact that in the election of 1784, immediately following the highly publicized controversy surrounding the council of censors, the constitutionalists overwhelmingly won the legislative elections. Also, between sessions, George Bryan won the vacant seat from Philadelphia, indicating that the supposed Republican stronghold itself had a substantial constitutionalist electorate. All the evidence indicates that the constitutionalists had a statewide majority, but also, like the Democratic party today, its supporters had a lower propensity to vote than republican voters. This is a typical pattern for lower socioeconomic groups such as those supporting the constitutionalists, and since they lost the 1785 legislative election, it is also apparent that the constitutionalists were not always able to turn out their statewide majority.

9. J. Paul Selsam, *The Pennsylvania Constitution of 1776: A Study in Revolutionary Democracy* (New York: Octagon Books, 1971), Chap. 1.

10. Estimates on the German population in Pennsylvania vary somewhat, but documents for public distribution typically were published in both English and German, with about a third coming out in German. The proceedings of the council of censors were published according to this ratio. Jackson Turner Main notes that legislators in Pennsylvania during the 1780s came almost equally from three groups—English, Scotch-Irish and German—and that the Pennsylvania assembly came as close to reflecting the state's society as any in the country (Main, *Political Parties*, 177). The Germans did not vote only for Constitutionalists, however. A substantial proportion did vote republican.

was substantial, and as long as the constitutionalists mobilized their supporters, they won.

Between the first and second sessions, the strength of numbers was tested again in the council of censors. The resignation of one of Philadelphia's censors brought on a direct test of the city's sentiment, and a hard-fought campaign resulted in the election of none other than George Bryan. Another censor died, and he, too, was replaced by a constitutionalist. This reversed the ratio to a 14–12 constitutionalist advantage.[11] At the same time, petitions with more than 18,000 signatures poured in opposing a new convention, and the republicans were beaten.

Now in control of the council of censors, the constitutionalists had no need to pursue the question of a new constitution any further, and they settled down to perform the rest of the duties for which the institution was designed. No one has ever considered the import of this second session because most historical analysis has been one-sided. In *The Federalist* 10, James Madison's delight in reiterating the list of legislative abuses compiled by the council in its 1784 report does not prevent his dismissing the institution in a lengthy section of *The Federalist* 50. Lewis H. Meader wrote the seminal analysis of the council in 1898. He nicely summarizes the events of the first sessions, largely ignores the second session, and spends the last three pages rejecting the utility of the institution with arguments that overlook the facts he has just finished outlining. Virtually every historian who mentions the council of censors merely cites Meader's conclusion without further analysis. Two important exceptions are Allan Nevins and Gordon S. Wood.

Nevins' book has been the standard source on the early state constitutions for half a century. It represents a considerable feat of scholarship but suffers from being more descriptive than analytic. Perhaps it is just as well, however, since some of the attempts at analysis miscarry. For example, in his discussion of the council of censors, Nevins engages in a polemic arising from an obvious dislike for anything that smacks of "leveling" (anything that en-

11. There was a thirteenth republican, but he failed to appear for a single roll-call during either session.

hances political equality). And he spends many pages quoting from documents and letters written by anticonstitutionalists, often treating propaganda as having factual content, yet he fails to cite constitutionalist propaganda. He thereby creates the impression that only a small, vociferous minority supported the 1776 Constitution. Supporters of the Constitution are labeled "blunderers," "reckless," "unscrupulous," "forgers," and are deemed to be consistently in error. Opponents, on the other hand, are called "sensible," "ablest members," and "careful thinkers," and are described as supporters of justice. When the radical supporters won a vote in the council by "*only* 14 to 9," he wrote, it was because their provision "embodied much Constitutional propaganda" (even though the 14 constitutionalists on the council at the time hardly needed any convincing). When opponents won 12 to 9, but failed to gain the necessary two-thirds (18 votes), the majority was being thwarted by a willful minority.

Nevins' characterization of the second session misses much of its significance because he spends most of his time being an apologist for the republicans.

> Bryan's Constitutionalists . . . labored ingeniously to do two incompatible things—first to whitewash the Constitution, and second, to show that it had been outrageously violated by the Anti-Constitutionalists when they had held the government . . . [The] list of infractions laid emphasis on those occurring in and after 1781, when the Anti-Constitutionalists had gained power [in the legislature]; this was manifestly unfair, for if the breaches made in the Constitution by its enemies were the more numerous, those by its friends were the largest.[12]

These two objectives are incompatible only from the point of view of someone opposed to the constitutionalist theory. The council of censors was designed to investigate the possibility of legislative errors under the assumption that the majority can sometimes be wrong in the short run. To find such errors is not to undercut the principle of legislative supremacy, but to attempt to check excesses

12. Nevins, *American States*, 189.

in direct majority rule. It was not expected that every time an abuse was discovered the council should propose an amendment, but rather that it would propose legislative solutions that would be enforced by an aroused electorate. It may or may not have been practical, but it was not illogical. That the constitutionalists were readily willing to concede errors on the part of the popularly elected unicameral legislature is a mark of their honesty.

Nevins says that the new constitutionalist majority on the council largely ignored the sins of the constitutionalist administrations. This was to be expected, given the probability that a majority within the electorate supported the constitutionalists at this point and, thus, were more concerned over anticonstitutionalist legislation which thwarted that majority. It is also to be expected because of a minor, though important, flaw in the institution of the council of censors. James Madison, with his usual perceptiveness, placed first in his list of flaws uncovered in the council's two sessions the fact that "at least some of its most active and leading members had also been active and leading characters in the parties which preexisted in the State."[13] In addition, too many members of the council had previously sat in the state legislature. The net result was the inevitable transfer of legislative controversies as well as factional disputes into the council. A simple provision excluding former legislators and governmental officials would have gone far toward alleviating this problem. The modern tactic of nonpartisan elections would have helped even more. That this possibility lay open was ignored by the anticonstitutionalists because they wished to kill the institution, not reform it, and subsequent historical analysis has, in important respects, failed to be sufficiently analytical because of ideological preferences brought to the subject.

Despite all these reasons for expecting the constitutionalists to ignore the errors of constitutionalist administrations, in fact during the second session when the constitutionalists were in control, the majority indicted the legislature over all seven years since the 1776 constitution had been adopted.[14] This span included both consti-

13. Jacob E. Cooke (ed.), *The Federalist* (Cleveland: Meridian Books, 1967), 345.
14. Council of Censors, "Proceedings and Minutes," 146.

tutionalist- and republican-dominated legislatures, and we are treated to the spectacle of George Bryan voting along with the majority to affirm that the legislature had been overstepping its bounds, regardless of which party was in power. The council did spend more time on specific issues resulting from the most recent session of the legislature, which was controlled by the republicans, but if this was understandable on political grounds, it was also understandable on practical grounds. The most recent violations were most subject to redress because the persons affected were still around and the damage was less likely to have become irreparable with the passage of time. Nevins never explains what he means by the constitutionalists making the "largest breaches." He cites no examples; there is nothing to indicate a difference between the activities of constitutionalist legislatures and republican legislatures, except for Nevins' admission that infractions were more numerous under the latter. And from its context, that statement appears to be an ideological statement on Nevins' part rather than a summary of the facts.

Gordon S. Wood has done by far the best job of analysis, making the only real contribution on the subject during the past seventy-five years. He establishes the fight between constitutionalist and republican in Pennsylvania as the paradigm of the shift from radical Whig to Federalist political thought. In a brilliant section entitled "Whiggism Against Itself," he shows that the thwarted republicans resorted to the tactic of using radical rhetoric against radical institutions.[15] Constitutionalist opposition to a new constitutional convention was depicted as fear of the people or as evidence of a constitutionalist attitude that the people were too stupid to elect good men to a new constitutional convention. The council of censors, designed as an instrument of popular control over the legislature, was pictured as an instrument blocking popular will. The argument was effective propaganda. This, plus the rising power of the highly organized Federalists, probably explains the loss of popular support for the council. The council, which was to have met again in 1790, never convened. The legislature authorized a constitutional conven-

---

15. Gordon S. Wood, *The Creation of the American Republic, 1776–1787* (Chapel Hill: University of North Carolina Press, 1969), 438–46.

tion in clear contravention to the 1776 constitution under which it was still operating.[16] The convention met and wrote a constitution very similar to that of Massachusetts, with two houses, a revised executive, and no council of censors. There was no constitutional provision for amendment. The people of Pennsylvania were never permitted to ratify the new document; the same convention proclaimed it adopted on September 2, 1790. To undercut undue popular opposition and justify the legislative action, Section 2 of the bill of rights stated: "That all power is inherent in the people, and all free governments are founded on their authority and instituted for their peace, safety, and happiness. For the advancement of those ends, they have at all times an unalienable and indefeasible right to alter, reform, or abolish their government, in such manner as they may think proper" (Thorpe, 3100). The rhetoric supporting direct, popular consent was there, but no institution for implementing that consent existed. That the instrument of adoption in this case was a convention called by the legislature strongly suggested what the republicans thought proper. This was still a Whig document in many respects, but far less radical than the earlier Pennsylvania Constitution. Significantly, the provision providing for instruction of representatives was softened. It now read: "Sec. 20 That the citizens may have a right, in a peaceable manner, to assemble together for their common good, and to apply to those invested with the powers of government for redress of grievances, or other proper purposes, by petition, address, or remonstrance" (Thorpe, 3101). The council of

16. The argument made by the 1789 legislative majority supporting their resolution is an interesting one. They held that the state bill of rights gave the people ultimate political power, that members of the legislature had "mixed" with the people and found them desirous of a convention, and therefore, by implication, the will of the people expressed through the legislature was superior to the will of the people as expressed through the constitution (see Meader, "Council of Censors," 296). The legislature was at this point in the hands of the republicans. Using essentially the same argument, the resulting convention wrote a new constitution which, among other things, eliminated the unconstitutionally bypassed council of censors. It is clear that at least in Pennsylvania as late as 1790, the doctrine of the constitution as fundamental law had not yet taken root. Even more interesting is the fact that the Pennsylvania republicans, who were almost all Federalists in national politics, supported the radical Whig principle of legislative supremacy at the state level and did not argue for the distinction between constitutional law and legislative law that Bernard Bailyn says had been accepted by 1776. The Pennsylvania delegation to the national Constitutional Convention of 1787, with the exception of Benjamin Franklin, was entirely republican.

censors died an unconstitutional death in Pennsylvania when its radical proponents lost the political battle to another group of men. This other group was not composed of traditional Whigs; they were mostly of a new breed that we now term Federalists.[17] The Federalists were in control at the national level and had also brought the most radical state constitution more into line with the others, thereby rejecting its radical theory. The Federalists, mostly in the person of James Madison, wrote the analysis of the council of censors that has survived to represent it. Overlooked by succeeding analysts, including Wood, was the fact that, despite a flaw that could have been corrected, the council of censors was a coherent and logically based institution that worked. During the second session the constitutionalist majority, having every reason to demonstrate the council's utility, made every effort to police the activities of government. There was a thorough examination of taxes and the majority reached the conclusion that some counties were in arrears. Significantly, the counties so admonished were, by and large, the very counties from which constitutionalists were elected. County commissioners were investigated to see if they had carried out their duties. Legislative bills of all types were considered for their constitutional propriety, and those singled out as improper were not only ones that would embarrass republicans. Indeed, while council votes often followed party lines, this was most true in beating back proposals made by the republican minority and designed to embarrass the constitutionalists. Otherwise, in contradiction to the first session, there were bipartisan motions to add republicans to important committees and constitutionalists often voted with republicans, and vice versa.[18] Although hardly providing a model of dispassionate debate, the constitutionalists attempted to make the council do the job for which it was intended, despite the highly partisan context.

17. Nevins, *American States*, 191; and Main, *Political Parties*, 181, 203, 406–407.

18. Most roll calls during the second session followed party lines, but there were frequent exceptions. The Proceedings and Minutes record cross-party voting on July 2, 3, 4, 7 and 9, for example, and throughout August there were crossings back and forth, depending on the issue. One should not conclude that matters were entirely open. In usual roll call votes, most members of each party voted together with a few crossing over. Nonetheless, there was a marked change from the first session, during which crossover voting was almost nonexistent.

No one has ever argued that the council was soft on the legislature, and in some respects the council was more fair in its deliberations. Win or lose, the republicans were always permitted to enter their reasoning into the official record, an opportunity they never missed. At one point, the republican-controlled legislature refused to turn over documents requested by the council, and while this was clearly contrary to Article 47 of the constitution, the council merely made note of the fact and carried out its investigation with a minimum of acrimony. Even under these trying circumstances, the council of censors was able to work in a reasonably effective manner.

Also overlooked by historians is the fact that the idea of a council of censors was not confined to Pennsylvania. Why the institution atrophied at the state level cannot be explained by events in Pennsylvania alone but requires a broader analysis.

The Institution Fails to Spread

Vermont had used the Pennsylvania Constitution as its model and, therefore, also had a council of censors. Significantly, there has never been any adverse criticism of the institution as it functioned in Vermont, and this despite its continued existence until 1869, providing many an opportunity to demonstrate the nature of its "faulty framework." Even Nevins states that it proved to be an effective body in Vermont. It successfully proposed amendments that were adopted by a convention and greatly improved the Vermont Constitution.[19] As in most states, the Vermont legislature tended to draw power unto itself, with a subsequent encroachment on what we would now consider the executive and judicial functions.

Why was the Vermont Constitution not considered flawed for the same reasons that Pennsylvania's was? The only explanation offered by Nevins is that Vermont had a more homogeneous population and milder party divisions, and thus the council was more effective.[20] This, at best, is a nonexplanation. In fact, Vermont was a combination of three major valleys, one opening to the north toward Quebec, one opening to the west toward New York, and one opening to the south toward Connecticut. Each section had histori-

19. Nevins, *American States*, 674–75.
20. *Ibid.*, 675.

cal and economic ties with its respective neighbors, and there was an additional source of faction in a considerable number of French-speaking people in the north. Internal Vermont politics were in fact characterized by considerable acrimony, and were not the least bit dull. There was, however, one element lacking. Vermont did not have the commercial centers that Pennsylvania had, or a large city with concentrated wealth. In short, Vermont lacked large numbers of the type that would later become Federalist and oppose excessive democracy.

In this sense, then, Vermont was more homogeneous, but Nevins' argument amounts to saying that the council of censors worked only where there were no strong mercantile interests. The implication is that the council of censors failed to develop elsewhere because most states, unlike Vermont, had deep economic divisions that reduced the prospects for reasoned discourse upon which the council had to depend for its effectiveness. The only problem with this is that legislatures also must depend upon reasoned discourse. Appropriately enough, the Pennsylvania legislature in the late 1770s was rendered inoperative by internal divisions, until the Continental Congress stepped in and threatened action unless matters were put to rest. The situation did ease somewhat as the republicans began cooperating with the constitutionalists, but with the end of the war, the legislature became a battleground again. It might be more accurate to say that divisions within Pennsylvania were so deep that no elected body could easily function effectively. The problem thus may have arisen, not so much from defective institutions, as from a badly divided electorate. Even with the adoption of the 1790 constitution, all that had been accomplished was the removal of the constitution itself as a focus for conflict. The divisions remained to convulse state politics.

During the 1780s, the division amounted to more than different economic interests competing for control of the legislature. Because the 1776 Pennsylvania Constitution had been written by an extremely radical group of Whigs, it was unusually responsive to the masses, meaning the less well-off. This situation was viewed as intolerable by the men of property, and thus reform of the constitution became their primary concern. Unfortunately, the council of censors, with its two-thirds requirement for calling a new convention, stood in the way. The republicans had power to win the legislature but not two-thirds of the council. The council, therefore, had to be branded a failure by the republicans for practical reasons. Some republicans probably opposed the council on theoretical or ideological grounds as well. Although the council was an instrument for democratic control, it was too extreme for their theory of republican government, which aimed at a mixed regime. On the other hand, some republicans could not have missed the obvious fact that the two-thirds requirement amounted to a long-term check on simple majority rule and could, with bicameral legislature and strengthened executive, serve as a barrier against a too-responsive legislature. One of the ironies of history may be that if the 1776 Pennsylvania Constitution had been a more standard Whig document, as was that of Massachusetts, the republicans-cum-Federalists might have been vigorous supporters of a council of censors for their own political reasons. The council was defective as far as the republicans were concerned, primarily because it protected too radical a constitution. A Massachusetts-style constitution with a council of censors would have produced different dynamics between the two parties.

Virtually every state had two parties in its legislature. Jackson Turner Main calls them "localist" and "cosmopolitan," regardless of the various names they went under. The cosmopolitans would become united at the national level as Federalists, and the localists would become united as the Antifederalists, later forming the core of the Jeffersonian Republicans.[21] If the division in Vermont was unusually mild because the state was mostly localist, that in Pennsylvania was deep and unusually bitter. The forces were relatively balanced in power, if not numbers, with a bloc of independents in the middle holding the balance.[22] Consequently, Pennsylvania politics lurched back and forth between the two. The overwhelmingly

21. Main, *Political Parties*, 406–407. The Jeffersonian Republicans were a national party and not to be confused with the republican party in Pennsylvania. The Pennsylvania republicans tended to become Federalists at the national level rather than Jeffersonian Republicans.
22. Main, *Political Parties*, 174–211.

constitutionalist legislature of 1784 was replaced by a mildly republican legislature in 1785, in much the way that the majority
within the council of censors shifted in the opposite direction between its sessions. To blame defective institutions for this unfortunate situation is to ignore political reality.

The idea for a council of censors also appeared in the 1784 New
Hampshire Constitution, which provided for a convention to be
called after seven years "to preserve an effectual adherance to the
principles of the Constitution and to correct any violations thereof,
as well as make any alterations . . . found necessary." The 1792
New Hampshire Constitution provided for an automatic poll of the
people every seven years at the town meetings electing senators. A
majority "aye" resulted in a convention. The 1785 constitution for
Frankland (later Tennessee) contained a council, but the idea died
with failure of ratification. The subsequent Tennessee Constitution
contained none. The 1789 Georgia Constitution provided for an
automatic amending convention in 1794 and then again in 1797.
More important, the idea appeared in Massachusetts. If it had become part of the highly influential 1780 constitution, it might have
become a familiar institution in state politics. Why it did not take
hold in Massachusetts provides an interesting insight into the development of republican government during the 1780s.

The town of Stoughton in Suffolk County instructed its delegates
to the convention that wrote the 1780 Massachusetts Constitution
to "spare no pain" in inserting a provision for a "Council of Censors and Controul."[23] The detailed description of their intent leaves
no doubt that it was the same institution found in the 1776 Pennsylvania document. Briefly examining the course of this proposal
will shed some light on how the idea came to be deflected, for later
constitutions in other states contain very similar institutional re-
placements.

The 1780 Massachusetts Constitution was the result of seven
months of deliberation by the convention, as well as a lengthy public debate surrounding the rejection of the proposed 1778 constitu-

23. Oscar Handlin and Mary Handlin, *The Popular Sources of Political Authority*
(Cambridge, Mass.: Harvard University Press, 1966), 426–27.

tion. A careful balance of colonial experience and newly formed but widely held political assumptions, the 1780 constitution was to become very influential and, in some senses, a working model for all subsequent state constitutions throughout the country. It did not contain a council of censors. The convention, in March of 1780, issued an address explaining the reasoning behind various provisions felt to be controversial, and the authors of the address did an unusual thing. They argued that the "Power of Revising . . . ought to be lodged in the hands of *one* person; not only to preserve the Laws from being unsystematical and inaccurate, but that a due balance may be preserved in the three capital powers of Government."[24] They added what has come to be a familiar argument in defense of executive power, that "The Governor is emphatically the Representative of the whole People." Programmatic consent by the people was thus transformed into executive veto. The office was strengthened to counterbalance the legislature, while the link with the consent of the people was retained by arguing that the executive, in a peculiar sense, embodied that general consent. It was a theoretical *tour de force* in that it materially contributed to a widely desired end, the strengthening of the executive, at the same time that it responded in part to the proposal raised by the Stoughton instruction.

The provision did not generate much opposition when the towns made their returns. Rather, controversy centered on another provision, Chapter VI, Article X, which provided for a constitutional convention in fifteen years to revise the document if two-thirds of qualified voters asked for one. This is in marked contrast to the Stoughton proposal, which would have automatically required a council of censors to be elected every three years. Furthermore, Article X mentioned only amendments to the constitution, not revision of laws or examinations of public officials. Out of the approximately 300 towns in Massachusetts at that time, a record of returns from 228 is still preserved in Handlin. Approximately 36 percent of these towns (83 out of 228) objected to Article X, but only one town, Petersham, suggested changing it to provide for a

24. *Ibid.*, 437.

council of censors. The rest commonly suggested that the fifteen years be changed to seven years, or perhaps five, and that the convention be more or less automatic. In short, the council of censors was transformed into the executive veto plus the amendment process.

Since the only other council of revision found in earlier constitutions was in the 1777 New York provision that, in effect, gave the executive veto to a council composed of the governor, chancellor, and the judges of the supreme court, there was a precedent for linking a council of revision with the executive veto. By following this precedent rather than that of Pennsylvania and Vermont, the highly influential Massachusetts Constitution of 1780 separated the notion of amendment from that of programmatic consent, and thus it preempted an institution embodying all four levels of consent.

This solution also failed to arouse Federalist concern for excessive democracy. Comparing Massachusetts towns supporting Federalist policies with the town returns on the 1780 constitution contained in the Handlin book, we find that 37 percent of the Federalist towns supported a change in Article X to make the time period less than fifteen years and more automatic. This compares favorably with the 36 percent average reported for all towns. Also, those towns identified as strongholds of Antifederalist sentiment had 37 percent negative returns. The format contained in the 1780 Massachusetts Constitution appears to have had equal appeal for all factions.

In summary, the council of censors, despite its theoretical coherence with respect to consent doctrine, appears to have been stillborn because Federalists opposed it as being too democratic and most radical Whigs did not consider it essential. An executive, also directly elected and representative of the people, could delay bad legislation with a veto but could not thwart a substantial majority for long. Amendments could be handled in another manner, one equally dependent upon the people. The legislature could be used to investigate and impeach governmental officials and police its own members. Experience with the council of censors in Pennsylvania may have also convinced the Whigs that it was simply redundant. Its advantage of bringing all the threads of consent together in one institution was not worth the needless political complications. Then, too, most states had upper houses that served, theoretically, as a check on the lower house. A council of censors looked doubly redundant with an upper house alongside it.

Both the 1780 Massachusetts and 1790 Pennsylvania constitutions were mainstream Whig documents. They retained legislative supremacy, but tried to moderate the extreme effects of direct popular consent through lengthy bills of rights, bicameral legislatures, and a strengthened executive. They did not satisfy the most radical Whigs, but they were not Federalist documents either. The Federalists would recognize the anomaly of an upper house that was indistinguishable from the lower. If radical Whigs, in recognizing the same problem, might suggest a council of censors, the Federalists would respond by making the upper house truly distinct. Rejecting the theory of mixed government, as well as the efficacy of making all legislators mere trustees of the people, the Federalists would define republican government as one in which all power is divided between three branches—two indirectly elected—each having some measure of influence over the other. The 1776 Pennsylvania Constitution, the 1780 Massachusetts Constitution, and the 1787 federal Constitution embodied different theories of republican government. Each was based on a different notion of consent. Pennsylvania's document took the relatively direct consent typified by the Massachusetts Constitution and pushed it to the limit. The federal Constitution was based on a relatively indirect form of consent by comparison. The rewriting of the Pennsylvania Constitution and the demise of the council of censors reduced the major alternative theories of republican government to two—one would reign at the state level and the other at the national level. In time, they would move closer together in a hybrid compromise, but in 1789 there was no denying the difference.

Before moving on to a more detailed examination of Federalist theory, one more aspect of republican government needs to be discussed. Despite the extended and often bitter political struggles between advocates of the three major theories of republican government, one aspect of republican government as it had developed in

America was not called into question but held in common by all parties. All through the era and for many years afterward, most government would take place, not at the state or national level, but at the local level. There, citizens developed and practiced republican virtue, and popular control was most complete, most effective, and most direct. At the local level we find the seeds for the self-guiding republic.

7

Local Government

During the past forty years there has been almost nothing written about local government in America prior to 1800. Aside from bits and pieces in histories of a more general nature, the current literature on the subject consists largely of reprints of volumes published long ago.[1] These works provide detailed and often fascinating summaries of how early local government operated, but they are largely devoid of analysis. That the subject is generally ignored today is regrettable, for at the local level we find, in their most vigorous form, the rule of law, republican virtue, representation, and direct popular consent—in short, all that we have come to associate with republican government. Most important, it is to the local level that we must look for the unique development of republican ideas and institutions in the United States.

Historians commonly say that Americans during the seventeenth and eighteenth centuries loved their towns and counties more than they did their colonies or states. It is not well understood that as late as the 1790s, most government took place, not at the state or national level, but at the local level. Town and county government was cherished, because here Americans expressed themselves most

1. Four recent reprints are: Edward Channing, "Town and Country Government in the English Colonies of North America," *Johns Hopkins University Studies in Historical and Political Science*, 2nd ser., X (1884), reprinted by Johnson Reprint Company, 1973; Ernest S. Griffith, *History of American City Government: The Colonial Period* (New York: Oxford University Press, 1938), reprinted by Da Capo Press, 1972; Anne Bush Maclear, "Early New England Towns," *Studies in History, Economics and Public Law*, XXIX (1908), reprinted in book form by AMS Press, 1967; and John Fairfield Sly, *Town Government in Massachusetts (1620–1930)* (Cambridge, Mass.: Harvard University Press, 1930), reprinted by Archon Books, 1967. A more complete bibliography on local government prior to 1800 will be found at the end of this book.

fully and most distinctively. Although institutions were based upon local government as it was found in England, conditions in America led to political forms that expressed an essentially new and uniquely American perception of politics. Indeed, it is no exaggeration to say that by 1665 New England towns and townships had set the pattern for local politics for the next century and half. Despite fluctuations in suffrage or in deference to local elites, the basis for radical Whig political theory was in operation long before the American Revolution, before the Glorious Revolution in England, and even before there was the word *Whiggism* to describe it. No discussion of republican government in America can ignore these local institutions, for they place the first state constitutions, consent doctrine, Federalist theory, and such institutions as the council of censors in an intelligible context.[2]

The Origin of Local Government in America

Some scholars have traced English town politics back through Anglo-Saxon history to the Teutonic *mark* or *markgenossenschaft*. This was a localized clan held together by the double tie of common religion and real or assumed blood relationship. Under an elected or hereditary chief, it assembled in the open air to constitute at once a judicial and a legislative body.[3] Since the village community held and cultivated the land in common, the assembled mark-men supposedly decided seed time and harvest, settled petty differences, determined who would be admitted to the *Genossenschaft*, and devised measures for securing the peace of the community, as well as managed all aspects of the common economic life.

Whether the attribution is an accurate one, local government in America did, from the beginning, use the offices, language, and institutions found in seventeenth-century England. It would be difficult to sustain the argument that Americans were not strongly in-

---

2. It would be incorrect to infer that local government at all times or in all places was so advanced. The point is that local government in most of New England was essentially the same in 1776 as it had been in 1665, despite perturbations during the intervening years.

3. George E. Howard, *An Introduction to the Local Constitutional History of the United States* (Baltimore: Johns Hopkins University Press, 1889), Chap. I; and Sly, *Town Government in Massachusetts*, Chap. III.

fluenced by English precedent. At the same time, English forms were so drastically altered in their American existence that it is easy to understand why historians of the nineteenth century viewed them as a revival of the primitive village communities of a thousand years earlier. To understand this transformation, a brief discussion of English local government is in order.

There is evidence that before the Norman invasion, many, if not most, townships operated more or less independently through a *tungemot*, or town meeting. Norman conquest, however, completed an already existing trend toward feudal organization, and townships became economically and politically dependent upon feudal lords. A complex and confused development had led, by 1600, to a set of overlapping jurisdictions with various names. There were manors, boroughs, townships, shires, and parishes.[4] The parish is of particular interest, for it had to combine many of the secular township functions with ecclesiastical functions. A minister—rector, vicar, or incumbent—was the spiritual head of the community, and he also presided at the vestry meeting, or local legislature. The constable was the head civil officer. Appearing under a number of names, his importance is reflected in the common-law maxim: Where there is a constable, there is a parish. Churchwardens were the lay guardians chosen by the vestry who, with both secular and ecclesiastical duties, connected the two sides of parish life. Guardians of the church building and property, they were also the parish fiscal officers. Minor offices of the parish included vestry messenger, sexton, waywardens, or surveyors of highways, collectors of taxes, auditors of accounts, common drivers (of animals), and watchers of bounds and enclosures.

All those who paid scot and lot could participate in the vestry meeting. Meetings, called by the constable, were usually held on Sunday after church, and the vote was taken by hand or by division of the house. This "open vestry" had, by 1600, commonly resorted to electing a committee called the "select vestry" to run the parish

4. Part of the confusion lies in overlapping terminology. Some parishes were larger than counties, but basically it was a subunit of the county, and the terms *parish*, *town*, and *township* were often used interchangeably. See Channing, "Town and County Government," 9. *Shire* and *county* were also used interchangeably, though there were exceptions to any usage of the term.

between meetings. In many instances this select body, usually composed of prominent leaders, superseded the open vestry, replacing a reasonably representative institution with an oligarchic one. While this change was occurring, temporal and ecclesiastical functions were gradually being separated until, in the nineteenth century, the parish came to be primarily ecclesiastical, with little secular power.

All of this, of course, refers to the organization of the Church of England. Dissenting congregations of Quakers and Presbyterians had much more democratic organizations, with church matters being in the hands of the congregation. That many early immigrants to the New World came from these dissenting groups helps explain their more democratic institutions; but the point should not be pushed too far, as even these congregations often deferred in their judgment to prominent leaders, resulting in oligarchic tendencies here as well.

Over all, during the early part of the seventeenth century, local government was still based partly on the feudal manor and partly on parishes and townships organized as subunits of counties or shires. There were some representative features in English local government, but more generally, local government officials were appointed by the lords or by self-perpetuating select vestries. Except for the southern colonies, where English social and political institutions were imported largely intact along with the Anglican church, American local government would not pursue these trends. Nor would it, for a long while, separate secular from religious institutions, but in some respects would intensify the connection.

In the southern colonies local government would follow the pattern of Virginia and be based on the county. The soil and geography in the South were conducive to large-scale plantations, and the population was sparse. These factors resulted in the West Indies pattern of settlement, with few towns and thinly settled counties organized around an Anglican-dominated parish government. The earliest settlements in Virginia were organized initially by public meetings of the settlers, but within a decade, the English system of local government was transferred to this part of America.

New England, on the other hand, was organized around the town. Geography prevented large-scale farming and forced settlers into small pockets of land along the coast and the banks of rivers. Unlike the South, where many settlers were from the lower classes and easily dominated by the gentry that migrated with them, those settling in New England came overwhelmingly from the English middle class and brought their ideas, energy, and organization with them. Essential to their organization was their dissenting religion, which not only served as a reason for migration, but also bound them closely into tight communities. There was good reason for their settling near one another. If nothing else, the need for proximity to the church guaranteed settlement into towns and villages.

The middle colonies were settled by a more heterogeneous population, including Dutch, Swedes, Catholics, Quakers, Puritans, and churchmen, and political organization was also mixed. But in the long run, New England political ideas exerted a powerful influence even into the Carolinas, and New York, New Jersey, and Delaware developed lively town meeting systems. Since the New England towns bred what we would come to call republican government, it is there that close attention most dramatically reveals the origin of consent-giving institutions in America.

It should be remembered that the original settlers in New England came to found colonies, not towns, but the colonists soon found themselves scattered into separate pockets within the same colony. In the Massachusetts Bay Colony, for example, by 1639, less than ten years after coming ashore under the 1629 charter, there were twenty towns named in the minutes of the general court.[5] Plymouth, of course, had been settled by the Pilgrims in 1620 but, contrary to popular belief, never developed into much of a colony. Nevertheless, by 1640, the minutes of its general court mention seven towns, though Plymouth the town had still not been distinguished from Plymouth the colony. Records for the latter colony have not survived from the earlier years, and we are dependent upon the records of the Massachusetts Bay Colony for documentation concerning the origin of local government.

Cambridge began the movement in 1632 by establishing a monthly meeting. "Agreed that every person under subscribed shall meet

5. Sly, *Town Government in Massachusetts*, 21.

every Monday in every month within the meeting-house in the afternoon within half an hour after the ringing of the bell and that every one that make not his personal appearance there and continue there without leave until the meeting be ended shall for every default pay twelve pence and if it not be paid, meeting then to double it and so on until it is paid."[6] The Dorchester town records begin two years after the 1630 settlement of the Massachusetts Bay Colony with entries relating to the allotment of land and the erection of fences. Presumably there had to have been informal meetings of the town earlier for there to be provisions for record keeping, but the third entry, dated October 8, 1633, is probably the earliest "home rule" document in American history, because it makes town meeting decisions binding on everyone.[7] Until this point, affairs had been under the control of the clergymen, aided by the advice of the colony magistrates. But on this date, the inhabitants of the town agreed to establish a regular Monday meeting of all the inhabitants "there to settle (and sett downe) such orders as may tend to the general good." The 8 A.M. meeting would be announced by a drum and attendance was strongly encouraged. A "steering committee" of twelve was selected to insure that at least those twelve would appear weekly, though there was reference to one meeting every month as being of greater importance—one that presumably all adults should attend.

On February 1, 1634, Cambridge elected a 7-man committee to carry on affairs between town meetings; on August 23, 1634, Watertown elected three town officials, and on February 10, 1635 Charlestown elected the first board of selectmen to be officially recorded.[8] The pattern quickly became common throughout New England. By 1650, the various colonies were composed of towns, each governed by its inhabitants through a town meeting, with a board of elected selectmen running affairs between meetings but still remaining subordinate to the majority at the town meeting.

Several things are remarkable in this development. It happened

6. Cambridge Town Records, 4.
7. *Dorchester Town Records*, in *City of Boston: Fourth Report of the Record Commissioners*. Vol. IV (Boston: Rockwell and Churchill, 1880), 3.
8. Sly, *Town Government in Massachusetts*, 31–32.

quickly throughout New England, which suggests common, strong inclination. Unlike those in England, the town meetings were not superseded by the selectmen, even though members of certain families tended to be elected. Deference to certain men was not a mark of subservience but of confidence in their abilities.[9] The first towns to create their own governments did so on their own initiative, without approval or incorporation by the general court. In 1636 the general court for the Massachusetts Bay Colony passed the first organic law for the organization and regulation of towns and began officially to incorporate new towns. It restricted local governments only by requiring that they not contradict laws passed by the court and by limiting the size of fines they could levy. In summary, local government developed quickly, surely, and with little controversy. Most important, it was based on direct popular consent.

The Basics of Local Government

Local government in New England had several characteristics that were important in structuring the subsequent development of republican theory. Town meetings were notable for exercising broad powers, blending judicial with legislative matters, regulating town life and morals in extraordinary detail, and electing an impressive number of officials. Also, despite a certain deference toward the gentry who were prominent among important officeholders, elected officials were effectively kept under control as town meetings developed the techniques of instructing delegates, initiating legislation, recalling elected officials at both the local and colonial levels, and holding referendums. In short, everything that the radical Whigs were to press for at the state level in the 1770s and 1780s had already been developed and tested at the local level during the previous century. The radical idea in the 1770s was to apply these local institutions to the state level.

In keeping with what would later be orthodox Whig political theory, the local assembly of the town meeting was unrestricted as to subject matter of legislation. There seems to have been a restless anxiety in these "little republics" to bring every possible subject

9. J. R. Pole, *Political Representation in England and the Origins of the American Republic* (Berkeley: University of California Press, 1971), 38–54.

within the purview of the majority or of the magistrates chosen by
it. This is reflected nicely in the list of officers elected by the various
town meetings, a list that will be reproduced at length as the quick-
est way to make the point. Aside from selectmen, usually running
from seven to twelve in number, there were: the constable, town
clerk or recorder, treasurer, assessors, collectors, surveyors of highways, clerks of the market, fence viewers, hog reeves, pound keepers, and common drivers.[10] These were the important officers that
were invariably found in New England towns. Virtually every aspect of town life had an officer elected to regulate it, however, the
number depending on the size of the population and the economic
diversity to be found in the town. Possible offices, all of which were
found in Boston before 1700, included water bailiffs, cow keepers,
town drummers and teachers of town drummers, tithingmen, per-
ambulators, ringers and yokers of swine, sealers of weights and
measures, keepers of ordinaries, town bellmen, cullers of staves,
measurers of corn and of boards, corders of wood and overseers of
wood corders, overseers of chimneys and chimney sweepers, overseers of almshouses, gaugers, viewers, surveyors of casks of tar,
fire wards, town criers, informers of offenders against the license
laws, scalers of leather, licensors and inspectors of brick makers,
cullers of fish, inspectors of hides for transportation, measurers of
salt, packers of flesh and fish, inspectors of the killing of deer, deer
reeves, school wardens, school teachers, truckmasters, brewers, re-
bukers of boys, sizers of meadows, warners of town meetings, scav-
engers, viewers of lands, lot layers, judges of delinquents at town
meetings, judges of boundary disputes, branders of cattle, pinders,
jurymen, town cannoneers, commissioners for equalization of assessment, town fishers, town deputies, town doctors, town grub-
bers, and persons to keep dogs out of church.[11] All this in a Boston
which, in 1700, had only 6,700 people. The list is not exhaustive. It
also fails to indicate that an office often had more than one individual assigned. For example, in 1679 Dorchester elected four yokers and ringers of swine, four men to look after boys in church,

10. Howard, *Local Constitutional History*, 91.
11. *Ibid.*, 83–84, and 97–99. See Jack P. Greene (ed.), *Settlements to Society: 1607–
1763* (New York: W. W. Norton, 1975), 249.

and eighteen fence viewers. In 1681, it elected thirteen tithingmen. That this army of town officials did not get in each other's way can possibly be explained by the unsurprising fact that towns usually had difficulty filling many of the positions. Being an inspector of bridges could not have taken up much time, fence viewers were usually paid well, and being town brewer had its obvious advantages; but most offices paid only a nominal sum and interfered with one's own livelihood. Keeping dogs out of church is not particularly uplifting, and not everyone could have enjoyed the role of informer.

Regulation of society was far more detailed than even the list of offices indicates. Most towns kept a night watch, organized by the constable, to which every able-bodied male was liable for duty at some time. It is worth citing portions of the instructions regulating the watch and adopted by the Boston selectmen in 1662, to illustrate the extent to which morals were subject to regulation by local government.

> 1. That they Silentlie but vigilantlie walke theire severall turnes in the several quarters and partes of Towne, two by two, a youth allwayes joyned with an elder and more sober person, & two be allwayes about the markitt place.
>
> 2. If after 10 of ye clocke they see any lights, then to make discreett inquiry, whether there be a warrantable cause, likewise if they heare any noyse or disorderlye carriage in any house wisely to demand a reason of it, & if it appeare a reall disorder, that men are danceing, drinckeing, a singinge vainlie &c, they shall admonish them to cease. . .
>
> 5. If they finde any younge men, Maydes, women or other persons, not of known fidellitie, & upon lawfull occation walkeing after 10 of the clocke at night, that they modestly demand the cause of theire being abroad, & if it appeare that they are upon ille minded imployment then to watch them narrowlye & to command them to repaire to theire lodginges. . .
>
> 6. For as much as the watch is to see to the regulating of other men's actions & manners, that theirfore they be exemplary themselves neither using any uncleane or corrupt language nor unmannerle or unbeseming tearmes unto any.[12]

12. *Report of the Record Commissioners*, in *Boston Records, 1660 to 1701*, Vol. III (Boston: Rockwell and Churchill, 1881), 8–10.

These rules were in effect until 1701, when a revision was made. If the instructions were unusual, it was only because they were more liberal than was often the case. Boston was already one of the more cosmopolitan towns in the colonies.

Because the selectmen were to act in behalf of the town meeting between sessions, they performed virtually every function that the meeting could, except electing the important officers. Town records contain minutes of the meetings of the selectmen and of the town meetings, and they are jumbled together as if indistinguishable in importance. These records show that the selectmen were given a myriad of powers and responsibilities, which really reflects the great power of the town meeting, since there is little evidence that selectmen ever seriously encroached on the prerogative of the body that elected them.[13]

A brief listing of a few duties assigned the selectmen is another way of viewing the nature and extent of local government. The entire financial administration was vested in the board of selectmen. They could assess, collect, and audit taxes. It was their job to let contracts for public works, lease town property, and order suits to recover debts or fines. The records also show them acting to admit newcomers as inhabitants of the town, regulate the temporary entertainment of strangers, set up cages for Sabbathbreakers, require idle persons to work, decide property disputes, settle newcomers in proper and diligent employment, appoint individuals to search out unlicensed houses of entertainment, license brewers and fix the price of beer, establish ferries, admit apprentices to their calling, superintend the paving of streets, regulate the height of fences, provide dinners for school visitors, regulate the price of wheat, censor private morals, relieve idiots and insane persons, and so on.[14]

Nor was this breadth of activity peculiar to a few New England colonies. In Virginia, the Carolinas, Georgia, and Maryland, local government was centered in the county due to the absence of population concentrations in significant numbers. The county court, while officially functioning as the judicial branch, effectively controlled local political administration and decision making as well.

13. Howard, *Local Constitutional History*, 88.
14. *Ibid.*, 79–82; and Sly, *Town Government in Massachusetts*, 76.

Despite the fact that the county court was composed of eight to thirty judges appointed by the governor, it still tended to represent the local oligarchy rather than the crown. As elsewhere in the colonies, political power flowed upward from county to province rather than outward from the provincial government. In addition to the normal adjudication of civil and criminal disputes expected of such courts, they involved themselves in every aspect of economic, social, and political life. Like town government in the north, county courts in the South had broad powers. They regulated the treatment of slaves and servants, built and maintained roads, bridges, streets, and wharves, regulated navigation on rivers and streams, nominated and oversaw commissioners and surveyors responsible for these duties, collected both local and general taxes, kept standard weights and measures, graded and inspected goods for export, served as a local conservation authority, ordered the destruction of pests and the observance of game regulations, provided relief for the poor, upheld public morals, took care of orphans, levied troops for the militia and supplied them with provisions, ammunition, and housing.[15] The list appears endless and, to a modern reader, somewhat disconcerting. If a government today were to have such complete powers, it would be termed totalitarian, regardless of whether it was being run directly by a majority of the citizens or by a small group of selectmen or judges. Yet for at least half of American history, most government was at the local level, and local government knew few bounds. Regulation of highways is one thing, but can one imagine a government today at any level passing the following ordinance? "Whereas great Inconvenience hath arisen by single p'sons in this Colonie being for themselves and not betaking themselves to live in well Governed famillies . . . henceforth noe single person be suffered to live of himself or in any family but such as the Celectmen of the town shall approve of."[16] And yet there were few complaints, not because men in those days did not understand the meaning of freedom, but because local communities were relatively ho-

15. George Dargo, *Roots of the Republic: A New Perspective on Early American Constitutionalism* (New York: Praeger, 1974), 44–45.
16. David Pulsifer (ed.), *Records of the Colony of New Plymouth* (Boston: William White, 1861–69), XI, 223.

mogeneous, and the laws were, in most cases, made by the majority of local citizens, who had common values. For this reason we find two outstanding features of local government. One was the constant and careful attempt to regulate who could or could not live in the town; the other was a relentless striving to keep political power in the hands of the town meeting, in the hands of the majority within the local community. The first trait has already been discussed in some detail earlier in this essay. The second deserves an extended discussion because it places the first state constitutions in a new perspective.

Popular Control at the Local Level

Records from all the New England colonies indicate that as much as the colonists cherished popular control through the town meeting, it took up a lot of their time. Consequently, weekly meetings became monthly, and some colonies were forced to resort to fines for those not attending.

The institution of selectmen eased the problem considerably by reducing the need for frequent meetings and helping to focus discussion at town meetings. Instead of having to thrash out every proposal, townsmen were then able to use their meetings to give instructions and pass judgment on the activities of the selectmen. On major issues, the town meeting would instruct the selectmen as to what to do and how to do it, and the selectmen were then required to make a detailed report of their actions to the town. Between town meetings, individuals or small groups of individuals might approach the selectmen on their own and receive a judgment, and this, too, would be subject to town review at the next meeting. In effect, the selectmen were acting as a small legislature representing the interests of the community, and representing the community in mirror-like fashion, as if the entire town were present. The town meeting (majority), through instructions and writing legislation (initiative), guided the selectmen (legislature), who were subject both to a review of their legislation (automatic referendum) and possible defeat at the next election. These institutions flowed from serious needs pragmatically met, instead of from any political theory. Not until a century later would the radical Whigs apply a coherent theory to state constitutions and strive to recreate at the state level what Americans had evolved at the local level.

The process of making colonial legislatures resemble selectmen in their relationship to town meetings began almost immediately, however. When the towns began to send deputies to the Massachusetts General Court, they treated their deputies just as if they were selectmen. The town meeting voted instructions for its deputy and required him, upon his return, to report on the business of the general court. Many towns in New England had *all* colonial legislation read to the citizenry, and Rhode Island, from 1647 to 1663, went so far as to require that all laws be referred back to the towns for their acceptance or rejection. As early as 1640, a law was passed in Plymouth Colony providing for instructions to the deputies.[17] The Massachusetts General Court, both in the June and October sessions of 1641, requested the towns to instruct their deputies on certain matters.[18] Instructions continued to be made periodically to colonial legislative representatives until 1776. At that point, instructions became much more frequent, far less humble in language, and more concerned with statewide matters than specific town problems. The practice of instructing delegates was by then at least 135 years old in New England. It was not until 1765, at the beginning of the American revolutionary era, that the freemen of the middle and southern colonies voted instructions to their delegates in the popular assembly on a regular basis; but by that time there was a political theory to justify what had grown up as a natural institution in New England.[19]

The referendum was also applied to the broader government. We have already noted the Rhode Island requirement, from 1647 to 1663, that all laws passed by the General Assembly be referred to the towns. The referendum was used as early as 1641 in Massachusetts, when a majority of towns rejected a general court plan for altering the procedure of collecting votes.[20] In the same year, a ma-

17. *Ibid.*, II, 36.
18. N. B. Shurtleff (ed.), *Massachusetts Colonial Records* (Boston: n.p., 1853–4), I, 33, 340, 346.
19. Kenneth Colgrove, "New England Town Mandates," *Publications of the Colonial Society of Massachusetts*, XXI (1919), 422.
20. Shurtleff (ed.), *Massachusetts Colonial Records*, I, 334.

jority of towns voted to adopt a new state code that we now know as the Massachusetts Body of Liberties. The referendum was frequently used during the colonial era; therefore, it was not out of the ordinary when, in 1776, the general court submitted to the town meetings a proposal on the question of independence from England. Throughout the colonial period there had been a tendency to limit the use of the referendum to constitutional questions. It was a logical step, therefore, both historically and theoretically, to have the constitutions themselves be adopted in statewide referendums. Once again, radical Whig theory pressed for an institution that had been developed in New England on practical grounds or had evolved as a natural development of local government by town meeting.

There was even an attempt to develop agency consent beyond sole reliance upon elections. In 1644, the town of Gloucester "dismissed" its representative to the general court and voted another in his place. The general court refused to accept the recall vote and, in this particular instance, prevailed.[21] However, in 1686, Salem recalled her deputies from the general court, and in 1687, Fairfield, Connecticut, recalled her deputies for having given in to the governor, Sir Edmund Andros.[22] The instrument of recall was used a number of other times with success during the colonial era and at least once during the revolutionary era, but annual elections made recall a relatively clumsy tool by comparison.

By 1776 there was a strong tradition of the popularly elected lower house being closely tied to the town meeting, at least in New England, New York, New Jersey, and Delaware. The relationship was also reasonably strong in Pennsylvania and Maryland. The onset of the Revolution resulted in local assemblies being activated in the southern states as well. It comes as no surprise, then, that the first state constitutions tended strongly toward direct popular consent. They rested heavily upon local government, and local government was based upon direct popular consent through town meetings. The manner in which these Whig documents embodied direct popular consent has already been discussed in great detail. What has not been mentioned is the extent to which the first consti-

21. *Ibid*., III, 3.
22. Colgrove, "New England Town Mandates," 426.

tutions embodied another aspect of radical Whig theory by leaving most governmental matters at the local level. They did not explicitly limit the power of the state legislature (although the 1789 Georgia document was amended in 1795 to limit powers to those expressly enumerated in the Constitution).[23] Rather, local power was preserved by the state constitutions' failing to regulate local government and then placing the state legislature at the mercy of local demands. Fourteen of the first eighteen state constitutions established at least one county office, usually the justice of the peace or the sheriff, but not one mentioned a town office as being subject to the legislature.[24] Six of these fourteen constitutions explicitly excluded some county offices from state control and made them subject to local election.[25]

Elsewhere, the creation of county offices meant only that the state legislature was establishing a police force and judicial system to handle cases that occurred outside town jurisdictions, a necessary function that had been handled similarly in colonial times and represented no serious diminution in the legislative or judicial powers of the town meeting.

To be sure, the fact that the state legislature was not limited in its powers per se but could involve itself where it wanted, posed a po-

23. Article VIII in "Amendments to the Constitution of 1789," in Thorpe, 790. Interestingly, the 1798 Georgia Constitution goes to the opposite extreme in Article I, Section 22. "The general assembly shall have power to make all laws and ordinances which they shall deem necessary and proper for the good of the State, which shall not be repugnant to this constitution" (Thorpe, 794). This section is interesting, not only for reversing the constitutional provision of only three years, but also because it uses "necessary and proper," taken from Article I, Section 1, Paragraph 18 of the United States Constitution. However, the phrase is used in a more expansive manner than in the federal document. Despite the familiar language, state government still was given and used broader powers than the national, Federalist-designed government. At the same time, the final clause in Section 22 indicates that the notion of a constitution as fundamental law has begun to take root at the state level.

24. These fourteen are 1776 South Carolina, 1776 Virginia, 1776 New Jersey, 1776 Maryland, 1776 Delaware, 1776 Pennsylvania, 1776 North Carolina, 1777 Georgia, 1777 New York, 1778 South Carolina, 1780 Massachusetts, 1784 New Hampshire, 1786 Vermont, and 1789 Georgia.

25. These six are 1776 New Jersey, 1776 Maryland, 1776 Delaware, 1776 Pennsylvania, 1776 North Carolina, and 1777 Georgia. There is a strong tendency for all the constitutions written during the second and third waves to place all major county officials under state control.

tential threat to local government. Local control of the legislature remained so strong, however, that interference in local prerogative without permission was politically dangerous. The danger really ran in the opposite direction. Local government was so influential, through the instruments of direct popular consent, that legislatures tended to involve themselves in legislation that had particularistic impact even in matters involving explicit state powers. Taxation and appropriations often favored certain groups of towns or counties, and the legislative reversals and instabilities that the Federalists abhorred often flowed from local governments competing for advantage at the state level.

Economic advantage was the usual concern. Sometimes competition was between towns in the same state, and sometimes between towns in different states. In either case, legislative support for one town over another was often the crucial variable in economic development. This was not a new situation but one that had existed in colonial days as well, especially since the rapid commercial expansion that began in the colonies during the 1750s. The war and independence accelerated economic development, or at least increased the stakes in a highly fluid situation. Anyone interested in a more detailed discussion need only consult Ernest S. Griffith's description of town and city competition during the 1750s and 1760s.[26] Albany and New York City continued to be locked in severe competition. The New Jersey colonial legislature supported Perth Amboy as a competitor to New York City for the major port in the region. Support was continued until well after 1776, despite the obvious disadvantages Perth Amboy had as a port. Money for this support had to be taken from elsewhere in the state, and one can only wonder to what extent the citizens of Perth Amboy used the hope of state economic advantage to secure their own goals. Annapolis and St. Mary's continued to maneuver for advantage in the Maryland legislature; Philadelphia and Baltimore competed for support from their respective legislatures in a battle for commercial supremacy, as did Wilmington and Brunswick. Western towns and coastal towns were

26. Griffith, *History of American City Government*, especially Chap. XIV.

often at odds, and instability in economic policy reflected particularistic goals here, as well. Federalist institutions would not and could not eliminate these problems.

Madison and others also mention involvement of the state legislatures in judicial and moral matters. Here we have the Whigs doing at the state level what they had been doing at the local level for a century and a half. The distinction between legislative and judicial matters was a relatively new one. Most early state constitutions made the judicial system the creature of the legislature, if for no other reason than it seemed the natural thing to do, given American political tradition. Constitutions toward the end of the second wave began the move toward an independent judiciary, but invariably only at the level of the state supreme courts. Most courts still remained subject to strong legislative influence. Involvement of the legislature in moral matters was also natural. The state constitutions often contained statements of fundamental moral values, as we have already seen, and most also contained provisions encouraging the elevation of public morals even to the point of openly encouraging church attendance. Again we have Whig political instruments at the state level merely reflecting and continuing what had been common practice at the local level since 1621. Every type of legislation that Madison decried at the state level had, in fact, been practiced at the local level. Read carefully in the context of his writing elsewhere, his list of "sins" comes down to two charges—the national government is ineffective and needs more power, and state government is far too involved in the details of life and should be curbed. Both problems had a common solution in an effective national government, truly superior to state government yet limited in the scope of its power. Madison and other Federalists may have been entirely correct in concluding that Whig political theory produced serious problems when applied at the state level, but it cannot be overlooked that the desire to eliminate such practices was completely contrary to the American political tradition that was still dominant in the 1770s. The Federalist position represented a fundamental change in political morality, and the enforcement of this new morality would require a new theory of republican government.

The Federalist emphasis on "interests," using the individual as the unit of analysis, ran counter to Whig emphasis on community and virtue. The growing strength of this doctrine of individualism could only undercut the town and county as the unit of representation. Federalists still expected most government to take place at the local level, but the role of local government was now subtly transformed. It was viewed as representing heterogeneous interests, with the result that the practice of local communities instructing state representatives was not as meaningful as it once had been. Now it was a matter of the poor having a common interest, regardless of their locale; and the same held true for merchants, large landowners, and creditors. Representatives would respond to interests instead of communities, and in doing so, the idea of the public good being sought by a disinterested legislature would be replaced by competition for votes based on appeals to pride and economic advantage. Virtue took on a different meaning and was relegated to a less important position in Federalist republican theory.

Radical Whigs unwittingly played into Federalist hands by pressing for political equality. Giving each town at least one representative created unwieldy legislatures. There was also the problem of differential town size, and rewarding larger towns with more than one representative in proportion to population seriously exacerbated the problem. The obvious solution to excessively large legislatures and unequal representation was to base representation on population using the county as the unit for apportionment. By 1787, only five states continued to use towns as the apportionment unit, five used the county, and four used the county plus the few major cities.[27] Only Massachusetts among the heavily populated states represented towns. The rest of the large states, those that would

27. Massachusetts, New Hampshire, Rhode Island, Connecticut and Vermont used towns. There is an obvious regional bias here. New Jersey, Delaware, New York, South Carolina and Pennsylvania basically used counties, although Pennsylvania made special provisions for Philadelphia; and New York, South Carolina, and Pennsylvania apportioned according to the population within a county instead of representing counties equally. Virginia, Maryland, North Carolina, and Georgia used a mixed system whereby a half-dozen or more major towns or cities were accorded the status of counties and explicitly given representation in their respective constitutions.

contain most of the population increases in the years to come, abandoned town representation. This being the case, it became increasingly difficult for any given town to exert influence on state legislators, since rarely did one town represent anything close to a majority of a county, and state representatives were usually elected countywide in multimember districts. Only when a matter aroused the united interest of an entire county would instructions prove effective. It was no accident that by the early part of the nineteenth century, instructions from town meetings to state representatives had become relatively infrequent.[28]

Even the town meetings themselves were beset by the problem of size. Kenneth Colgrove reports one instance, in 1821, when the problem of fitting even a significant minority into the town meeting hall had reached such absurd dimensions that the lamplighters of Boston were in a majority at a town meeting and carried the vote to raise their own wages.[29] John Fairfield Sly follows the history of town government in Massachusetts from 1620 to 1930 and describes in detail the problems the town meeting had in adjusting to increased population in the state with the strongest and most enduring attachment to radical Whig principles. Certainly, many Americans were cognizant of the problems connected with applying these principles to state government, and as logically as the council of censors flowed from radical Whig principles and the assumptions of local governmental practice, its failure to take hold may reflect an indifference born of a growing skepticism.

The town meeting played an important role in organizing and conducting the American Revolution. The English constantly complained that the Boston town meeting was the source of much unrest. In 1774, the towns of Massachusetts established the first Provincial Congress through the votes of instruction. Throughout the transition from colonies to states, the revolutionary leaders relied upon the town and county meetings as the constitutional basis for their extralegal state legislatures and their political actions. By this time, town meetings had been activated in the northern states, and

28. Colgrove, "New England Town Mandates," 446.
29. *Ibid.*, 447.

county organizations established in the South. State institutions were thus constructed from below quite rapidly, and because state institutions rested upon these mini-republics, they naturally embodied the principles that the townsmen took for granted. The strength of the radical Whigs is to be sought here, rather than in the inherent power of any theory. The theory had pragmatic power because it supported and justified a form of republican government that had existed at the local level for almost 150 years.

The strength of radical Whig politics was also its weakness, for it rested upon and supported localism and particularism. Radical Whigs thus had no plan for a national government and did not know how to respond to nationalism.[30] Provincialism did not die out, but the strong nationalistic fervor that swept America in the 1770s and 1780s increasingly undermined Whig attempts to maintain a weak central government. There was also the obvious fact that Whig principles could not overcome the weaknesses inherent in the Articles of Confederation, for to strengthen the national government threatened popular local control. In a certain sense, three alternatives were available. Radical Whig principles could be applied at the national level to create a very democratic government, but it would be distant from the people and would also undercut the power of local and state government. The Articles of Confederation could be kept, but they were patently ineffective, especially with state provincialism creating all the problems that James Madison so incisively listed. A third alternative was presented by the Federalists. Aside from the familiar language and institutions, their proposed national constitution had the strong virtue of creating an effective national government with limited powers, a point they continually stressed. This meant that most government would remain at the local level. The gain in national power was only at the expense of state power. That the proposed Constitution was federal in nature would permit the radical Whigs to retain their state governments relatively intact, as well. Overlooked for the moment was the fact

30. The view of the relationship between state and local government developed in this chapter leads to the conclusion that the Articles of Confederation best expressed Whig sentiments and Whig political theory when it came to a national government.

that the Constitution was constructed according to a different political theory resting upon considerably different assumptions than those of state and local government. Equally important, there was no way to predict that the document contained the potential institutional and legal tools for greatly expanding the powers of national government at the expense of the other levels of government. It is time to analyze more carefully the Federalist theory of republican government and the assumptions that contained this potential.

8

Federalist versus Antifederalist

Few people today realize how close the national Constitution came to being rejected. Americans of that era were almost evenly divided between the Federalist and Antifederalist persuasions. More than a constitution was at stake. Powerful forces invested the acceptance or rejection of the proposed constitution with drastic implications for the future form of American civilization. It was more than a matter of economics. Embedded in the struggle between Federalist and Antifederalist was a clash between the two cultural traditions that had grown up in America. One was over a century-and-a-half old, based on religious tradition and rooted in the habit and custom of local control. It emphasized the majority and the community. The other tradition was more recent and was derived from the formal and intellectual "liberal" perspective that grew out of the Enlightenment. Less inclined to emphasize democratic institutions, this second tradition was more attuned to progress, secularism, and individual freedom. Neither tradition has died out in American political theory, but the fact that the United States Constitution is based on the second, the Federalist tradition, has had a profound impact on American politics to this very day. The older tradition has been cast in the role of perpetual opposition in American political history, sometimes in religious form from the Right, and sometimes in secular form from the Left. Because both traditions remain prominent in American political thought today, and because the roles could easily have been reversed, the dichotomy requires a closer examination. Understanding this theoretical division is important because, despite the apparent congeniality of the two traditions in 1776, the Federalists were to write a national constitution in 1787 that was in some respects fundamentally at odds with the Whig tradition that had predominated in the state constitutions and Articles of Confederation.

Two Political Factions

Federalist strength was concentrated along the coast and in the major cities. Antifederalist strength was located in the interior counties and in towns that were not major commercial centers. Generally speaking, that is also how the vote on the Constitution divided.[1] Estimates vary somewhat, but it is generally agreed that the Antifederalists were in a majority in at least six and possibly seven of the thirteen states, and that, overall, approximately 50–52 percent of the voters were Antifederalists.[2] Furthermore, the delegates elected to the various state conventions appear to have reflected the state-by-state ratios fairly accurately (see Table 9). Of course, the Federalists required ratification by nine states, not just seven, and that meant mustering more than a simple majority of the convention delegates. Throughout the thirteen states the Federalists had 835 delegates, and the Antifederalists had 763; but by July 26, 1788, they had induced at least 60, perhaps 75, Antifederalist delegates to vote for the Constitution and had produced ratification by eleven states. How the Federalists were able to achieve victory from a minority position reveals a great deal about the evolution in political thinking that had occurred since 1776, and illuminates the fundamental theoretical split that has enlivened American politics since 1789.

Current scholarship on politics during the last half of the eighteenth century can be grouped into two broad categories. The first, developing out of the response to Charles A. Beard's classic, *An*

---

1. For documentation see Jackson Turner Main, *The Antifederalists: Critics of the Constitution, 1781–1788* (Chapel Hill: University of North Carolina Press, 1961); Jackson Turner Main, *Political Parties Before the Constitution* (Chapel Hill: University of North Carolina Press, 1973); Van Beck Hall, *Politics Without Parties: Massachusetts, 1780–1791* (Pittsburgh: University of Pittsburgh Press, 1972); and Orin Grant Libby, *The Geographical Distribution of the Vote of the Thirteen States on the Federal Constitution, 1787–8* (Madison: University of Wisconsin Press, 1894).

2. Main, *The Antifederalists*, 249.

Table 9
CHRONOLOGY AND SUPPORT FOR RATIFICATION*

State	Convention met	Federalists†	Antifederalists	Ratification vote	For	Against
1. Del.	Dec. 3	30	0	Dec. 7	30	0
2. Pa.	Nov. 21	46	23	Dec. 12	46	23
3. N.J.	Dec. 11	39	0	Dec. 18	39	0
4. Ga.	Dec. 25	‡		Jan. 2	26	0
5. Conn.	Jan. 1	128(?)	40	Jan. 9	128	40
6. Mass.	Jan. 9	170	190	Feb. 16	187	168
7. N.H.	Feb. 13	30	77	June 21	57	47
8. R.I.	(In March the towns voted not to call a convention, 16–48 (?))					
9. Md.	April 21	62	12	April 26	63	11
10. S.C.	May 12	126(?)	98	May 23	149	73
11. Va.	June 2	84(?)	84	June 25	89	79
12. N.Y.	June 17	19	46	July 26	30	27
13. N.C.	July 21	75	193	Aug. 4	75	193

*Based on Appendix D in Jackson Turner Main, *The Antifederalists: Critics of the Constitution, 1781–1788* (Chapel Hill: University of North Carolina Press, 1961), 288.

†The division into Federalist and Antifederalist is approximate. When a figure is tenuous it is followed by a question mark.

‡A large Federalist majority was reported, but accurate figures are not available.

Economic Interpretation of the Constitution of the United States (1913), has stressed the socioeconomic basis of politics.[3] Although Beard's extreme position is now largely rejected, Jackson Turner Main is the most prominent and most effective spokesman for those who interpret the politics of the era in much the same manner that behavioral political science does, by stressing the importance and differential behavior of political elites.

The second group, largely proceeding from Bernard Bailyn's seminal analysis in *The Ideological Origins of the American Revolution* (1967), represents a highly sophisticated return to an earlier tradition that stresses the importance of ideas, belief systems, and culture for political behavior during the era. Gordon S. Wood is the most successful spokesman for this approach. Wood's approach parallels a growing resurgence of interest in the same variables within current political science.

Political theory does not operate in a vacuum. Ideas arise from material circumstances and, in turn, help to shape those circumstances. The interaction is a complex one and from time to time one or the other may appear to be decisive for affecting human motivation and behavior. Throughout this book the analysis has blended the behavioral with the traditional approach and the socioeconomic with the cultural perspective, and not unexpectedly, material circumstances and ideas combine to provide an explanation for the Federalist victory. Given the superb efforts of historians in both categories, it is now difficult, if not impossible, to neglect either in analyzing political theory between 1776 and 1789. Together, they permit a coherent and complete analysis of developments in consent theory and, thus, of the self-guiding republic in its final form.

Jackson Turner Main's essential thesis is stated at the end of his first book. "But after all these facts have been taken into account, we can return to the major generalization: that the struggle over

3. In addition to the books by Jackson Turner Main, the major works in the controversy being considered here include Charles A. Beard, *An Economic Interpretation of the Constitution of the United States* (New York: Macmillan, 1913); Lee Benson, *Turner and Beard: American Historical Writing Reconsidered* (Chicago: Free Press, 1960); Robert E. Brown, *Charles Beard and the Constitution: A Critical Analysis of "An Economic Interpretation of the Constitution"* (Princeton, N.J.: Princeton University Press, 1956); and Forrest McDonald, *We the People: The Economic Origins of the Constitution* (Chicago: University of Chicago Press, 1958).

ratification of the Constitution was primarily a contest between the commercial and the non-commercial elements in the population. This is the most significant fact, to which all else is elaboration, amplification, or exception."[4] The evidence provided by Main and others does establish that economic factors were important, but major amplification undercuts the simplicity and force of his thesis and results in the same data supporting both an economic and cultural interpretation. In short, the commercial-noncommercial interpretation cannot explain, by itself, either the pattern of electoral support for the Constitution or why some Antifederalist delegates switched sides; therefore, it does not explain why the Federalist faction was able to win ratification.

Main has provided impressive evidence that during the 1780s almost every state legislature had two loose coalitions that formed protoparties.[5] Furthermore, the issues that divided them were similar from state to state, resulting in a nationwide two-party system in embryo. On one side were the merchants and the farmers with farms large enough and situated so that they could transport crops along lines of transportation to commercial centers. On the other side were primarily farmers who either were unable to grow a surplus or, if they could, lacked transportation facilities. The former group also included many professional and educated people, and because their outlook was broader, Main terms them "cosmopolitans." The latter group, generally limited in their concerns to their immediate vicinity, he calls "localists."

Whereas Main derives most of his conclusions from studying the legislative roll calls and the socioeconomic background of legislators during the 1780s, Van Beck Hall did an intensive study of Massachusetts towns themselves and developed a ranking index based upon economic variables such as vessel tonnage, money lent in interest, and town wealth, and social variables such as number of newspapers, age of town, and number of lawyers and ministers.[6] The result is an index that ranks towns according to their level of

---

4. Main, *The Antifederalists*, 280.
5. Main, *Political Parties*, 87.
6. Hall, *Politics Without Parties*. The author very courteously makes his index and town rankings available by mail.

176

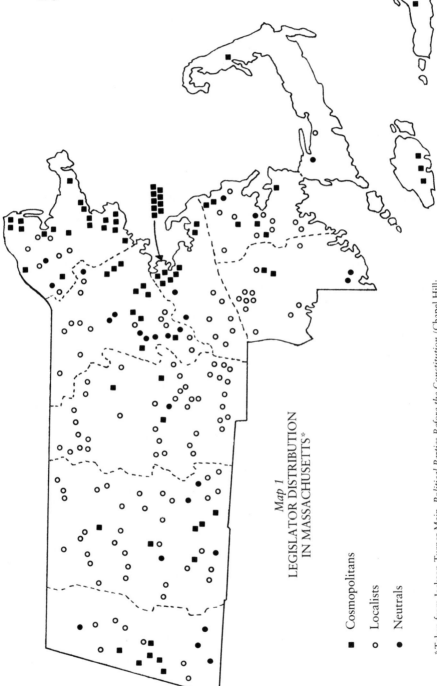

Map 1
LEGISLATOR DISTRIBUTION
IN MASSACHUSETTS*

■   Cosmopolitans

o   Localists

●   Neutrals

*Taken from Jackson Turner Main, *Political Parties Before the Constitution* (Chapel Hill:
University of North Carolina Press, 1973).

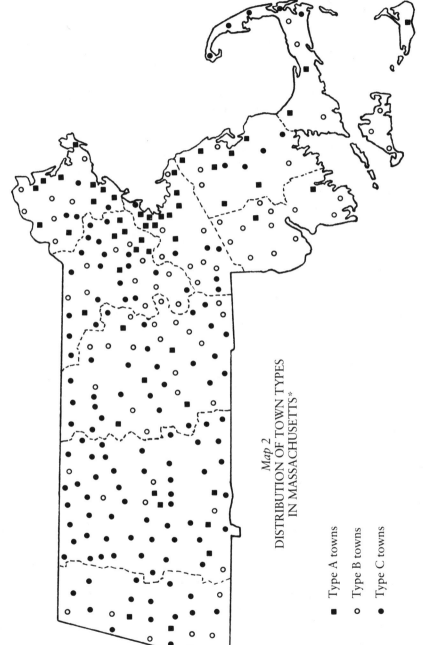

Map 2

DISTRIBUTION OF TOWN TYPES
IN MASSACHUSETTS*

■ Type A towns

○ Type B towns

● Type C towns

*Taken from Van Beck Hall, *Politics Without Parties: Massachusetts, 1780–1791* (Pittsburgh: University of Pittsburgh Press, 1972).

economic and cultural development. Dividing the towns into three categories, each containing an equal number of people, we have Type A towns being most developed, Type C towns least developed, and Type B towns in the middle. Comparing Maps 1 and 2, we can see the marked tendency for Main's cosmopolitan legislators to come from Hall's Type A towns. Both were generally found along the coast, along the road leading northwest out of Boston through Concord and Lexington to Leominster and then in an arc south to Worcester, along the banks of the Housatonic River running due south in westernmost Berkshire County, and along the banks of the Connecticut River running south through Hampshire County, the next most western county. Type B towns in the same geographic pattern also produced cosmopolitan legislators. Localists tended to come from Type C towns, and the bottom half of the Type B town category. Hall has, in effect, identified Main's cosmopolitan towns using another method. A third map shows that support for the Constitution came heavily from those areas where cosmopolitan legislators and Type A towns predominated. The basis of the Federalist-Antifederalist split is thus apparent, although the situation is still a bit more complex than this.

Aside from the towns along the coast and those along navigable rivers that opened them up to commercial trade with Connecticut towns and the coast to the south, forty-four Type C towns voted for ratification of the Constitution. This matches the forty-four Type B towns and forty Type A towns doing the same. While Type A, highly cosmopolitan towns were more than twice as likely to support ratification of the Constitution as localist Type C towns, one-third of the towns that did support the Federalists were economically marginal, with little or no surplus, no minister, no tonnage, no newspaper, and almost no money lent at interest (see Table 10). Without the support of these western, noncommercial towns, the Federalists would have been swamped. Type A towns are clearly skewed toward the Federalists, and Type C toward the Antifederalists, but the important support from western noncommercial towns cannot be explained simply on the basis of their economic ties to commercial ones. In many cases, they engaged in no commerce whatsoever.

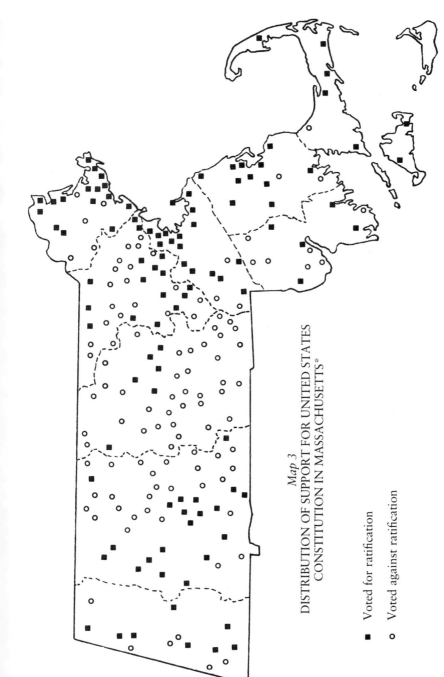

Map 3

DISTRIBUTION OF SUPPORT FOR UNITED STATES
CONSTITUTION IN MASSACHUSETTS*

■ Voted for ratification

○ Voted against ratification

*Based on data from Orin Grant Libby, *The Geographical Distribution of the Vote of the
Thirteen States on the Federal Constitution, 1787–8* (Madison: University of Wisconsin
Press, 1894).

Table 10
TYPE OF TOWN SUPPORTING RATIFICATION IN MASSACHUSETTS

Town vote	Types of towns			Totals
	Type A	Type B	Type C	
For ratification	40 (74%)	44 (51%)	44 (32%)	128 (46%)*
Against ratification	12 (22%)	39 (45%)	94 (68%)	145 (52%)
Divided	2 (4%)	3 (4%)	0 (0%)	5 (2%)
	54 (100%)	86 (100%)	138 (100%)	278 (100%)

* There were 360 delegates elected to the ratifying convention. One hundred and seventy of them were Federalists (47 percent of the total), and 190 of them were considered Antifederalist (53 percent).

The pattern is repeated elsewhere. In New Hampshire, for example, Federalist support came heavily from small towns, considerably inland from the major centers of trade, with little or no commercial potential (see Map 4). True, many Federalist towns were found clustered on the coast or along the Connecticut River in the west, but small frontier-type communities were even more numerous. This is the only way to explain how, even though the Federalists won 101 towns as opposed to 79 for the Antifederalists, the apportionment by population resulted in a 77 to 30 delegate advantage for the Antifederalists at the ratifying convention. Obviously the latter faction took the lion's share of the medium-sized towns with most of the state's population, and the Federalists had many small towns.

In Pennsylvania and Virginia there was the same combination of eastern commercial towns and western frontier towns, but here the evidence is even more dramatic because there was no possible commercial connection to explain the phenomenon. In both states they were separated by mountains and the Antifederalist counties (see Maps 5, 6, and 7). Again, the area in the middle of the states formed the core of Antifederalist opposition. New York and the Carolinas fit the commercial-noncommercial division Main describes, but New Jersey, Maryland, and Delaware went completely Federalist. Since commercial and noncommercial areas in these states went Federalist, Main's distinction explains little. There are other exceptions. For one thing, Georgia had no commercial centers, yet it went

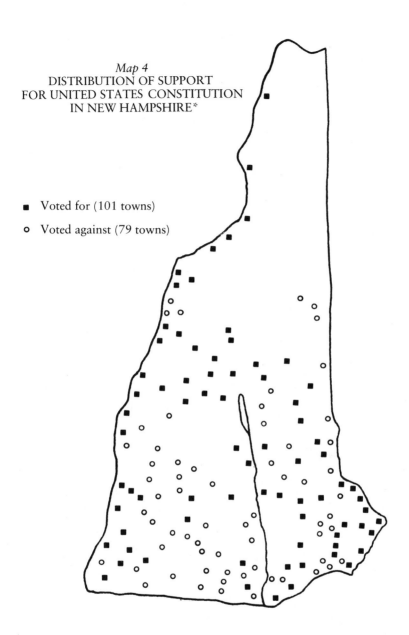

Map 4
DISTRIBUTION OF SUPPORT
FOR UNITED STATES CONSTITUTION
IN NEW HAMPSHIRE*

■ Voted for (101 towns)

○ Voted against (79 towns)

*Based on data from Orin Grant Libby, *The Geographical Distribution of the Vote of the Thirteen States on the Federal Constitution, 1787–8* (Madison: University of Wisconsin Press, 1894).

completely Federalist. For another, the only area in Maryland that did not vote Federalist was the region immediately adjacent to Baltimore, Maryland's primary commercial center. Connecticut was overwhelmingly Federalist, and Rhode Island was overwhelmingly Antifederalist. Both are on the coast, and both had a majority of their population in noncommercial towns.

In summary, while the commercial towns and cities overwhelmingly supported the Federalist-penned Constitution, about a third of its support across the country came from noncommercial towns, especially on or near the frontier. The economic hypothesis does not explain their support, yet without their votes the Federalists would never have come close enough to winning to worry about converting delegates at the state conventions.

In the cases of western Pennsylvania, western Virginia (now West Virginia), and Georgia, the frontier was insecure in the face of hostile Indians and foreign settlements, British in the north and Spanish in the south. This local concern may have been strong enough in itself to induce support for a stronger central government that could supply protection, something the government under the Articles could never successfully provide. There was, however, no frontier problem in New Hampshire, Massachusetts, Connecticut, or Rhode Island. Here, another explanation may prove useful. One thing distinguishing Type 3 towns that supported the Federalists from Type 3 towns that supported the Antifederalists was the age of the town. Federalist towns were generally quite young, whereas opposition towns of Type 3 had usually been settled for long periods. It is possible that an intangible aspect of political culture was at work in the form of the tradition of local community control. The older Type 3 towns, while not prosperous, still had much longer experience living under their town meeting and may have been more resistant to a perceived threat to local control, whereas frontier Type 3 towns had not yet developed that sense of community. This hypothesis, though useful, is speculative and cannot explain why extreme western Virginia and North Carolina (now Kentucky and Tennessee) remained Antifederalist. The matter is a complex one, and regardless of how limited the political culture hypothesis is, the com-

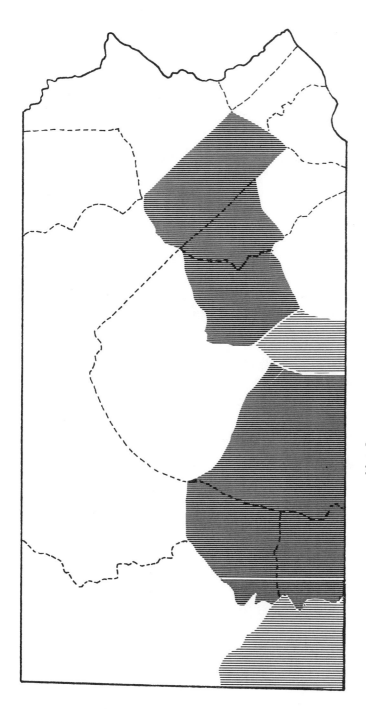

Map 5

DISTRIBUTION OF SUPPORT FOR UNITED STATES
CONSTITUTION IN PENNSYLVANIA*

* Based on data from Orin Grant Libby. Compare this map with Map 6, which shows that
the support of the northern and western counties could not have been predicted by the type
of legislators they sent.

☐ Federalist counties

▮ Antifederalist counties

▤ Divided counties

184

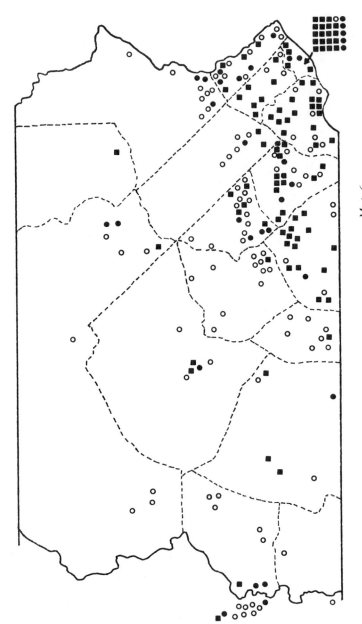

Map 6
LEGISLATOR DISTRIBUTION
IN PENNSYLVANIA*

■ Republicans (mostly to become Federalist)

○ Constitutionalists (mostly to become Antifederalists)

● Neutrals

*Taken from Jackson Turner Main, *Political Parties Before the Constitution.* Residences
are geographically approximate.

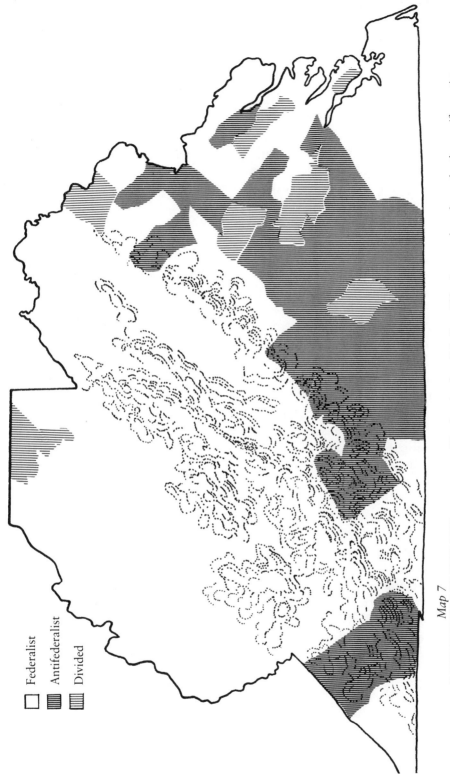

Map 7
DISTRIBUTION OF SUPPORT
FOR UNITED STATES CONSTITUTION
IN VIRGINIA*

☐ Federalist

▨ Antifederalist

▤ Divided

*Based on data from Orin Grant Libby. Areas are shown here rather than specific counties to simplify the visual presentation. There were approximately two dozen counties west of the Shenandoah Valley, and approximately seventy-five counties in the eastern portion of the state.

mercial-noncommercial analysis is also limited in its explanatory power.

The economic approach also suffers when used to explain the phenomenon of delegates switching sides. Here, considerable elaboration is required to sustain the argument, and one is on firmer ground when it comes to alternative explanations. In his own amplification, Main suggests that the Federalists won because the great majority of newspapers circulated throughout the states were published in the Federalist urban strongholds and, thus, were sympathetic to their cause; Federalist leaders were more prestigious than Antifederalist leaders; the initial ratifications came so quickly that a psychological momentum was developed which favored the Federalists; the Antifederalists were "unable to unite, even within a particular state, in order to concert their efforts"; and many Antifederalist leaders were from the same socioeconomic background as Federalist leaders and therefore were more open to compromise than the rank-and-file Antifederalists.[7] Main argues that this last fact was exploited heavily by promising the lukewarm Antifederalist leaders that a bill of rights would be attached to the Constitution, thus reassuring them and winning their grudging "conversion." He does not explain, however, why this particular proposal was appealing to them.

The arguments concerning newspapers and leadership are true enough, but they pertain more to the selection of convention delegates than to the crucial "conversion" phenomenon. These advantages, superior organization, and "dirty tricks" such as disrupting the mail between the Antifederalist leaders certainly had some impact, but the approximately 835 to 763 delegate advantage that the Federalists mustered over the twelve state conventions was not really an impressive one, especially when one considers that the Federalists controlled all the delegates in three states, leaving them in an approximate 737 to 763 minority throughout the other nine states. The Federalists did not win ratification only by outcampaigning the Antifederalists in the convention elections (although their superior

7. Main, *The Antifederalists*, 249–55.

organization did turn an approximate 40 percent electoral minority into a delegate tie in Virginia).

As for psychological momentum, this may have been an important factor in New York's ratification, but it does not explain why North Carolina and Rhode Island continued to hold out after ratification was assured, nor does it explain events in Massachusetts and New Hampshire, where well-informed delegates were probably not surprised by the first five ratifications. This is, at best, a slippery argument.

Main's last two arguments are more to the point, and he rightly places greatest emphasis upon them. The Antifederalist delegates seemed unable or unwilling to work together in many instances, and this hurt them badly. There is, however, no economic explanation for this phenomenon—at least Main advances none. The best explanation is probably related to the last phenomenon that he describes. There was an apparent disparity between what some Antifederalist leaders espoused and the demands of the Antifederalist rank and file. More important, there was considerable disparity between one set of leaders and another. Some leaders evidenced a lukewarm attachment to the democratic principle and were more concerned with sound currency and civil order than others.

In a more careful examination of those Antifederalist delegates who switched, Main discovers that a minority of the fifty-six he examined came from regions near the coast and from the upper socioeconomic stratum of society.[8] From this he derives an essentially economic explanation for their defection by arguing that these characteristics tended to separate such Antifederalist leaders from the noncommercial-oriented and less well off rank and file. Since most Antifederalist leaders, as well as supporters, clearly did not have such characteristics, the distinction is a potentially important one, but is not in itself a sufficient explanation. "They frequently defended views somewhat less democratic than those of their constituents, and they were often out of sympathy with the economic demands of

8. The last chapter in Main's book on the Antifederalists is reproduced in a somewhat different form in Stephen G. Kurtz (ed.), *The Federalists—Creators and Critics of the Union, 1780–1801* (New York: John Wiley and Sons, 1972), 61–75.

the rank and file. . . . As a result, Antifederalism as formulated by its most prominent spokesman *sometimes* lacks the democratic overtones we have attributed to it" (emphasis added).[9] In reality, some Antifederalist leaders were less than enthusiastic about direct popular participation, but most Antifederalist leaders *were* enthusiastic. In fact, the relative absence of direct popular participation formed the core of Antifederalist criticism of the proposed Constitution, as Main notes in his next paragraph. The Antifederalists were, after all, Whigs, and throughout the 1770s and 1780s they had relentlessly pressed for direct popular participation in state government. It would be surprising if Whig leaders suddenly changed their minds, or the rank and file started electing a different kind of leadership. At the same time, Antifederalist leaders did not emphasize direct popular control at the state level as much as they had in the past; but this is perfectly understandable in light of the political theory to which they were generally committed.

The point to remember is that there was a split in the Antifederalist leadership. The split was not primarily economic in origin, although economics played its role. Instead, the split was between the radical Whigs and the more traditional Whigs, between men like Samuel Adams and John Adams. If the crucial variable was one of economics, and if the defectors had the requisite socioeconomic characteristics, then Main must explain why the defecting Antifederalists did not become Federalists in the first place. They did not because, despite their disagreement with many radical Whigs' eco-

9. Main, *The Antifederalists*, 281. On page 130 of the same volume, Main provides an ingenious noneconomic explanation for the relative absence of economic overtones. In essence, he argues that almost all the delegates to the state ratifying conventions, Federalist or Antifederalist, were of "the better sort," and, therefore, constrained by social mores from being abusive or unpleasant. For the Antifederalists to accuse their Federalist brethren of being elitists and uninterested in the welfare of the people would not have been permissible, and so the Antifederalists were forced to walk on eggshells when discussing this central issue. Perhaps this explains much, but legislators in Pennsylvania, for example, had not been loathe to verbally abuse each other in the past. The interested reader may satisfy himself on this point, as well as obtain a good feeling for the progress of the controversy by consulting Jonathan Elliott, *The Debates in the Several State Conventions on the Adoption of the Federal Constitution* (5 vols.; Philadelphia: J. B. Lippincott, 1901). Also of interest are Samuel B. Harding, *The Contest Over the Ratification of the Federal Constitution in the State of Massachusetts* (New York: n.p., 1896), reproduced by University Microfilms, Inc., Ann Arbor, Michigan, 1964; and Theodore Foster (ed.), *The Minutes of the Rhode Island Convention of 1790* (Providence: Rhode Island Historical Society, 1929).

nomic policies, they nonetheless found them more congenial than the Federalists on the crucial matters of local control, the relative importance of majority rule, and emphasis upon community and virtue, rather than on individualism and interests.[10] What, then, caused their "conversion" if not economics? A probable answer is multifaceted and includes consideration of the theoretical developments outlined in this volume. These developments produced strong cross-pressures and considerable theoretical ambiguity, which made some Antifederalist delegates more susceptible to Federalist overtures. Let us try to reconstruct the situation.

Wilson Carey McWilliams notes that "the doctrines of the Enlightenment entered America through the port cities and great plantations, the 'ports of entry' for ideas as well as trade."[11] The coastal and major river towns shared not only an interest in commercial matters but also a common exposure to the wave of ideas emanating from Europe. Here were concentrated the men of commercial wealth and the men with education and European contacts. H. Trevor Colbourn has documented the impressive commonality of library holdings among educated Americans of the period, and Jackson Turner Main has established the dramatic difference in average education between Federalist and Antifederalist.[12] The more educated a man was, the more likely he was to be exposed to the literature of the Enlightenment. The closer he lived to the commercial and cultural centers, the more often he interacted with those espousing Enlightenment ideas.

The educational distinction between Federalist and Antifederalist should not be pushed too far. The more traditional Whigs were often members of the educated elite that predominated before 1776. Many, like John Adams, continued to inject the pre–1776 values into Whig political discourse. Many also injected Enlightenment ideas, especially when it came to justifying bills of rights that tended to hem in majority rule, and traditional Whigs were prominent in

10. For an impressive analysis of the history of American political thought, especially as it involves the idea of fraternity, see Wilson Carey McWilliams, *The Idea of Fraternity in America* (Berkeley: University of California Press, 1973).

11. *Ibid.*, 170.

12. H. Trevor Colbourn, *The Lamp of Experience* (Chapel Hill: University of North Carolina Press, 1965).

supporting bills of rights during the 1780s for this very reason—to moderate majority rule. Prominent Whig documents such as the Essex Result, quoted at length in an earlier chapter, neatly blended traditional Whig thought with Enlightenment ideas. John Locke was often quoted with approval, regardless of the fact that his assumption of individualism was at odds with Whig attachment to community. Never completely happy with the extremes to which radical Whigs had taken their principles, many traditional Whigs like John Adams lacked the fervent attachment to the democratic principle. Unless care was taken, some Federalist ideas could be construed as supportive of a mixed regime, especially since Federalists, as we have already seen, often used traditional Whig terminology, and also because many of the traditional Whigs had, themselves, uncritically absorbed Enlightenment ideas in their education and associations. As Gordon S. Wood so ably illustrates, John Adams could become a Federalist despite his continued attachment to traditional Whig principles because he did not recognize the implications of Federalist political theory.[13] Adams was almost certainly not alone in his confusion or in his desire to balance and offset the democratic principle through a mixed government; and as Paul Eidelberg shows, it is still possible today to interpret the American Constitution as embodying the Whig theory of a mixed regime.[14] Certainly many traditional Whigs became Federalists, but many remained in the Whig fold and became Antifederalists. Those in the latter group would be prominent, educated leaders, available as delegates to ratifying conventions. They would generally come from the more cosmopolitan eastern towns and would be wealthier than most Antifederalists. These characteristics were, after all, typical of the traditional Whigs prior to 1776, and there is no reason to suspect that they had moved or become impoverished.[15]

13. Gordon S. Wood, *The Creation of the American Republic, 1776–1787* (Chapel Hill: University of North Carolina Press, 1969), 567–92.

14. Main, *The Antifederalists*, 131; and Cecilia M. Kenyon, "Men of Little Faith: The Anti-Federalists on the Nature of Representative Government," *William and Mary Quarterly*, 3rd. ser., XII (1955), 3–43; Paul Eidelberg, *The Philosophy of the American Constitution* (New York: Free Press, 1968).

15. In addition to theoretical confusion, Antifederalist leaders were subjected to social cross-pressures from the Federalists with whom many of them shared common educational

Aside from the split leadership, two more reasons can help explain the seeming inability of the Antifederalists to organize. First, some Antifederalists agreed that changes in the Articles of Confederation *were* necessary. The Federalist proposal was too extreme for them, but the unwillingness to defend the Articles deprived them of their easiest alternative to the Federalist proposal. Second, the Antifederalists (Whigs) had always been most concerned about local political control and thus had no theoretical answers for the problem of a national government beyond desiring it to be relatively weak. To extend direct popular control to the national level would be to concede the importance of the central government as well as expand its powers. Local control of state government, with a loose confederation to coordinate the continent, was their natural inclination, and this was no basis upon which to construct their own alternative plan, even if there had not been a split in the leadership. Jackson Turner Main argues persuasively that, if anything, the Antifederalists would have logically pressed for a plan of government quite similar to the Paterson, or New Jersey, Plan that was advanced by the small states at the Constitutional Convention.[16] Regardless of specifics, it would have created a government only slightly more powerful than that created by the Articles of Confederation.

There is one more possible facet to the situation that might help explain the defection of about 10 percent of the delegates. The Federalist plan, while too strong for most Antifederalists' tastes, did leave local government and local control of state legislatures intact. Furthermore, the national government was limited to the enumerated powers, and the promise of an amendment to reserve all other powers to the states and the people might have seemed to minimize the problem. Superficially, it left state government and those care-

---

and social experiences. During the convention, many Antifederalists were wined and dined, not in an attempt to bribe them, but in an attempt to activate natural social ties that already existed, and to reassure such Antifederalist leaders that the Federalists were trustworthy. Most susceptible to this tactic would be the more traditional Whigs with a college education and social ties to the seaboard towns. Of course, all these characteristics were most common in representatives from towns relatively near the commercial centers in the east, since frontier and subsistence towns did not produce or support such men.

16. Main, *The Antifederalists*, 184–5.

fully fashioned Whig constitutions basically unaltered. Lacking an alternative, confused by Federalist use of words, sharing a concern for the excesses of democracy exhibited by state government, and reassured by the promise of amendments that would both hem in the majority and leave local and state governments essentially unchanged, it is perhaps not surprising that some traditional Whigs decided to vote for ratification. The utter reasonableness of the Federalist position is nowhere better summarized than in Madison's *The Federalist* 46.

> If therefore, as has been elsewhere remarked, the people should in future become more partial to the federal than to the state governments, the change can only result, from such manifest and irresistible proofs of a better administration, as will overcome all their antecedent propensities. And in that case, the people ought not surely to be precluded from giving most of their confidence where they may discover it to be most due; But even to that case, the state governments could have little to apprehend, because it is only within a certain sphere, that the federal power can, in the nature of things, be advantageously administered.[17]

Madison noted that even in the good days under the Articles of Confederation, the people were more attached to their local governments for the simple reason that the flaws in the Articles made national government less effective.[18] The worst that could be expected was that, under the proposed Constitution, national government would become as effective in its own sphere as local government was in its sphere; but because the national government was limited

17. All quotes from the Federalists papers will be taken from J. E. Cooke (ed.), *The Federalist* (Cleveland: Meridian Books, 1961). This citation is from page 317. Paper number 27 is also relevant. *The Federalist* is an unusual blend of propaganda and political theory. Despite the fact that the two major authors, James Madison and Alexander Hamilton, disagreed on many matters, the collection of papers nonetheless emphasizes their common beliefs and, more important, is a relatively coherent and concise summary of the core theory then current among supporters of the Constitution. The arguments found in *The Federalist* did not spring suddenly from the heads of these two men. They can be found rehearsed in newspapers, letters, and minutes to meetings involving many people over a number of years. It is the clarity of expression, coherence, and comprehensiveness, as well as the sparks of original thought, that make these papers such an impressive project.

18. This is reflected in the fact that until at least the 1820s turnout for national elections was significantly lower than for state and local elections. This is precisely the opposite of today's pattern. See J. R. Pole, *Political Representation in England and the Origins of the American Republic* (Berkeley: University of California Press, 1971), 543–64.

in its powers, the people's affections could change but the status of state power could not.

Today, we use the term *federalism* to describe the division of power between national and state governments. Vincent Ostrom has more accurately labeled it the theory of a "compound republic."[19] Under this arrangement, most government would still take place at the state and local levels, free from national interference, but on matters beyond the competence of a single state the national government would be supreme. The self-guiding republic was compound in a deeper sense than multiple levels of government. It was compound from its inception in the sense that one theory of republican government was operating at the state level and another at the national. The radical Whig theory of politics, so arduously developed in the quarter-century prior to 1787 and so logically related to the American political theory of the previous century and a half, was not extended to the new national government. Instead, the capstone of the self-guiding republic was drawn from a different political culture with different goals and assumptions that were, in many respects, inimical to the older political culture enshrined at the state level. While not a theoretically coherent package, it nonetheless had a socioeconomic neatness that has never been explored. The Federalists had the national government they needed and wanted for continental commercial development. The Whigs, more interested in local control of their communities, retained their state governments essentially free of national interference in cultural, moral, religious, or police matters. With a population that was almost evenly divided between the two political cultures, the compound nature of the self-guiding republic must be considered to have a certain political elegance.

Two Political Cultures

It would be a mistake to press the Whig-Federalist dichotomy too far. Then, as now, there were many stripes of each belief system shading into one another so that if social scientists had been around in the 1780s, they probably would have had great difficulty deciding

19. Vincent Ostrom, *The Political Theory of a Compound Republic* (Blacksburg: Center for Study of Public Choice, Virginia Polytechnic Institute and State University, 1971).

where to draw the line of demarcation between the two groups. Whiggism and Federalism were coherent political theories, but Americans did not always reach consistency in their belief patterns and often blended elements of each. Also, to say that the population was about evenly divided between the two persuasions is to speak of voting behavior and not necessarily of theoretical commitment. Political scientists find today that, at best, approximately 10 percent of the electorate has a reasonably coherent ideological basis for voting the way they do.[20] The 1780s were times of extraordinary political interest that make the 1960s look pale by comparison, yet it is unlikely that more than 15 percent of the voting population acted on the basis of a coherent Whig or Federalist theoretical commitment. Probably, at best, three times that number regularly supported one faction or the other on the basis of commitment to certain symbols or local leaders, but they probably had no more than a minimum of intellectual content to their support. The rest of the population was probably not so much neutral as indifferent and had to be wooed with promised benefits.[21] For example, throughout the 1770s and 1780s, artisans and laborers in major cities and towns supported the Whigs in state politics mainly because Whig politicians spoke to their needs. The Whigs rarely delivered, however, probably because they disliked cities and what they stood for, and the Federalists were able to enlist the support of this laboring class for the federal Constitution.

As a working approximation, about 15 percent of the voters were full intellectual participants in the Whig or Federalist political cultures, another 45 percent regularly supported one faction or the other, and the remaining 40 percent was evenly split but gave its

20. Angus Campbell, *et al.*, *The American Voter* (New York: Wiley, 1960).

21. These approximations are based upon commonly repeated historical estimates plus the findings of modern political science about voting patterns. We find today, for example, that even with a much more educated population, the proportion of those having ideological or near-ideological bases for voting is around 10 percent, and about 25 percent vote on the basis of group benefits. We find also that when it comes to politics, people do not change their minds easily or often. That is, there is a stability to voting patterns that changes slowly. The main difference between current political identifications and those in the 1780s is that the absence of mass-based political parties then made identification with certain leaders a more potent source of political organization. Jackson Turner Main, in his *Political Parties Before the Constitution*, documents the extent to which politics revolved around certain leaders at the state level, as well as around clusters of issues.

support for specific promised benefits. These estimates pertain to those who regularly voted, and since this constituted only about 60–70 percent of the adult male population, the actual numbers are smaller than they appear at first.

If electoral support was almost evenly split, for whatever reason, the hard-core cadres were about equal in numbers as well. As always, from among the 15 percent with a coherent theoretical commitment came the vast majority of political activists and leaders. These men developed the institutions, adjusted theoretical reasoning, set the issues, activated the followers, and made the offers to the uncommitted. They defined the politics of their day; therefore, the content of their respective belief systems was crucial.

Vincent Ostrum identifies four assumptions underlying Federalist political theory—the principles of individualism, self-interest (or relative advantage), human fallibility (with a capability for learning), and political constraint.[22] Contrary to Whig inclinations, Hamilton and Madison argued that the federal government must carry its agency to the individual person of the citizen rather than to communities in their collective capacities. This, in turn, rested upon the assumption that actions resulted from individual volition rather than social need, and that individual satisfaction, not collective evaluation, was the measure of good government. Undoubtedly, some Federalists took the principle to the extreme, considering individuals self-sufficient in moral as well as political matters. But the essential difference from Whig thought was the insistence that, although human behavior takes place in a social context, the basis of social organization lies in the way every individual relates himself to others. Thus, since individuals act, they are *individually* responsible and cannot be governed by laws that apply benefits or sanctions to communities.[23]

This attachment to individualism did not preclude governmental response to collectivities, nor did it imply that laws applying to specific individuals could or should be made. The Federalists were very much against the practice of Whig-dominated state legislatures in which specific persons were singled out for differential tax benefits

22. Ostrom, *Political Theory of a Compound Republic*, 17–25.
23. Cooke (ed.), *The Federalist*, 102–103, 95. See also 94, 105, 349.

or penalties, or the legislature made ruling on specific legal cases. On the contrary, the Federalists desired what we now term political equality, or equality under the law. This was in keeping with their "mechanistic" view of politics—the view that there could be a science of politics that studied political phenomena in terms of interchangeable "atoms" (individuals) subject to universal laws of behavior.[24] Although individuals differed in wealth, ability, and interests, they all based their actions on the same motivations, the primary one being that of self-interest. Laws, therefore, must be universal in their application rather than local in impact if they were to be effective.

At the same time, the Federalists recognized that legislation, especially legislation involving appropriations, often had a differential impact. Certain collectivities, termed "factions," would benefit more than others. These factions, however, would not be local communities, but rather collections of individuals with common interests constructed from many individual decisions. It was perfectly possible that the individuals of one community would choose to seek advantage over the individuals in another community; but it was more likely that one set of individuals in Town A would join with like-minded individuals in Town B to seek relative advantage over other sets of individuals in the two towns. The Federalists were thus opposed to localism because it interfered with the natural forces governing politics.[25] Individualism, on the other hand, was useful both as a unit of analysis and as a principle of governmental response to the real source of political conflict.

The apparent contradiction between equality under the law and the differential impact of legislation was bridged by a theory quite familiar to students of American political theory. Equality under the law was to insure that all factions had the same opportunity to press for their relative advantage and that out of the competitive struggle would emerge a balance of benefits from which the entire society would benefit. This equilibrium would emerge through a process

24. *Ibid.*, 1, 51, 84, 195, 196, 235.
25. The opposition to localism is stated vigorously and often. Cooke (ed.), *The Federalist*, 5, 35–36, 106–107, 116–17, 128–29, 102–103, 146, 306, 420–22, 425.

equivalent to Adam Smith's invisible economic hand, an idea well known to Enlightenment theorists.

Although the Enlightenment emphasized rationalistic analysis, it did not assume that men were generally guided in their actions by reason. On the contrary, *The Federalist* reflects a relatively pessimistic view of human nature, derived from Enlightenment theorists, that strikes at the very heart of the Whig notion of political virtue. The "reason of man continues fallible," so that "the latent causes of faction are thus sown in the nature of man." Man's propensity for peace is overshadowed by his inclination to violence; ambition overarches cooperation; and self-interest undercuts community. Hamilton could argue elsewhere that a certain class was much more inclined to political virtue, but it was a relative advantage rather than an absolute one. Regardless of class, "No man is allowed to be a judge in his own cause; because his interest would certainly bias his judgment, and, not improbably, corrupt his integrity."[26]

Even if these self-centered feelings were not inherent, the fundamental political reality would encourage them. If resources are sufficient for necessities, they are never sufficient for wants, and in either case, individuals must always choose among a set of imperfect options.[27] There is a natural tendency to make the best of a bad situation, which produces the striving for relative advantage. The extent to which human nature and the requirements of the human environment are taken as "givens" is striking. It stands in stark contrast to the opposed political culture. Whigs, and those communitarian conservatives carrying on the tradition today, put great hope in the power of religion to soften, if not transform, human nature. Many on the left of the political spectrum today also hold out the hope of changing human nature and modifying the human environment to minimize self-interested behavior. The Federalist perspective rejects the possibility of either. Instead, it seeks to transform momentary passion and immediate interest into more long-term considerations of justice that will create the greatest good for the

26. *Ibid.*, 58, 59. See also 211–12, 178–79, 235–37, 297, 349, 350–52.
27. *Ibid.*, 190, 269.

greatest number.[28] There is an implicit sense of possible progress, of
the continued improvement of the human condition, but no chance
of ever approaching perfection or constructing a utopia.[29] There is
hope, however moderate, and it is based upon the belief that men
can learn from their mistakes.

In an analogy drawn from medicine, Madison suggests that government should be based first upon the advice of those with a reputation for being most knowledgeable; then a careful weighing of the
alternatives in light of their probable consequences must be made;
then the course of action taken must be viewed as an experiment,
with the real possibility that an error may have been committed
which will require future amendment or replacement.[30] At the
same time, frequent change is to be avoided. Laws that are too
mutable often create more problems than they solve, and the Federalist warns especially against too frequent a reconsideration of
constitutional questions.[31] The mutability of state law, as we have
seen, was a primary source of anxiety for Madison and other Federalists. To control the effects of ill-considered majorities, Madison
constructed the now-famous theory of the extended republic, coupled with the fracturing of government itself into competing factions through the separation of powers, and checks and balances.[32]
In addition, the Federalists emphasized the distinction between a

28. Ostrom, *Political Theory of the Compound Republic*, 23.
29. For evidence of opposition to utopian thinking, see Cooke (ed.), *The Federalist*, 28
and 35–36.
30. *Ibid.*, 242–43. See also 231.
31. *Ibid.*, 340, 234.
32. The theory of the extended republic is found in Federalist paper 10, and the discussion of the theory underlying separation of powers and checks and balances is found in
papers 47–51. Robert Dahl has engaged in a formal analysis of Madison's theory and concluded that it has several serious logical errors which undermine its utility. See Robert Dahl,
Preface to Democratic Theory (Chicago: University of Chicago Press, 1957), Chap. 1.
However, Dahl made the mistake of failing to distinguish the two forms of tyranny that
Madison does, majority tyranny and tyranny of the government over the people. Paper 10
deals with the first form of tyranny, and papers 47–51 deal with the second. By confusing
the two forms, Dahl has been able to render Madison inconsistent. Since Dahl's interpretation is the most widely read by political scientists, his confusion is especially regrettable. For
a fuller discussion see Donald S. Lutz, "James Madison as a Conflict Theorist: The Madi-
sonian Model Extended" (Ph.D. dissertation, Indiana University, 1969); M. J. C. Vile,
Constitutionalism and the Separation of Powers (Oxford, England: Clarendon Press,
1967), Chap. XI.

constitution and statutory laws.[33] This distinction, never quite made in the state constitutions, placed the Constitution above the majority, at least in the short run. Requiring an extraordinary majority to approve amendments retained the people as the ultimate power but mitigated the impact of short-term passion in evaluating the success of the political experiment. The principle of political constraint required the institutional binding of both those in government and the majority within society. Either may be a source of tyranny, for in both cases human nature is still at the helm. Forcing delay, enhancing due deliberation, replacing quick decision making with a slower system that permits all factions to bring their interests to bear, enhances the probability that the experiments undertaken will be well-considered and conducive to the long-run interest of the entire nation.

The idea of government by deliberative process had been central to the American political tradition since the early 1600s.[34] The Federalist approach represented a deflection of the tradition insofar as the deliberative process was no longer housed in the legislature but was expanded to include three branches of government and the state governments in a federal structure. Deliberation was also removed somewhat from direct popular control. Under the traditional Whig theory of republican government the emphasis had been upon a legislature deliberating for the good of the community without interference by the executive. Radical Whigs had shifted a significant portion of the responsibility for deliberation to the people meeting at the local level. The Federalists emphasized constraint both on the legislature's role and the people's role in the deliberative process, for they had discovered republican government to be prone to a special malady, the republican disease of majority tyranny. Neither the people nor the legislature, whether free from interference or not, could be trusted, alone, to conduct deliberations for the good of the whole.

The problem lay not only in flawed human nature. It lay also in

33. Cooke (ed.), *The Federalist*, 360 and 543.
34. See Willmoore Kendall and George Carey, *The Basic Symbols of the American Political Tradition* (Baton Rouge: Louisiana State University Press, 1970).

the absence of true community. Traditional Whigs could trust a
legislature to deliberate dispassionately because of the community
ties that were assumed to bind legislator and constituency. Federalists paid lip service to community and the spirit of fraternity binding the community together, but invariably such passages in *The
Federalist* are contained in blatantly propagandistic sections and are
jarringly contrary to the view of human nature expounded at length
throughout the papers.[35] The Federalists inverted the role of fraternity in American political theory. Whereas the Whigs, both traditional and radical, viewed fraternity as an ethic in intrapersonal
relations that was instrumental to the goal of human excellence, the
Federalists conceived it as an end to be approximated through historical progress.[36] Fraternity became separated from the political
process, something unlikely to prosper among the heterogeneity of
interests until long years of competition and compromise had uncovered a political equilibrium in which the sense of mutually productive relationships would create the basis for a nationwide community. *The Federalist* fails to promise that such an equilibrium
will ever be reached, spends no time describing what successful republican government would look or feel like, and by implication,
shoves fraternity into the category of pleasant, irrelevant topics.

There is a more sinister aspect to the Federalist treatment of fraternity. Removing it from the political process permits Madison to
hold that "no axiom is more clearly established in law, or in reason,
than that wherever the end is required, the means are authorised;
wherever a general power to do a thing is given, every particular
power necessary for doing it, is included."[37] Read one way, this
passage supports inclusion of the "necessary and proper" clause in
the Constitution. Read another, it implies that the end justifies the
means.[38] A corollary is that good methods which have bad results
are not justified by rule or reason. "It will be of little avail to the
people that the laws are made by men of their own choice, if the
laws be so voluminous that they cannot be read, or so incoherent

35. Cooke (ed.), *The Federalist*, 9, 72–73, 88.
36. This is the essential thesis in McWilliams' *Idea of Fraternity in America.*
37. Cooke (ed.), *The Federalist*, 304–305.
38. McWilliams, *Idea of Fraternity in America*, 187.

that they cannot be understood."[39] As Wilson Carey McWilliams puts it, the Federalists believed that "Fraternal unity cannot be established by expecting men to behave fraternally. Attaining the goal may require unfraternal means."[40] If national "fraternity" is achieved in the remote future, it must preclude local affections or loyalties to anything but the entire society. McWilliams concludes, "*The Federalist*, in that sense at least, foreshadows mass society, a world of superficial relations where all bonds are reduced to the 'diffuse' and 'diminished'' affection that is tied to interest."[41] This is a far cry from Whig attachment to the town meeting, an implication that was probably seen by few men, for the Antifederalists took their defeat with surprising grace, given the bitterness of the fight over ratification. As is often the case in politics, the struggle was probably viewed as a factional one rather than a clash of political cultures. Objections were invariably offered as opposition to a specific constitutional provision or institution, rather than as a critique of assumptions and basic principles.

But cultural clash it was, and the Whigs lost. There is reason to doubt that Federalist ideas could have been resisted in the long run anyway. The localists regained control in 1800 with Jefferson's election; but despite his theoretical and political commitments, he supported and justified the Louisiana Purchase, which only increased the political, social, and economic forces undermining localist support. Individualism also increased its hold on the American mind, whether through the influence of the frontier, the growth of capitalism, or some combination of any other number of possibilities. In short, there is danger in giving too much weight to the Federalist victory in 1787, but thus far in the literature the tendency has run in the direction of giving it too little. Aside from 1776–1787, there have been few major turning points in the history of American political thought. There may have been one in the 1860s, and certainly there was one in the 1930s; but none are of such lasting significance as the first, for it divides our political history into two bicentennials, each lived under a different political theory. Shifts in

39. Cooke (ed.), *The Federalist*, 421.
40. McWilliams, *Idea of Fraternity in America*, 187.
41. *Ibid.*, 193.

thought during the 1860s and 1930s, and possibly the 1960s, are relatively minor adjustments within a framework of two competing political cultures that together constitute the definition of American political thought.

Two Political Theories

It is time to bring together the various theoretical strands that have been examined and developed elsewhere in this essay. Once we understand the two political cultures contending for supremacy, it is possible to appreciate the systematic differences separating Whig and Federalist political theory. At the same time it is possible to grasp the thread of underlying continuity that permitted the Federalists to sell their ideas to many Whigs. If our understanding the discontinuities is important for our appreciating Federalist creativity, then our understanding the continuities is also important if we are to fully appreciate Federalist genius in factional politics. In what follows, the reader is referred to sections of Gordon S. Wood's *The Creation of the American Republic* because most of Whig theory can be abstracted from his discussion. It should be noted, however, that the work of other historians, including Bernard Bailyn, could be used to support this propositional abstraction. And, although Wood has drawn together the various sources into the most complete discussion, the deductive model that follows is itself an abstraction from Wood as well as a reordering of his argument.

Whig political theory, as explicit theory, can be summarized in four sets of assumptions. The first set of assumptions flowed from the belief that the people were a homogeneous entity. Despite gradations and ranks within the population, all people had the same rights and thus were politically indistinguishable.[42] In the American Whig view, politics were an inevitable and perpetual battle between the people, who were trying to protect these rights, and the rulers, who were constantly trying to extend their power. This traditional dichotomy between the people and their government was joined with a belief that when conflicts arose between the desires of an

42. Wood, *Creation of the American Republic*, 18.

individual and those of the community at large, the community should get its way. Thus, the interests of the community were considered superior to those of any individual, especially if the individual held political power. From this general perspective we derive three related assumptions:

A1 The population is homogeneous with respect to rights.

A2 The population has a community of interests in protecting and preserving these rights.

A3 Community interests are superior to individual interests.[43]

The second set of assumptions flowed from the American belief that they were a virtuous people. Virtue was defined in the double sense of possessing superior moral qualities (in the Christian sense) and of possessing to a greater extent those qualities necessary for self-government (the Greek notion of virtue).[44] European commentators merely reinforced American beliefs when they spoke of the "natural man" living on American shores in possession of the "manly virtues" found in the "state of nature." The flight from European decadence had been prominent among the motivations for religious emigration to America during the 1600s. This tendency for Americans to view themselves as a chosen people brought to the promised land to escape the evils and temptations of the luxury in England would surface again in the 1770s as one of the major justifications for breaking with England, as Wood points out. Although seeing "through a glass darkly," these Americans with their pristine, republican virtues had a peculiar ability to govern themselves in a manner congruent with the good. Significantly, it was assumed that the good in a moral sense would always be congruent with the in-

43. These propositions are derived from discussion in Wood, *Creation of the American Republic*, 18–28, 53–65, 70–75.

44. By "Greek" notion of virtue is meant a rather prosaic version of *arete* as transmitted by Renaissance and Enlightenment writers to Americans, who in turn were inclined to use the concept roughly. In brief terms, a person who possessed the abilities to saw a straight line, drive a nail quickly and cleanly, and had a good eye for right angles possessed the "virtues" necessary to be a good carpenter. Likewise, a person who was thrifty, hard working, was financially independent, had an emotional and financial stake in the community, sufficient intelligence to understand the complexities of issues larger than his own family problems, and was reasonably sober in judgment had the essential virtues to be a good citizen and participate in self-government.

terest of the entire community. It was simply a matter of moving slowly enough to insure that the community interest had been properly ascertained. This led to the following logic:

B1 'The American people are a virtuous people in both the Christian and Greek senses (and thus peculiarly capable of self-government).

B2 If given enough time, the people will recognize the good.

B3 Once the good is distinguished from the bad, the American people will choose the good.[45]

The peculiar situation as of 1776 was that a Calvinist could read *virtue* and *good* exclusively in the Christian sense, and a rationalist could read these words exclusively in the sense taught through the pagan classicism of the Enlightenment; yet both would come to precisely the same conclusion:

B4 Government should be based upon, and beholding to, the deliberate sense of the community (derived from propositions A1–3 and B1–3).

That is, combining the assumptions under A, which rested upon a traditional view of political equality, with the assumptions under B, which justified popular sovereignty, leads to the deliberate sense of the community as the basis for politics. How this deliberate sense of the community was to be determined is the object of the next set of assumptions.

American Whigs retained the classical English view of politics insofar as the crown *was* government. The crown embodied the monarchic principle, it was the executive, it acted, and thus it was the essence of government. The legislature, on the other hand, was not part of government. It was indistinguishable from the people in that its members were drawn directly from the general population and then returned to experience the laws that they had approved. In this sense, and this sense only, did they represent the people. They literally re-presented the consent of the people to the proposals for action made by the crown as if the people were themselves all present in the chamber.

The assumptions under A meant that it made little difference

45. These propositions are derived from discussions in Wood, *Creation of the American Republic*, 28–36, 57–59, 93, 97–107, 117–24.

which individuals actually sat in the legislature, as long as they were returned to the people at the end of the session. Members of American legislatures generally came from the more propertied classes for reasons that were simple and obvious to the Whigs of the day. These men had more leisure time for such activities, they were familiar with the financial and legal complexities that a legislator faced, they had demonstrated a stake in the community by owning property in it, and they had demonstrated superior virtue by being able to amass and retain a certain amount of property. This presumably took discipline, sobriety, hard work, and a certain amount of intelligence—all of which were essential civic virtues. There was the additional belief that men of property could not easily be bribed by the executive and thus were more likely to retain their political independence because of their economic independence.[46]

The more radical Whigs differed precisely on this matter of representation. They pushed for something more akin to our current notion by seeking a more accurate mirroring of the community. That is, the wealthy in the legislature should be proportional to the wealthy in the general population, the frontier towns would be represented proportionally, and so on. In any case, the third set of assumptions are as follows:

C1 The crown (executive) is government. It acts.

C2 The legislature protects the people from government. It stands between the people and government and is not distinct from the people.

C3 The legislature embodies popular consent. It represents the community.

C4 The legislature produces the deliberate sense of the community (combining propositions C3 and B4).[47]

The fourth set of assumptions are already familiar either from what has been said earlier, or because they have been handed down to us intact by the Federalists.

D1 While people are equal in rights, they are not equal in abilities.

46. *Ibid.*, 237–38, 244–55.
47. *Ibid.*, 18–19, 24–26, 139, 162–63.

D2 Differential abilities lead to social and economic inequality (there is a "natural" aristocracy based upon virtue).

D3 Both the wealth of the community and the rights of the people need to be protected.

D4 There is no inherent conflict between the interests of wealth in the community and the interests of people in the community.[48]

This last proposition is a restatement of assumption A2 in a new context. It means that wealth should be put to work for the community, and as long as the community benefits, there is no reason to worry about accumulation. Such accumulation permits investment for economic expansion, which in turn provides jobs and a rising standard of living in the community. The logic connecting these assumptions also implied that there should be some legislative means for distinguishing financial matters from nonfinancial matters.

The institutional deduction from C4 is quite straightforward. There would be legislative supremacy. In the colonial context this meant that the crown-appointed governor should not be able to act on any matter without the consent of the popularly elected legislature. After the Revolution began and independent state governments were brought to power, this meant a greatly diminished executive and a dominant legislature. Since the legislature produced the deliberate sense of the people and was not distinguished from the people, it could be trusted in any matter; and state legislatures were soon involving themselves in every aspect of life.[49] This incipient "legislative tyranny" made many Whigs uneasy, but aside from trying to balance the power of the legislature with the power of a strengthened executive, and creating stronger bills of rights, the restraints placed upon state legislatures were surprisingly few in num-

48. *Ibid.*, 57–59, 71–72, 237, 218–19, 410–11.
49. James Madison documents what he calls "legislative tyranny" in his "Vices of the Political System in the United States," and Edward S. Corwin has verified that what Madison described actually occurred. See Edward S. Corwin, "The Progress of Constitutional Theory Between the Declaration of Independence and the Meeting of the Philadelphia Convention," *American Historical Review*, XXX (1924–25), 533. It should be remembered that these legislatures were not doing anything that local government had not done for over a century. What Madison objected to was the attempt to regulate every aspect of life at the state level, where particularistic legislation was much more likely to appear arbitrary.

ber and predictably ineffective as long as assumption C4 was not seriously modified or rejected.

In short, the general response was to continue holding assumption C4 while emphasizing assumption C3. Emphasis upon popular consent had already led to the obvious institutional deductions of frequent (usually annual) elections, a broadly defined suffrage, relatively low property requirements for holding office, and a habit of relying upon petitions and instructions from the people to the legislature. This direct consent relationship between the people and the legislature was simply intensified in its directness. More and more offices were subject to direct election, the suffrage was broadened, petitions and instructions became more frequent and more insistent; but by 1787 the Federalists viewed the Whig experiment in self-government as a failure. Also, whereas the Whigs had logically felt it acceptable for legislatures to write and approve constitutions or amendments to constitutions, there was a growing demand that constitutions and amendments be written by specially elected conventions and ratified by popular referendum. This development reflected a weakening in the Whig belief that the legislature was not part of government. Gordon Wood shows how the legislature slowly came to be viewed as separate from the people and therefore just as dangerous to liberty as the executive.

From assumptions C4 (the legislature produces the sense of the community) and D3 (both the wealth and numbers of the community should be represented) we derive the institution of a bicameral legislature. The upper house would represent the majority of property, and the lower house would represent the majority of the people. This would be produced by requiring a much higher amount of property for those running for the upper house. However, assumption D4 (that there is no conflict between wealth and numbers) would result in most states having the same property requirement defining suffrage for both the upper and lower houses. The result, as both Wood and Jackson Turner Main point out, was the electorate in each state elevating the same kind of people to both houses.[50]

50. See Jackson Turner Main, *The Upper House in Revolutionary America, 1763–1788* (Madison: University of Wisconsin Press, 1967), 188–91; and Wood, *Creation of the American Republic*, 206–14.

Members of the senates behaved in a manner indistinguishable from those in the lower houses, even on financial matters, which in turn weakened the rationale for having two houses. The Federalists would make the United States Senate representative of the states, and the House representative of people, although their essential argument would be that by requiring passage by two houses the resulting legislation would be more deliberate. Since this Federalist argument is logically deducible from the Whig assumption of the deliberate sense of the community being central to the political process (assumption B4), the Whigs could hardly argue with it. As Wood is fond of pointing out, Federalists often coopted Whig assumptions or concepts and placed them in a new context to alter the operation of Whig institutions.

Between 1776 and 1787 Americans lived under their state constitutions based upon Whig political theory. In the absence of a strong executive they experienced the legislatures *acting*, and acting in a manner affecting virtually every aspect of life. They experienced the bitter factionalism in their state legislatures and in the general population. They found growing economic inequality, were exposed to a stronger influx of Enlightenment ideas from continental Europe (especially in the cities and commercial towns), and found religion to be less and less important in their lives. There was also the problem of how to govern diverse populations spread over several states, as well as the problem of bicameral legislatures not acting according to Whig theory. The Whigs were sometimes puzzled, often dismayed, and frequently prone to disagreement over how to proceed, but they continued to evolve solutions based upon an essentially intact Whig political theory.

The Federalists were more radical in their theory making if not in their economics. They rejected the Whig "tinkering" approach and went back to the basic assumptions underlying American politics. Their most breathtaking move was to reject completely the first set of Whig assumptions. Instead of assuming a natural community of interests arising from a homogeneous population, they assumed that factions and political conflict have their roots in human nature and are thus inevitable. Some, like James Madison, went even further and argued that factions should be encouraged rather than eliminated so as to better control their effects through mutual check and balance. Federalists replaced homogeneity with heterogeneity. The Federalist assumptions are outlined in a manner parallel with those of the Whigs to illustrate similarities and differences.

A1 While the population is homogeneous with respect to rights, it is naturally heterogeneous with respect to interests.

A2 Government involves the regulation of these various interests to prevent any one from dominating. All factions are equal.

A3 The community interest will emerge from the interaction of these various factions through a political process that respects the equal rights of all to participate in that process.

A4 The "good" is that which emerges from the political process.[51]

The assumptions under B were retained with two important additions:

B1 The American people are a virtuous people (in the Greek sense).

B2 Some people are more virtuous than others.

B3 If given enough time, the people will recognize the good.

B4 It will take a long time for many to recognize the good.

B5 Once the good is distinguished from the bad, the American people will choose the good.[52]

The net effect is to require that the deliberative process be very deliberate. Still, the deduction from these Federalist assumptions is that:

B6 Government should be based upon, and beholding to, the deliberate sense of the community.

The fundamental Whig deduction that government should be based upon the deliberate sense of the community is retained, though deduced from a different set of assumptions. The Whigs saw collective decisions emerging from the cool, calm deliberations of men seeking the community of interest by looking to some standard of goodness that transcends individual and factional interests. The Federalists, on the other hand, saw collective decisions as emerging from the interaction of factions in a multi-institution arena where more able men respond to factions in a frankly political manner.

51. Wood, *Creation of the American Republic*, 519–62.
52. *Ibid.*, 471–518.

The deliberate sense of the community is not discovered through debate only. Rather it emerges from the political process. Delay is even more important to the Federalist, not only because it takes time to mechanistically produce the fair sense of the community, but also because in the short run many people will be slow to recognize what is a fair balancing of interests.

It is worth pausing here to ask how fundamental is the change wrought by the Federalists. As Kendall and Carey have pointed out, basing government on the deliberate sense of the community has been the fundamental American political symbol since the signing of the Mayflower Compact.[53] The continuity between Whig and Federalist political theory is here quite basic. If anything, the Federalists have simply become more insistent that the process be deliberative. On the other hand, a political culture is defined, not only by a set of institutions and political principles, but also by the widely held assumptions and arguments supporting these institutions and principles. In this respect the Federalists have made a clear break with the past. Theoretically we have moved from an essentially organic theory with roots deep in the Middle Ages and the Reformation to a modern, mechanistic theory securely rooted in the Enlightenment.

This theoretical shift does not result in the rejection of old political institutions and the creation of new ones so much as it redefines the relationships between them. Government now is any institution having political power. Political power still rests in the hands of the people, but as Wood points out, power is now viewed as homogeneous in that it can be parceled out to more than one institution. The legislature is thus by definition as much a part of government as the executive. Both embody popular consent, but both are dangerous to the rights of the people. The deliberate sense of the community is now arrived at by a government separate from the people, and the relationship between the various branches of government should be such as to produce the deliberate sense of the community while protecting the people from the government. The assumption that power can be separated or divided into different parts provides a solution to both problems.

53. Kendall and Carey, *Basic Symbols of the American Political Tradition.*

C1 Power is homogeneous. It can be parceled out.
C2 The legislature is as much a part of government as the executive (and the judiciary).
C3 All branches of government embody popular consent.
C4 The various branches of government together produce the deliberate sense of the community.[54]

The final set of Whig assumptions (under D) are retained, with the exception of the last. There *is* an inherent conflict between wealth and numbers.[55] The institutions deduced from these four sets of Federalist assumptions are too familiar to require extensive comment. However, it is worth considering for a moment what the Federalists have done to the upper house, since it illustrates once again the difficulties faced by Whigs when opposing the proposed United States Constitution.

In one respect the Federalists had solved a Whig problem by finding a role for the upper house—that of representing the states. At the same time they enhanced the deliberative process by requiring that legislation be passed twice. Furthermore, by electing senators through state legislators, the Federalists had refined that body to contain people of prominence and probably of greater wealth. Whigs could view this upper house as coming closer to their goal of representing the wealth of the community.[56] When Whigs spoke of representing or protecting the wealth of the community, they meant the sum of all property and production, and thus they saw wealth as a shared entity that everyone in the community had an interest in protecting and expanding. The Federalists, on the other hand, used the term *wealth* to refer to that minority of individuals who had a special interest as a result of having much more property and income than most citizens. This subtle but important difference was often missed by the Whigs. In the refashioning of the upper house we have the epitome of Federalist appropriation of Whig symbols for their own (Federalist) use, as well as an elegant theoretical wedge to divide and confuse Whig opposition to the Constitution. Not only did many Whigs not understand the new way that Federalists were

54. Wood, *Creation of the American Republic*, 447–48.
55. *Ibid.*, 475–79, and especially 491–92.
56. *Ibid.*, 557–58.

using the term *wealth*, but many Whigs were comfortable with having the Senate indirectly elected and thus were divided from the more radical Whigs who emphasized direct elections.

It is a crucial point that the Federalists were able to retain the Whig assumption of a virtuous people while making the connection between government and these virtuous people less direct. In effect, the federal Constitution became the instrument for creating "a republic which did not require a virtuous people for its sustenance." Gordon S. Wood sees the Federalists as evolving "an elitist theory of democracy" out of a more truly democratic Whig theory of politics.[57] On one hand, the Federalists were prevented from going too far down this path by the universal and prevailing American beliefs in republicanism, the sovereignty of a virtuous people, and the centrality of government based on the deliberate sense of the community. On the other hand, Whig political theory was flexible enough to permit the Federalists to use the same basic symbols and ideological inclinations as those men they were trying to overcome politically. This goes a long way toward explaining the seeming impotence of Antifederalist arguments against the Constitution.

57. *Ibid.*, 517.

Conclusion

What We Have Lost

The Federalists won the struggle for ratification of the federal Constitution, and with it they won center stage in history. The Whigs were increasingly consigned to the distant wings, trotted out only occasionally to play the role of short-sighted, obstructionist opposition to the Federalists. In our failure to treat the Whigs seriously, we have not only lost the earlier tradition of American political theory that dominated our shores for over a century and a half, we have also lost the roots of Federalist thinking, and thus, ironically, the full measure of Federalist brilliance, originality, and subtlety.

Textbooks in American political theory continue to treat colonial political thought in an indifferent manner, and relegate Whig political theory to a short page or two, if it is even mentioned. The failure of political scientists to respond to the outpouring by historians on this subject in recent years results primarily from a misconception about American political history that is so old and so widespread that it is almost a core assumption in the discipline. A student of American political theory stated the matter baldly. "For theoretical as well as practical purposes the origin of the American track can, therefore, be assumed to begin in 1776. The thinkers, issues, and events prior to 1776 have never really had a central impact on the conduct of American politics."[1]

However, agitation for direct election of the United States Senate during the nineteenth century was based heavily on the fact that al-

---

1. Gordon Lloyd, "Textbooks in American Political Theory," *Political Science Reviewer*, V (Fall, 1975), 314.

most all states directly elected their upper houses. This situation at the state level was a direct result of Whig political theory developed before 1776. Much of the so-called democratic impulse in American politics had its origin in Whig thought, even though this impulse was later associated with movements having other names.

Do we look to the federal Constitution to understand why there has been an antagonistic relationship between the American executive and Congress, or do we seek explanation for this relationship being written into the Constitution in the traditional colonial antagonism between elected legislatures and crown-appointed governors? Why didn't the Federalists design a British-style parliamentary government at the national level? Is it not possible to seek the roots of our continued distrust of distant, big government in the American preference for independent local government that goes back to the 1620s? It is not reasonable to trace our continued moralistic and "chosen people" stance in foreign policy back to the colonial belief that Americans were a "natural" people with uncorrupted, pristine virtues? While it is true that the issues and events between 1776 and 1789 have profoundly affected how we conduct politics in America today, those issues and events were generated and structured by what came before. Furthermore, those issues and events between 1776 and 1789 to a significant degree revolved around the writing, adoption, and operation of state constitutions. The "American track" did not begin in 1776 but a century and a half earlier.

The picture that emerges from reading colonial documents, the early state constitutions, pamphlets, newspapers, and what historians have to say about all of these is one of America dominated in 1776 by a Whig political theory derived from English Whig theory rooted in the seventeenth-century commonwealth experience. Between 1776 and 1787 Whig political theory was found to have serious problems in generating effective institutions at the state and national levels, and by 1787 it was superseded, at least at the national level, by Federalist theory. In some respects Federalist theory is derived directly from Whig theory. In other respects it departs from Whig theory in response to problems experienced living under Whig institutions. Thus, even Federalist innovation is linked to the earlier mode of thought.

The work of Bernard Bailyn and Gordon S. Wood provides an efficient means for sketching this new picture with greater accuracy. Bailyn found that American political theory was a combination of several theoretical strains. "Most conspicuous in the writings of the Revolutionary period was the heritage of classical antiquity." The pamphlet authors, however, had a very restricted knowledge of the ancients insofar as they drew from a restricted set of works by the ancients. "What gripped their minds, what they knew in detail, and what formed their view of the whole of the ancient world was the political history of Rome." Plutarch, Livy, Cicero, Sallust, and Tacitus dominated their footnotes on the ancients. "More directly influential in shaping the thought of the Revolutionary generation were the ideas and attitudes associated with the writings of Enlightenment rationalism."[2] Bailyn found an astonishing number of citations to leading secular thinkers of the Enlightenment such as Voltaire, Rousseau, Montesquieu, Locke, Pufendorf, Vattel, Beccaria, Grotius, Hume, Bolingbroke, Delolme. Although the range of authors cited was impressive, pamphleteers often had only a superficial knowledge of most, and failed to distinguish between important figures like Locke and secondary figures like Burlamaqui. Also prominent were major figures in English common law such as Coke and Blackstone. There were frequent references to trial reports, but Bailyn notes that the "offhand familiarity" that pamphleteers used in drawing from this third intellectual tradition did not reflect great knowledge. Citations were often imprecise and inappropriate, and although the common law was influential in shaping the minds of revolutionary leaders, it did not determine their conclusions. A fourth tradition affecting the ideas of the revolutionary pamphleteers derived from the political and social ideas of New England Puritanism, especially the ideas associated with covenant theology. While this was in a sense the most limited and parochial tradition, contemporary texts in American political theory often emphasize Puritan thought as the most important antecedent to American revolutionary thought. Or, as Gordon Lloyd points out, there is at best the tendency to list all these intellectual traditions in historical se-

2. Bernard Bailyn, *The Ideological Origins of the American Revolution* (Cambridge, Mass.: Belknap Press, 1967), 23, 25, 26.

quence without explaining how these various, disparate sources fit into the history of American political theory in any coherent fashion.[3]

Bailyn's essential contribution is to show that there is a coherent pattern brought to all these intellectual strands by a fifth aspect of the American colonial heritage, and that this last tradition is far more important than has been recognized before.

> But important as all of these clusters of ideas were, they did not in themselves form a coherent intellectual pattern, and they did not exhaust the elements that went into the making of the Revolutionary mind. There were among them, in fact, striking incongruities and contradictions. . . . What brought these disparate strands of thought together, what dominated the colonists' miscellaneous learning and shaped it into a coherent whole, was the influence of still another group of writers, a group whose thought overlapped with that of those already mentioned but which was yet distinct in its essential characteristics and unique in its determinative power. The ultimate origins of this distinctive ideological strain lay in the radical social and political thought of the English Civil War and of the Commonwealth period; but its permanent form had been acquired at the turn of the seventeenth century and in the early eighteenth century, in the writings of a group of prolific opposition theorists, 'country' politicians and publicists.[4]

Prominent names were John Trenchard, Thomas Gordon, Algernon Sidney, Henry Neville, Bishop Benjamin Hoadly, John Milton, Robert Viscount Molesworth, Viscount Bolingbroke, and a host of lesser names. These men, whose writings are today long forgotten, were often regarded as equal to or better than John Locke in their respective abilities at political analysis. As Bailyn says, "More than any other single group of writers they shaped the mind of the American Revolutionary generation."[5] These men called themselves Whigs, and many American pamphleteers also termed themselves Whigs after their English and Scottish exemplars. For a variety of reasons American political thinkers appropriated Whig ideas and used them

3. Lloyd, "Textbooks in American Political Theory," 314.
4. Bailyn, *Ideological Origins*, 33–34.
5. *Ibid.*, 35.

selectively to draw upon the other traditions listed above. It is the prominence of Whig theory that brought coherence to these five strands, and if any name should be attached to the first American political theory, Whig is as good a name as any.

The matter of names is not unimportant. Because there was diversity among them, and because they lost the struggle to define the form of national government we adopted, defenders of this earlier tradition have come to be known as Antifederalists. This name connotes mere opposition and little sense of their having a positive, coherent theory of their own. Perhaps because they are portrayed only negatively as Antifederalists, American Whig political theorists have been ignored and their intellectual roots forgotten. At the same time, we have forgotten the meaning and consequences of the first two hundred years of our American experience.

Gordon Wood takes up where Bailyn leaves off. Bailyn demonstrates that Whig thought dominated American political theory in 1776, but Wood shows the interaction of Whig theory and Federalist theory (which drew most heavily upon Enlightenment thinkers) in the context of events between 1776 and 1787. Bailyn has reoriented the historian's view of the Revolution by forcing another look at English Whig thought, but his perspective remains that of an historian looking at English intellectual history. Wood, on the other hand, keeps his eyes firmly set on our own shores.

It is Wood's conviction that it was the Americans' "habit of thinking" that created their Revolution. Social and economic factors may have conditioned these habits of thought, but ultimately an analysis of the era must come to terms with the "distinctiveness of the political culture in which the Revolutionary generation operated." The differentness of the eighteenth-century world cannot be ignored. It was a world in which familiar words like *liberty*, *democracy*, *virtue*, and *republicanism* had meanings quite different from those we attach to them today. A careful look at eighteenth-century American politics leads us to conclude that Americans at that time took their political theory very seriously, that there was a coherence in American political theory before 1776, that the political culture defined by this theory shifted significantly between 1776 and 1787, and that events during the period can be made comprehensible and be partly explained by the struggle between adherents of the old political culture and those who sought to replace it with a new one.

American Transformations of English Thought

In a review written by Richard D. Brown, Bernard Bailyn is taken to task for being his own revisionist.[6] Bailyn argued in the introductory essay to his earlier book *Pamphlets of the American Revolution* that "The Revolution was in the minds of the people, and this was effected, from 1760–1775. . . . This radical change in the principles, sentiments, and affections of the people was the real American Revolution." However, when Bailyn expanded that essay into the book *The Ideological Origins of the American Revolution*, he concluded the following: "I discovered that the configuration of ideas and attitudes I had described in the General Introduction as the Revolutionary ideology could be found intact—completely formed—as far back as the 1730's."[7] The problem here is that if the distinguishing ideology of the revolutionary period was "completely formed" in the 1730s, how can Bailyn speak of a revolutionary "transformation" of ideology in the 1760s and 1770s? Brown suggests that Bailyn's evidence leads to an obvious conclusion that Bailyn himself never draws. "The revolutionary change was not the fusion of partially recognized ideas into an ideology: that was already complete. Rather, it was the extension of this ideology to greater numbers of people, who stretched it to its logical conclusions in applying it to immediate political questions."[8] In another review, Lawrence H. Leder makes a similar point. "On almost every occasion when some local crisis arose, the colonists sought for and found theoretical justifications for their own positions in the older English political and legal theorists. . . . Much of what Americans wrote in the heat of the 1760s and 1770s had been written earlier by their fathers and grandfathers. The earlier expositions may have been less sophisticated and even contradictory to

---

6. Richard D. Brown, book review, in *New England Quarterly*, XL (December, 1967), 577.

7. Bailyn, *Ideological Origins*, xi.

8. Brown, review in *New England Quarterly*, 579.

their over-all effect, but that was because the problems to which they related were local rather than imperial."[9] In the 1760s political interest shifted to a new level, that of imperial and colonial relations. This forced many people to appropriate more Whig theory than they had in the past, and to apply it to the solution of new problems. In the process of stretching English Whig theory to apply to their immediate political questions, Americans did an interesting thing. They transformed Whig political theory to fit American experience.

Concepts like representation, consent, constitution, rights, and sovereignty were not transformed in meaning from what Americans had previously meant by them. Rather, they were either appropriated for the first time or applied to imperial politics for the first time; in so doing, Americans transformed English Whig thought to produce concepts that were different with respect to England, but congruent with the dominant American ideology.

For example, in the earlier years of colonial history, Americans had in fact re-created a kind of representation that had flourished in medieval England, though not for any theoretical reasons.[10] Originally, elective representation to Parliament had meant bringing local-minded men together as attorneys for their respective electors. A representative's business began and ended with the interests of the constituency. Local communities tried to bind their representatives to local interests through every means. A representative was required to have local residency or own land locally so as to have a stake in the community. His wages were closely controlled, he was provided minute instructions as to his powers and the limit of concessions he could make, and he was held strictly accountable for all actions taken in the name of his constituents. As a result, a representative did not speak for an estate, a class, or a specific interest. Instead he spoke for that entire local community and its collective interests.

This form and practice of representation had been considerably altered through changing circumstances by the time Americans rose to challenge imperial policy. Parliament had become representative

9. Lawrence H. Leder, book review, in *New England Quarterly*, XXXIX (June, 1966), 39.

10. Bailyn, *Ideological Origins*, 162–65.

of a nation, and members stood for the interest of the realm more than for particular local communities. Members of Parliament did not even necessarily live in the districts they represented. As Edmund Burke had it, Parliament was a deliberative assembly of one nation with one interest, that of the whole rather than the many local prejudices. But colonial America had reproduced English institutions in miniature and were led by circumstances in another direction. Specifically, they placed the locus of community in the town and in the county instead of in the nation. Americans were most devoted to their local governments, and like their medieval counterparts they kept these towns and counties largely autonomous. Americans were thus inclined to keep the voices of local interests clear and distinct, and to consider colonial legislatures as creatures of local government, designed to protect local communities from interference by the crown's representative, the governor. "The Massachusetts town meetings began the practice of voting instructions to their deputies to the General Court in the first years of settlement, and they continued to do so whenever it seemed useful throughout the subsequent century and a half. Elsewhere, with variations, it was the same; and elsewhere, as in Massachusetts, it became customary to require representatives to be residents of, as well as property owners in, the localities that elected them, and to check upon their actions as delegates."[11] What of the Whig assumption of a community of interests? Building upon the work by Bailyn and others, we can see that the potential contradiction between this assumption and the colonial penchant for locally controlling legislators was masked by a number of circumstances. First of all, Americans assumed that the community of interests lay in the *local* community. This is where that assumption most directly applied. Second, colonial legislatures spent most of their time fighting to check, if not dominate, the crown-appointed governors. This meant that all local communities automatically shared one major interest, and this was to keep the governor out of local affairs as much as possible. Colonial legislatures were thus put in the position of making relatively few laws for the entire colony, thereby having few

11. *Ibid.*, 164–65.

opportunities for fighting among themselves, and of spending most of their time defending the one interest all local communities held in common.

After independence, state legislatures became much more active as they became the focus of government. The contradiction between local interests and state interests was immediately apparent. The towns and counties responded by tightening the control over their representatives. The result was a plethora of particularistic legislation respecting not only individual towns but also individual persons. The more radical American Whigs kept pressing for tighter and tighter control over state legislatures and applied the assumption of homogeneous community primarily to local communities. The more moderate Whigs saw the problem inherent in this and pressed for a broader perspective, with the state being recognized as a potential community. Neither radical nor moderate Whig, however, could develop a plan for a strong national government. Each preferred a weak national government, much like the Articles of Confederation, with strong constituency control.[12] The Federalists saw clearly that a contradiction was present not only in Whig theory as Americans practiced it, but also in the theory as applied to any large, diverse group of people. They rejected the assumption of a homogeneity of interests at any level of political organization.

Note that there is first a transformation of English Whig thought to a peculiarly American form. Then there is a post-1776 transformation in theory, wrought by the Federalists and based upon the experience of American Whig theory operating in a new, nonimperial context. Where, then, is the origin of American Whig thought to be found? The answer seems to be that colonists had, over the two hundred years preceding the federal Constitution, developed a set of political institutions that were Whig-like in their operation. These institutions had developed for other than theoretical reasons. Starting in about 1730 the colonists began explicitly appropriating English Whig political theory to justify what they wished to do locally in governing themselves. They chose Whig theory because it was most congruent in its implications with the kind of institutions

12. Gordon S. Wood, *The Creation of the American Republic, 1776–1787* (Chapel Hill: University of North Carolina Press, 1969), 486.

already developed and preferred by the colonists. In the process of appropriating this theory, the colonists bent it to shape meanings and concepts suited to their own needs and experiences. Beginning in the 1760s there was a quickened appropriation of this theory as a host of new political problems arose fairly suddenly. Again Whig thought was most congruent with the kind of political solutions preferred by the colonists. Again the theory was bent to suit their experiences. In summary, the origin of American Whig theory, and thus the origin of American revolutionary ideology and the state constitutions it spawned, is to be sought in the institutions unfolded and evolved by Americans during the seventeenth and early eighteenth centuries. We should look to England only for the terms and concepts used to bring theoretical coherence to this experience of living together on American shores.

Political theorists and historians have usually overlooked the importance of the early colonial experience and emphasized European theoretical origins simply because any exercise in political theory leans naturally toward a history of ideas approach. The history of ideas approach in turn leans upon treatises and tracts identified with coherent and prominent ideational traditions. In the context of American political theory, this means pamphlets, letters, sermons, and newspaper articles with reasonably sustained political discourse. One problem with this approach is that one has difficulty determining when an idea has become prominent or determinate as opposed to merely stated. More important, one is led to ignore the more formal political documents written by Americans, and these documents often tell more about the history of political thought than the most logical and well-written pamphlets. A key example of this is found in the early state constitutions, which embody the final form of ideas and institutions evolved over a great number of years, and "freeze" for us the dominant institutions, ideas, and political factions of a particular instant in a particular place. It is in attempting to understand the evolution of these formal documents that we come face-to-face most starkly with American political thought, and it is in trying to understand these documents that we are led most directly to American political theory.

George Dargo, one of those who demonstrates the usefulness of this approach, shows how the Massachusetts Body of Liberties (1641) expanded upon and developed ideas first found in the Magna Carta. The Body of Liberties was a response to the fear of unbridled power being placed in the hands of the Bay Colony magistracy. Responding to their own political needs, the colonists wrote a document derived from English political history, but containing refinements, improvements, and innovations that made it singularly American and extremely advanced theoretically. This development led to the Laws and Liberties of 1648, which George Haskins calls "the first modern code of the Western world."[13] George Dargo concludes that "the Massachusetts code of 1648 sounded the note that was to be struck repeatedly in the seventeenth century, one that would resonate many years later in the Antifederalist claim that a constitution without basic liberties was not a constitution at all."[14] Although Dargo claims that this aspect of American political thought was complete by the end of the seventeenth century, we have shown that the constitutional development of bills of rights continued on through the state documents of the 1770s and 1780s.[15] Among other things, bills of rights shifted their use of *ought* to *shall*, came more explicitly to limit legislative will, and expanded to define longer and longer lists of rights. In the context of Whig theory and Whig opposition to the federal Constitution, we can at last understand the theoretical reasons for inclusion of the Bill of Rights in the federal Constitution, and why that inclusion is fundamentally at odds with Federalist theory.

The formal documents available, besides helping us to uncover in detail the core American political tradition as it developed between 1587 and 1787, also lead us inevitably to look more carefully at the origin of American political thinking, which is located in the founding and operation of local government. If there is anything more ignored than formal documents, it is the history of local government in America before 1800. A search for work on local gov-

13. George Lee Haskins, *Law and Authority in Early Massachusetts: A Study in Tradition and Design* (New York: Macmillan, 1960), 120.
14. George Dargo, *Roots of the Republic: A New Perspective on Early American Constitutionalism* (New York: Praeger, 1974), 61.
15. *Ibid.*, 65.

ernment reveals very few books, and most of those were written more than half a century ago and are still being reproduced as primary works. Yet it is in local government that we find in full operation institutions and theories that were later to be dignified with the name *Whig*. For example, legislative supremacy was operative at the local level in the form of the town meeting and the small interim body between town meetings, the selectmen. The colonists patiently, persistently, and cunningly pressed the same idea in their development of colonial legislative power in opposition to the governors.

Homogeneity of interests was not only assumed, it was enforced. It was assumed insofar as any freeholder could hold office, though it was not considered pernicious that most elected officials were wealthy. The interests of the average voter were not considered markedly different from those of the more wealthy. Since there were no factions, there was no basis for appealing to one part of the electorate over another. This made public political campaigning unneeded and undesirable. A candidate ran on his good name from his front porch. Homogeneity was enforced in most communities through careful control of who could live there. Even travelers who stayed in the community overnight had to vouch for their financial independence and good behavior so as not to put a strain on the community or create disorder. Political faction was looked upon as the greatest danger to these communities, and extraordinary means were taken to prevent it.

Community interests were considered superior to those of individuals. The community could expropriate land and property to pay debts or for community purposes. Virtually all those rights to which we now attach such great importance could be abridged by the local or colonial legislature for the good of the community; all colonists were subject to inquiry and possible penalty.

The complete set of Whig assumptions could be found operative in colonial America well before 1730, although there was no coherent, widely held theory justifying them. When English Whig theory became available, it was quickly and easily appropriated and then transformed to justify what was already common practice. One of the most crucial transformations, and one that has been overlooked, is that undergone by the concept of consent. Here, as with the notion of representation, the process begins with government at the local level, but in the case of consent the implications are more central to the theoretical changes wrought by the Federalists.

The Transformation of Consent

In modern discussions of consent, the concept is invariably linked with the discussion of political obligation. Two points need to be made immediately. First of all, this linkage, this use of consent, has resulted from the rise of contract theory. Putting the question in the form "What obliges people to obey any government?" implies that there is a condition of no government, which can be used for comparison. Only since Hobbes and Locke developed the notion of a state of nature has it made sense to ask the question in this way. The second point is that modern analyses of consent, having this contractarian bias, fail to press the investigation to explore what the term meant before the rise of contract theory. This omission is unfortunate because it fails to come to terms with the uses and meaning originally associated with the term, and thus it fails to demonstrate that the concept is a much richer one than the linkage with political obligation implies. Part of the Federalist legacy to us is the transformation of consent to a modern format in American political thought.

During the Middle Ages, one could find three related words to describe agreements between two or more people: contract, compact, and covenant. These words were somewhat interchangeable, but each implied a different form of agreement. A contract usually implied an agreement of mutual responsibilities on a specific matter. It carried with it a restricted commitment, such as in a business matter or a marriage contract, and involved small groups of people. The contract would be enforceable by law but did not itself have the status of a law.

A compact, on the other hand, was a mutual agreement or understanding that was more in the nature of a standing rule, which, if it did not always have the status of a law, often had a similar effect. A compact implied an agreement that affected the entire community in some way, or relations between communities. The word had the root meaning of knitting together or bringing the component particles closely and firmly into a whole. Because a compact was not as specific as a contract, and was more like a settled rule than an agreement with specific responsibilities, we do not find talk of a marriage compact or a Mayflower contract.

A covenant could be viewed as having two distinct though related meanings. As a legal term in England, it referred to a formal agreement with legal validity, made under the seal of the crown. This denoted an agreement of a serious, legal nature witnessed by the highest authority. Covenant also referred to any agreement established or secured by the Divine Being. The formal agreement made and subscribed to by the members of a congregational church in order to constitute themselves a distinct religious society had God as the witness and securer of the agreement.[16] The covenant between God and his chosen people in the Old Testament was, of course, the paradigm for this usage. Note that both the secular and religious meanings are characterized by being witnessed and therefore secured by the highest relevant authority.

A covenant could be made by an entire community or by a portion of the community. This means that a compact between the members of a community could be witnessed by God and therefore become a religious covenant, witnessed by the crown and thereby become a secular covenant, or made without any higher witness and thus be a simple compact. Presumably any compact with both God and the crown as securers would be simultaneously a civil and a religious covenant. This is precisely the format used in the Mayflower Compact, most of the colonial charters and organic documents, and many of the early state constitutions. When we look at American

16. Americans are familiar with covenants made to establish a congregation, but in England and Scotland they were usually applied to larger associations. For example, bonds of agreement signed by the Scottish Presbyterians for the defense and furtherance of their religion and ecclesiastical polity were usually termed "covenants." The National Covenant was signed at Edinburgh on February 28, 1638 for the defense of Presbyterianism against the episcopal system introduced by James I and Charles I, and the Solemn League and Covenant was accepted by the General Assembly of the Church of Scotland on August 17, 1643 and the English Parliament on September 25, 1643. Such usage dates back to at least a century before. The covenant subscribed to by the Lords of the Congregation and their followers at Edinburgh on December 3, 1557, and at Perth on May 31, 1559, was for carrying out the Protestant Reformation.

documents, from the first foundation document of 1620 to the state constitutions of the 1780s, they were invariably either a mixed religious-civil covenant form of compact, a civil covenant form of compact, or a simple compact. In this context the role of consent is somewhat different from what we usually assume.

Take, for example, the most common form of compact written before 1776, the mixed religious-civil covenant. Calling upon God to witness and bless a civil union was to ask Him to sanction the union as being in accord with the broader covenant found in the Bible. Giving one's consent to join a community with this kind of covenant, for example, was in part a religious act of commitment, and elections to choose "the elect" were also acts of consent with religious overtones. Note that in this context there was no question of consent itself providing the basis for obligation. Rather, consent was the instrument for establishing authority in the community and expressing the sovereignty of God. If God transmitted his sovereignty to the people by making each of them in His image and likeness, they in turn were the conveyers of this sovereignty to the rulers, who had authority because it had been sanctioned by God. The people's consent is the instrument for linking God with the rulers, but because this authority comes through the people, the rulers are beholding to God through them. Thus, political obligation in this setting was activated through consent, but obligation rested upon an oath, implied or explicit, to follow God's will.

A number of early state constitutions required oaths of those voting and those elected to office. Most of them, however, required oaths only of those elected to office, since voters had usually taken an oath to uphold the laws upon being admitted to the community. Today we still require new citizens to take an oath instead of signing a contract. In this regard, as in many others, Whig political theory developed in a straightforward fashion from the Mayflower Compact to the early state constitutions. The signers of the Mayflower Compact knew that they were signing a religious compact, more properly a mixed religious-civil covenant, not a contract. They did "covenant and combine" themselves into a "civil body politic" in "the presence of God" and "in the name of God," which not only carried with it the force of an oath, but also activated the obligations to be rendered by Christians. More than a century and half later, their political descendants all over the country would write state constitutions that called upon God for witness and sanction, required oaths of those holding office to activate their Christian obligations, and required that men elected to office be members of Protestant religions that adhered to covenant theology, thus insuring their proper response to the oaths. Elections gave consent for certain individuals to represent the interests of the community, and such consent also established the locus of civil authority. If citizens had rights, no one had the right to place their individual interests above that of the community. To do so would be false pride, and therefore rights were alienable by the community or its representatives. Representatives were to be men of virtue, because this would enhance the community's hewing to the terms of the compact, and if representatives came from the wealthier portion of the community, was this not a reflection that they were more likely to be among the elect? However, since no particular subset of individuals had greater access to the inner Divine Light through which men discovered God's will, all men of known virtue with a stake in the community could participate in politics, just as everyone could read the Bible on their own. Catholics, with their priests and pope, were suspected of not having independent wills. Dissidents within a community, if they did not leave, were cast out, because challenging authority and disagreeing over religious doctrine both implied a rejection of the covenant.

All this, of course, was most prominently held in New England. However, the same form is found in local- and colony-level documents throughout the colonies. Although God's name continued to be evoked right into the 1780s, there was an unmistakable trend toward secularization; but at most this meant a shift to a purely civil or simple form of compact. These formal documents were still viewed as knitting together the community into a whole governed by the majority. A completely secular compact cut the people loose from the Divine Being and created the question of how obligation was now activated toward government. It was a question that no one seemed to ask, perhaps because the continued use of oaths could be used as a convenient fiction for achieving the desired end.

And, of course, until 1776 there was still the crown to secure any covenant.

For Americans, then, the idea of republican government had roots partly in religious doctrine that evolved during the late Middle Ages. Republican government rested upon popular consent, partly because under the radical Protestant version of covenant theology all had equal access to God's will. If covenants resulted of necessity from the calm deliberation of an entire community, why should not strictly civil compacts as well? It is one of these wonderful accidents of history that consent by a deliberative majority of Christians, which rested upon popular sovereignty derived from equal participation in the Divine Light, should imply political institutions that were also implied by a mercantilist people who believed that stockholders should control the affairs of the corporation through elections and majority rule. If the religious minority suggested the pattern for political institutions in colonial America, the nonreligious majority had little reason to suspect the essential fairness and efficacy of these institutions. Increasing secularization would not undermine the inclination toward republican government based upon popular consent and popular control. On the contrary, the appropriation of English Whig ideas, and their transformation into American forms, would provide an umbrella theory that would easily satisfy religious and secular Whigs alike. English Whigs could trace their ideas to similar religious roots in the seventeenth century, but the situation in America and the experiences held in common by those who lived in the colonies permitted full expression of ideas that in England were hemmed in by a developed society with a long history.

Even the highly secularized Federalist theory could build upon these foundations. Of course, a new basis for political obligation was now needed, since government was no longer based upon a covenant sanctioned by God or the crown, but upon a contract among men. This contract had specified limitations and mutual responsibilities, and Sections 8, 9, and 10 of Article I of the federal Constitution read more like a contract of particulars than anything found in the state constitutions. With these explicit limitations and grants of power in the Constitution, it is no wonder that tne Federalists saw no need for a bill of rights. Government was already explicitly limited by the political contract. A new doctrine was also needed for explaining how we were to operate in a political system in which the rights of the community were no longer considered superior to the rights of individuals. The American newspapers in the late 1780s were full of letters to the editor from Federalists who increasingly resorted to a Lockean formula of deriving civil rights from the natural rights of individuals who have freely given their consent. The implications of these theoretical developments were largely missed by the Whigs.

The Whigs missed these shifts in the concept of consent because there was an apparent continuity between the United States Constitution and what came before. There was, first of all, institutional continuity. The bicameral legislature was prominent in this regard, as was a separate executive checked by the legislature in each of its essential functions. There was also continuity between Whig and Federalist symbols. The idea of rule by a deliberate majority was apparent in the system of checks and balances as well as in the bicameral legislature. The design of the federal system, with limited national powers, clearly implied retention of local control. Having the states determine who could and could not vote preserved the role of elections, and insured that local majorities could enforce community values and police community virtue. The institutional changes made by the Federalists did make consent at the national level less direct, less active, and less continuous. However, this resulted from the states serving as intermediaries for consent giving in many cases, and thus constituted an argument in favor of continued state power and thus local control. Direct election of the lower house was in line with the Whig preference for popular control of the legislature, while indirect election of the Senate and president could be justified by the Federalists as filtering upward more virtuous men, an argument understood by the Whigs. In regard to this last point, the Whigs had themselves been unsuccessful in their state constitutions when it came to differentiating between the two legislative houses. The Federalist solution not only had the virtue of promising to restore the distinction between the two houses, it also placed Senate elections in the state legislatures, which had to be re-assuring to both state- and local-oriented Whigs. In short, the institutions and basic symbols of the federal Constitution were quite continuous with what the Whigs had developed, and most of what was new appeared to preserve state power at the expense of the national government.

There was, however, considerable discontinuity with respect to the theoretical explanations underlying these symbols and institutions. These theoretical shifts were important, not for the variations they immediately produced in Whig institutions, but for the direction in which these institutions would develop in the future. A contract is always viewed more legalistically than a compact, and the precise wording of the federal Constitution contained possibilities not perceived by the less legalistically inclined Whigs. The localist-minded Whigs, having less interest in serving at the national level, left the way open for national-minded men to do much of the institutional development. Finally, because it was essentially their document, the Federalists captured the field when it came to explaining what the various provisions of the Constitution meant. The newspaper essays by Madison, Hamilton, and Jay, later collected as *The Federalist*, were only a small part of the outpouring of Federalist essays, pamphlets, and speeches that disseminated and popularized Federalist thought.

Popular sovereignty, political equality, and majority rule would rest upon new theoretical explanations derived, not from covenant theology and transformed English Whig ideas, but from the secular, rationalistic ideas of the Enlightenment. Oaths would be secularized, the bicameral legislature would serve a new purpose, and courts would have a new status. But above all, the doctrine of consent that underlay the Whig theory of republican government would be replaced. This makes our understanding of Whig political theory doubly important. First, through understanding Whig theory we come to understand the origin and development of the political institutions and symbols eventually adopted by the Federalists. Second, Whig political theory provides a template against which to measure Federalist ingenuity. What this comparison tells us is that the Federalists significantly shifted American political theory from what it had been prior to 1787.

Popular Consent and Popular Control
in the Federalist Constitution

The task remains of evaluating one final aspect of the Federalist victory, for it lies at the core of a continuing debate that has generated considerable heat in recent years. It is the debate as to whether the American Constitution is an instrument for popular control or elite control. The problem is more complex and subtle than this simple question indicates. Part of the frustration lies in the enormous change our political system has undergone since 1787. The question really should be a two-fold one. Does the American Constitution today support elite rule? The answer to this question is beyond the scope of this book. The second question—whether the Constitution was *designed* to support elite rule—though not necessarily related to the first one, can be answered on the basis of our investigation.

Did the Federalists, in their design of the national Constitution, attempt to remove government from popular control? The evidence indicates that the answer to this question is no. The federal Constitution limited the power of the national government and thereby kept as much power as possible at the state and local level, where there clearly was popular control. Delegates to the Constitutional Convention often spoke in terms of keeping government close to the people. When reading Madison's notes on the convention, we are looking back over a history that includes a bitter struggle over states' rights, and we are often induced to read that struggle into the convention proceedings. It is more likely that the delegates were speaking the plain truth. Most government in the 1780s took place at the state and local level, where many delegates wished it to remain. To the extent that this demand was met, government remained in the hands of the people, regardless of what institutions were adopted at the national level.

Even at the national level, the powers that were expressly delegated were centered in the legislature, a fact which is often overlooked. Discussion at the convention, as well as political discourse in other forums, clearly indicated that three specific powers were considered most important for the national government—the taxing power, the power to disburse money, and the power to declare war. All three were given to the legislature, the lower house of which was popularly elected and embodied popular control in the most direct sense. Furthermore, the lower house was elected every two years so as to keep it close to the people. There was no attempt to restrict suffrage in any way. On the contrary, the first paragraph of Section 2, Article I of the Constitution specifies that, when it comes to electing members to the House, "electors in each state shall have the qualifications requisite for electors of the most numerous branch of the state legislature." As shown earlier, these qualifications were for the most part minimal. This provision is also significant because delegates to the Continental Congress had consistently been elected by the state legislatures. There was, therefore, no constitutional precedent for having national representatives elected directly by the people. If the Federalists had followed the constitutional practice of the day—the practice outlined in the state constitutions written by the Whigs—they would have had the House of Representatives elected by the state legislatures instead of directly by the people. In this context, having the United States Senate elected by the state legislatures was not unusual, whereas having the House elected directly *was*. This departure from earlier constitutional practice was thus a move toward greater directness in consent. In *The Federalist*, James Madison repeated a view commonly held at the convention, namely, that the new national government must be "erected on the great body of the people." Having the lower house of the most powerful branch of the national government elected directly by an electorate that was defined by the very liberal state suffrage requirements did not indicate a desire on the part of the Federalists to remove government from popular control.

A better question, one that goes to the heart of the matter, is: Did the Federalists attempt to make popular control less direct than had come to be the case at the state level? The answer to this question is probably yes. The trends embodied in the state constitutions written between 1776 and 1787 reflected a shift in the definition of republican government from one in which the people collectively *share* in sovereignty (see John Adams' definition, page 16, herein) to one in which the *whole* sovereignty is essentially vested in the people (Samuel Adams' definition, page 17, herein). Furthermore, there was a serious attempt at the state level to make all four types of consent so direct as to approach Jefferson's definition: "a government by its citizens in mass, acting directly, according to rules established by the majority." Madison's definition of republican government, on the other hand, explicitly permits indirect as well as direct consent. To repeat Madison's words (page 00, herein), republican government is "a government which derives all its powers directly or indirectly from the great body of the people, and is administered by persons holding their office for a limited period, or during good behavior. . . . It is essential to such government that it be derived from the great body of the society, not from an inconsiderable portion, or a favored class of it." Madison's definition is disarmingly honest in describing the types of institutions designed by the Federalists.

Article VII of the federal Constitution required that the document be ratified by conventions elected for that purpose in at least nine states. However, some states had earlier developed the practice of submitting proposed constitutions directly to the people in a referendum. Specifications for amending the national document are even less direct. One method requires two-thirds of the state legislatures to apply for a national convention which, in turn, submits proposed amendments to either state conventions or state legislatures for approval, requiring three-fourths of either set of bodies. The other method is for two-thirds of both houses of Congress to propose an amendment, subject to three-fourths of either set of bodies. Again, societal and governmental consent cannot be given directly by the people in a referendum, as had been practiced in some states.

The United States Constitution, itself indirectly approved and amended, uses the word *consent* eight times in the body and once in the Bill of Rights, and uses *concur* twice in the body. Interestingly, this is almost the exact average for such usage in the second wave of state constitutions. However, in the federal document, the context is always one of Congress, or one of its two houses, giving consent on some matter acted upon by another branch of government. Only in the Bill of Rights are the people mentioned as giving consent, and that is in the case of an individual's giving consent for quartering troops in his home. Although the word is present in the federal Constitution, the usage reflects the Federalist concern for institutional checks between the various branches of government rather than the Whig concern for the relationship between government and the people.

With respect to agency consent, the Federalist document is distinctive in that the upper house and executive are elected in a manner that permits only indirect participation by the people. Even though this is consistent with the practice under the Articles of Confederation, it is contrary to the direct election practiced by the states. The broad suffrage defined by the state documents is retained for the House of Representatives but is made irrelevant for the other institutions at the national level. Both the House and the Senate have longer terms of office than was usually the case at the state level. The net effect, regardless of intent, is to place programmatic consent on a different footing from that found in the states. Indeed, there is no mention in the United States Constitution of that frequently repeated right of the people to instruct their representatives.

The problem here is in distinguishing the *consequences* of Federalist institutions from Federalist *intentions*. Whether the Federalists intended to enshrine a form of republican government at the national level that embodied less-direct consent than that found at the state level can never be answered with certainty. There is no doubt that the Federalists had to solve crucial political problems not encountered at the state level. The need to create a government that would act directly on individual citizens and at the same time protect the political reality of existing states created a novel situation not faced before. The need for an effective national government was also paramount, given some of the experiences under the Articles of Confederation. At the same time, senators and the president could have been popularly elected, as they are today, without interfering with either of these goals.

There is evidence that Federalists and non-Federalists alike were very concerned with the danger of unbridled majorities acting directly on legislatures. The Federalists were especially sensitive to instability in legislative policies and the legislative encroachment on the other branches. Furthermore, there were many examples of civil unrest to which Madison and others often referred. North Carolina and Massachusetts had both experienced serious insurrections. The Wyoming Valley in Pennsylvania had threatened to secede from the rest of the state. Sometimes civil unrest was less spectacular, but closer to home. John Jay, one of the three authors of *The Federalist*, was himself felled during a riot in lower Manhattan, which forced him to withdraw from further writing for medical reasons. That Jay had developed a reputation for successfully quelling the very kind of riot in which he was injured indicates the frequency of such outbursts.[17]

Madison and Hamilton considered the control of factional violence as their main theoretical goal in *The Federalist* (see, for example, the opening sentence of *The Federalist* 10). Majority tyranny was the specific form of faction that most interested them. It is tempting to draw the conclusion that these preoccupations reflected an intent on their part to remove decision making from the majority. On the other hand, why worry about majority tyranny unless planning majority rule? Federalist concern over the possibility of majority tyranny may not be so much a sinister sign as an indication of their commitment to making majority rule work.

Regardless of intent, it is probably accurate to characterize their institutions in the following manner. The Federalists did not remove government from popular control, but based it ultimately on the consent of the majority. The involvement of the majority in decision making was made less direct than it was at the state level, not to prevent majority rule, but to slow it down. The president and Supreme Court were so weak in the early years, that there was doubt they could survive in the face of the very powerful Congress. At

---

17. The reader should not conclude that all or even most of the unrest had specifically political causes. The riot that forced Jay to withdraw from writing more of *The Federalist* resulted from the discovery that a body had been stolen from a grave in a lower Manhattan cemetery. An outraged mob attempted to storm King's College under the assumption that medical students had stolen the body for use as a cadaver. While the causes for this pedestrian riot were not political, it does say something about the state of forces for securing civil order as well as the potential for political unrest.

best, they could delay congressional will, causing the decision-making process to be more deliberate. The mixing of direct with indirect consent can be viewed as a series of stumbling blocks in the path of the majority, forcing it to be more careful and less capricious, and thereby minimizing most of the problems experienced with the state legislatures operating under conditions of direct consent. Government, theoretically, would still be by majority rule; but the combination of an extended, diverse republic impeding the formation of majorities, and the institutions of delay placed in the path of Congress helping to screen out majorities based upon emotion or short-term interests, would presumably produce a more stable and effective government.

Critics of the American political system have often contended that it moves too slowly, is responsive to interest groups rather than to the majority, and is often not responsive at all. It is possible that the Federalist framers, if they were around today, would agree with such an assessment. After all, they did not foresee that the president and the Supreme Court would become so powerful. They had no concept of mass-based political parties or the myriad of highly organized committee systems. As can be expected, the institutions they designed have evolved, expanded, and been altered in ways the framers could not predict, whatever their intent. But our job here is not to assess the United States Constitution in terms of what it has become. Rather, it is to understand the extent to which it represents a deflection of constitutional trends during the 1770s and 1780s.

The Federalists chose a different version of republican government than that developed between 1620 and 1776 in America. Their version may or may not be explained and justified by the conditions and problems they faced. What is clear is that the Federalists broke in important ways with the definition of republican government that was embodied in the early state constitutions. The key to understanding this theoretical discontinuity lies in the shift in the conception of consent. The political forces that led to the design of the early state constitutions eventually induced changes in the federal Constitution toward more direct agency consent with respect to the president and Senate; but part of the Federalist legacy is a doctrine of consent that lacks coherence. Americans are still fighting today over how direct majority consent should be, and the United States Constitution contains conflicting directions for us. It is not unfair to say that American contributions to consent theory, through the design of consent-giving institutions, reached a peak in the 1780s, but these developments were deflected by the design of the United States Constitution and consequently never brought to completion.

Establishing the importance of Whig thought in the history of American political theory means that instead of focusing upon the American Revolution in our theory textbooks, we should concentrate upon the American Evolution—the evolution that began in 1620, not in 1776. Future research may increase or diminish the role assigned to Whig theory in the history of ideas associated with the American experience, but Whig political theory, and the early state constitutions that most completely represent that theory, should never be ignored again.

Selected Bibliography

This list is selective in that it does not contain all the sources consulted in the writing of the book, and it is far from including all the relevant work on American political thought during the colonial and revolutionary eras. At the same time, the list contains enough citations so that a serious student could use it as a guide for moving quickly and deeply into the mass of information available. For easier use, the bibliography has been divided into a number of subsections. Several key topics, such as local government and the history of suffrage in America, have been separated, and the most important or useful works identified. The remaining material has been divided into two categories, those works that the author feels any serious student of American political thought should read, and those that are of related interest.

Primary Material

Adams, Charles Francis, ed. *The Works of John Adams*. Boston: n.p., 1850–56.

Bailyn, Bernard, ed. *Pamphlets of the American Revolution*. Cambridge, Mass.: Belknap Press, 1965.

Bartlett, John Russell, ed. *Records of the Colony of Rhode Island and Providence Plantations in New England*. Providence, R.I.: A. Crawford Greene and Brother, 1856.

Bates, S. A., ed. *Town Records of Braintree, 1640–1793*. Randolph, Mass.: n.p., 1886.

Browne, William Hand, ed. *Proceedings and Acts of the General Assembly of Maryland, Jan., 1637/8–Sept., 1664*, in *Archives of Maryland*. Vol. II. Baltimore: Maryland Historical Society, 1883.

Carroll, Bartholomew, ed. *Historical Collections of South Carolina*. New York: Harper, 1836.

Chafee, Zechariah, Jr., ed. *Documents on Fundamental Human Rights*. New York: Atheneum, 1963.

Cooke, J. E., ed. *The Federalist*. Cleveland: Meridian Books, 1961.

Court Records of Essex County, Massachusetts, 1636–1641, in *Historical Collection of the Essex Institute*. Vols. VII–VIII. Salem, Mass.: Essex Institute Press, 1865–69.

Dorchester Town Records in City of Boston. Fourth Report of the Record Commissioners. Vol. IV. Boston: Rockwell and Churchill, 1880.

Early Records of the Town of Portsmouth. Providence, R.I.: E. L. Freeman and Sons, 1901.

Elliott, Jonathon, ed. *The Debates in the Several States Conventions on the Adoption of the Federal Constitution*. Philadelphia: J. B. Lippincott, 1901.

Farrand, Max, ed. *The Records of the Federal Convention of 1787*. Rev. ed. New Haven, Conn.: Yale University Press, 1937.

Force, Peter, ed. *American Archives: Fifth Series, A Documentary History of the United States of America*. Washington, D.C.: n.p., 1848.

Ford, Paul Leicester, ed. *Pamphlets on the Constitution of the United States*. New York: Da Capo Press, 1968.

Foster, Theodore, ed. *The Minutes of the Rhode Island Convention of 1790*. Providence: Rhode Island Historical Society, 1929.

Gerlach, Larry R. *The American Revolution: New York as a Case Study*. Belmont, Calif.: Wadsworth, 1972.

Greene, Jack P., ed. *Settlements to Society: 1607–1763*. New York: W. W. Norton, 1975.

Hammond, Isaac W., ed. *Documents Relating to Towns in New Hampshire*. Concord, N.H.: Parsons B. Cogswell, 1882.

Handlin, Oscar and Mary Handlin, eds. *The Popular Sources of Political Authority*. Cambridge, Mass.: Harvard University Press, 1966.

Hoadly, C. J., ed. *New Haven Colonial Records*. Hartford, Conn.: n.p., 1857–58.

Hunt, Gaillard, ed. *The Writings of James Madison*. New York: G. P. Putnam's Sons, 1901.

Hyneman, Charles S., and George Carey. *The Second Federalist*. New York: Appleton-Century-Crofts, 1967.

Jacobson, David L., ed. *The English Libertarian Heritage*. Indianapolis: Bobbs-Merrill, 1965.

Jefferson, Thomas, *Writings of Thomas Jefferson*. Washington, D.C.: n.p., 1907.

Jensen, Merrill, ed. *English Historical Documents: American Colonial Documents to 1776*. Vol. IX. New York: Oxford University Press, 1955.

Kavenagh, W. Keith, ed. *Foundations of Colonial America: A Documentary History*. New York: Chelsea House, 1973.

Lewis, John D., ed. *Anti-Federalists Versus Federalists: Selected Documents*. San Francisco: Chandler, 1967.

Larabee, Leonard W., comp. *Royal Instructions to British Colonial Governors, 1670–1775*. New York: n.p., 1935.

McCloskey, Robert Greene, ed. *The Works of James Wilson*. Cambridge, Mass.: Belknap Press, 1967.

Pulsifer, David, ed. *Laws, 1623–1682*, in *Records of the Colony of New Plymouth*. Vol. II. Boston: William White, 1861.

Reed, George Edward, ed. *Papers of the Governors, 1759–1785*, in *Pennsylvania Archives*. Vol. III. Harrisburg: State of Pennsylvania, 1900.

Second Report of the Record Commissioners of the City of Boston, Vol. II. Boston: Rockwell and Churchill, 1881.

Shurtleff, N. B., ed. *Massachusetts Colonial Records*. Boston: n.p., 1853–54.

Thorpe, Francis N., ed. *The Federal and State Constitutions, Colonial Charters, and Other Organic Laws of the United States*. Washington, D.C.: Government Printing Office, 1907.

Thornton, John Wingate, ed. *The Pulpit of the American Revolution*. Boston: Gould and Lincoln, 1860.

Town Records of Boston, 1634–1777, in 2nd, 7th, 8th, 12th, 14th, 16th, and 18th *Reports of Boston Record Commission*. Boston: Rockwell and Churchill, 1880–88.

Town Records of Newark, New Jersey, 1666–1836, in *Collections of the New Jersey Historical Society*. Vol. VI. Newark: *Daily Advertiser*, n.d.

Trumbull, J. Hammond, ed. *The Public Records of the Colony of Connecticut*. Hartford, Conn.: Brown and Parsons, 1850.

Upham, W. P., ed. *Town Records of Salem: 1634–1659*, in *Historical Collections of the Essex Institute*. Vol. IX. Salem: Essex Institute Press, 1868.

Whitehead, W. A., F. W. Ricord, and W. Nelson, eds. *New Jersey Archives, 1631–1776*. Newark: Daily Journal Establishment, 1880–86.

Early State Constitutions

BOOKS

Dodd, Walter Fairleigh. *The Revision and Amendment of State Constitutions*. Baltimore: Johns Hopkins Press, 1901.

Erdman, Charles R. *The New Jersey Constitution of 1776*. Princeton, N.J.: Princeton University Press, 1929.

Fisher, Sydney George. *The Evolution of the Constitution of the United States*. Philadelphia: J. B. Lippincott, 1897.

Green, Fletcher M. *Constitutional Development in the South Atlantic States, 1776–1860*. Chapel Hill: University of North Carolina Press, 1930.

Nevins, Allan. *The American States During and After the Revolution, 1775–1789*. New York: Macmillan, 1924.

Peters, Ronald M., Jr. *The Massachusetts Constitution of 1780: A Social Compact*. Amherst: University of Massachusetts Press, 1978.

Selsam, J. Paul. *The Pennsylvania Constitution of 1776: A Study in Revolutionary Democracy*. New York: Octagon Books, 1971.

ARTICLES

Corwin, E. S. "The Progress of Constitutional Theory Between the Declaration of Independence and the Meeting of the Philadelphia Convention." *American Historical Review*, XXX (1924–25), 511–36.

Dodd, W. F. "The First State Constitutional Conventions, 1776–1783." *American Political Science Review*, II (1908), 545–61.

Morey, William C. "The First State Constitutions." *Annals of the American Academy of Political and Social Science*, IV (1893), 201–32.

Webster, William C. "Comparative Study of the State Constitutions of the American Revolution." *Annals of the American Academy of Political and Social Science*, IX (1897), 380–420.

Wright, Benjamin F., Jr. "The Early History of Written Constitutions in America." Chap. XII, in *Essays in History and Political Theory in Honor of Charles Howard McIlwain*. Cambridge, Mass.: Harvard University Press, 1936.

Local Government

BOOKS

Akagi, R. H. *The Town Propiretors of the New England Colonies*. Philadelphia: n.p., 1924.

Cook, Edward. *Fathers of the Towns: Leadership and Community Structure in Eighteenth Century New England*. Baltimore: Johns Hopkins University Press, 1976.

Griffith, Ernest S. *History of American City Government: The Colonial Period*. New York: Oxford University Press, 1938.

Howard, George E. *An Introduction to the Local Constitutional History of the United States*. Baltimore: Johns Hopkins University Press, 1889.

Maclear, Anne Bush. *Early New England Towns*. New York: AMS Press, 1967.

Porter, A. O. *County Government in Virginia: A Legislative History, 1607–1904*. New York: Columbia University Press, 1947.

Sly, John Fairfield. *Town Government in Massachusetts (1620–1930)*. Cambridge, Mass.: Harvard University Press, 1930.

Webb, Beatrice, and Sydney Webb. *English Local Government from the Revolution to the Municipal Corporations Act*. London: Longman, Greens, 1906.

ARTICLES

Andrews, C. M. "The Genesis of the Massachusetts Town, and the Development of Town-Meeting Government." *Massachusetts Historical Society Proceedings*, 2nd Series, VII (1818), 174–211.

————. "The River Towns of Connecticut: A Study of Wethersfield, Hartford, and Windsor." *Johns Hopkins University Studies in Historical and Political Science*, VII (Nos. 7–9).

Channing, Edward. "Town and County Government in the English Colonies of North America." *Johns Hopkins University Studies in Historical and Political Science*, 2nd Series, X (1884).

Colgrove, Kenneth. "New England Town Mandates." *Publications of the Colonial Society of Massachusetts*, XXI (1919), 411–49.

Ferguson, Isabel. "County Courts in Virginia, 1700–1830." *North Carolina Historical Review*, VIII (1931), 14–40.

Guess, William C. "County Government in North Carolina." *James Spruant Historical Studies*, XI (1911), 5–39.

McCain, Paul M. "The County Court in North Carolina Before 1750." *Trinity College Historical Papers*, XXXXI (1954), 37–51.

Worcester, Alfred. "The Origin of the New England Town Meeting." *Waltham Historical Society Publication*, No. 2 (1925).

Elections and the Suffrage Before 1800

BOOKS

Bishop, Courtland F. *History of Elections in the American Colonies*. New York: Burt Franklin, 1968.

Bonomi, Patricia U. *A Factious People: Politics and Society in Colonial New York*. New York: Columbia University Press, 1971.

Brown, Robert E. *Middle Class Democracy and the Revolution in Massachusetts, 1691–1780*. Ithaca, N.Y.: Cornell University Press, 1955.

Brown, R. E., and B. K. Brown. *Virginia, 1705–1786: Democracy or Aristocracy?* East Lansing: Michigan State University Press, 1964.

Chute, Marchette. *The First Liberty: A History of the Right to Vote in America, 1619–1850.* New York: E. P. Dutton, 1971.

McCormick, Richard P. *The History of Voting in New Jersey: A Study of the Development of Election Machinery, 1664–1911.* New Brunswick, N.J.: Rutgers University Press, 1953.

Sydnor, Charles S. *American Revolutionaries in the Making: Political Practices in Washington's Virginia.* New York: 1965.

Williamson, Chilton. *American Suffrage from Property to Democracy: 1760–1860.* Princeton, N.J.: Princeton University Press, 1968.

ARTICLES

Brown, Robert E. "Democracy in Colonial Massachusetts." *New England Quarterly,* XXV (1952), 291–313.

Buel, Richard, Jr. "Democracy and the Revolution: A Frame of Reference." *William and Mary Quarterly,* 3rd Series, XXI (1964), 165–90.

Cohen, Norman S. "The Philadelphia Election Riot of 1742." *Pennsylvania Magazine of History and Biography,* XCII (1968), 306–19.

Klein, Milton M. "Democracy and Politics in Colonial New York." *New York History,* XL (1959) 221–46.

Langdon, George D., Jr. "The Franchise and Political Democracy in Plymouth." *William and Mary Quarterly,* 3rd Series, XX (1963), 513–26.

Leonard, Sister Joan de Lourdes, C.S.J. "Elections in Colonial Pennsylvania." *William and Mary Quarterly,* 3rd Series, XI (1954), 385–401.

Lokken, Roy N. "The Concept of Democracy in Colonial Political Thought." *William and Mary Quarterly,* 3rd Series, XVI (1959), 568–80.

Murrin, John. "The Myths of Colonial Democracy and Royal Decline in 18th Century America: A Review Essay." *Cithara,* V (1965), 53–69.

Pole, J. R. "Historians and the Problem of Early American Democracy." *American Historical Review,* LXVII (1962), 626–46.

———. "Suffrage Reform and the American Revolution in New Jersey." *New Jersey Historical Society Proceedings,* LXXIV (1956), 173–94.

———. "Suffrage and Representation in Massachusetts: A Statistical Note." *William and Mary Quarterly,* 3rd Series, XIV (1957), 560–92.

Varga, Nicholas. "Election Procedures and Practices in Colonial New York." *New York History,* XLI (1960), 249–77.

Zuckerman, Michael. "The Social Context of Democracy in Massachusetts." *William and Mary Quarterly,* 3rd. Series, XXV (1968), 523–44.

Best General Works

Bailyn, Bernard. *The Ideological Origins of the American Revolution.* Cambridge, Mass.: Belknap Press, 1967.

———. *The Origins of American Politics.* New York: Alfred A. Knopf, 1969.

Chute, Marchette. *The First Liberty: A History of the Right to Vote in America, 1619–1850.* New York: E. P. Dutton, 1971.

Colbourn, H. Trevor. *The Lamp of Experience.* Chapel Hill: University of North Carolina Press, 1965.

Conkin, Paul K. *Self-Evident Truths.* Bloomington: Indiana University Press, 1974.

Dargo, George. *Roots of the Republic: A New Perspective on Early American Constitutionalism.* New York: Praeger, 1974.

Douglass, Elisha P. *Rebels and Democrats.* Chicago: Quadrangle Books, 1955.

Ferguson, E. James. *The Power of the Purse.* Chapel Hill: University of North Carolina Press, 1961.

Greene, Jack P. *The English Colonies in the Eighteenth Century: 1689–1763.* New York: Oxford University Press, 1969.

———. *Quest for Power.* Chapel Hill: University of North Carolina Press, 1963.

Hall, Van Beck. *Politics Without Parties: Massachusetts, 1780–1791.* Pittsburgh, Pa.: University of Pittsburgh Press, 1972.

Howard, George E. *An Introduction to the Local Constitutional History of the United States.* Baltimore: Publication Agency of the Johns Hopkins University, 1889.

Kammen, Michael. *Deputyes and Libertyes: The Origins of Representative Government in Colonial America.* New York: Knopf, 1969.

Kendall, Willmoore, and George W. Carey. *The Basic Symbols of the American Political Tradition.* Baton Rouge: Louisiana State University Press, 1970.

Kammen, Michael. *People of Paradox.* New York: Vintage Books, 1973.

Kellogg, Louise Phelps. *The American Colonial Charter.* New York: Da Capo Press, 1971.

Kenyon, Cecilia. *The Anti-Federalists.* New York: Bobbs-Merrill, 1966.

Konvitz, M. R., and C. Rossiter, eds. *Aspects of Liberty.* Ithaca, N.Y.: Cornell University Press, 1958.

Kurtz, Stephen G., ed. *The Federalists: Creators and Critics of the Union, 1780–1801.* New York: John Wiley and Sons, 1972.

Levy, Leonard W. *Freedom of Speech and Press in Early American History.* New York: Harper and Row, 1963.

Libby, Orin Grant. *The Geographical Distribution of the Vote of the*

Thirteen States on the Federal Constitution, 1787–8. Madison: University of Wisconsin Press, 1894.

Lovejoy, David S. *Rhode Island Politics and the American Revolution.* Providence, R.I.: Freeman, 1958.

Mason, Alpheus. T., and Gerald Garvey, eds. *American Constitutional History: Essays by Edward S. Corwin.* New York: Harper and Row, 1964.

McDonald, Forrest. *We the People: The Economic Origins of the Constitution.* Chicago: University of Chicago Press, 1958.

McLaughlin, Andrew C. *Foundations of American Constitutionalism.* New York: New York University Press, 1932.

McWilliams, Wilson Carey. *Ideas of Fraternity in America.* Berkeley: University of California Press, 1973.

Merritt, Richard L. *Symbols of American Community, 1735–1775.* New Haven, Conn.: Yale University Press, 1966.

Morgan, Edmund S. *Puritan Political Ideas.* Indianapolis: Bobbs-Merrill, 1965.

Oberholtzer, Ellis Paxson. *The Referendum in America.* New York: Charles Scribners Sons, 1912.

Olson, Alison Gilbert. *Anglo-American Politics, 1660–1775.* New York: Oxford University Press, 1973.

Pitkin, Hanna Fenichel. *The Concept of Representation.* Berkeley: University of California Press, 1972.

Pole, J. R. *The Seventeenth Century Sources of Legislative Power.* Charlottesville: University Press of Virginia, 1967.

Roche, John P., ed. *Origins of American Political Thought.* New York: Harper and Row, 1967.

Ward, Harry M. *Statism in Plymouth Colony.* Port Washington, N.Y.: Kennikat Press, 1973.

Williams, E. Neville. *The 18th Century Constitution, 1688–1815.* Cambridge, England: Cambridge University Press, 1971.

Zemsky, Robert. *Merchants, Farmers and River Gods: An Essay on Eighteenth Century American Politics.* Boston: Gambit Press, 1971.

ARTICLES

Adams, W. Paul. "Republicanism in Political Rhetoric Before 1776." *Political Science Quarterly,* LXXXV (September, 1970), 397–421.

Dutcher, George M. "The Rise of Republican Government in the United States." *Political Science Quarterly,* LV (1940), 199–216.

Katz, Stanley N. "The Politics of Law in Colonial America: Controversies over Chancery Courts and Equity Law in the 18th Century." *Perspectives in American History,* V (1971), 257–84.

Kenyon, Cecilia M. "Men of Little Faith: The Anti-Federalists on the Nature of Representative Government." *William and Mary Quarterly*, 3rd Series, XII (1955), 3–43.

Kirby, John B. "Early American Politics—The Search for Ideology: An Historiographical Analysis and Critique of the Concept of Deference." *Journal of Politics*, XXXII (November, 1970), 808–38.

Meader, Lewis H. "The Council of Censors." *Pennsylvania Magazine of History and Biography*, XXII (1898), 265–300.

Morgan, Edmund S. "The Political Establishment of the United States, 1784." *William and Mary Quarterly*, 3rd Series, XXIII (1966), 286–308.

Murrin, John C. "The Myth of Colonial Democracy and Royal Decline in 18th Century America: A Review Essay." *Cithara*, V (1965), 53–69.

Pargellis, S. M. "The Procedures of the Virginia House of Burgesses." *William and Mary Quarterly*, 2nd Series, VII (1927), 73–86.

Shoemaker, Robert W. "'Democracy' and 'Republic' as Understood in Late Eighteenth-Century America." *American Speech*, XIV (May, 1960), 83–95.

Surrency, Erwin C. "The Courts in the American Colonies." *American Journal of Legal History*, XI (1967), 253–76, 347–76.

Leder, Lawrence H. *Liberty and Authority: Early American Political Ideology, 1689–1763.* Chicago: Quadrangle Books, 1968.

Main, Jackson Turner. *The Antifederalists: Critics of the Constitution, 1781–1788.* Chapel Hill: University of North Carolina Press, 1961.

———. *Political Parties Before the Constitution.* Chapel Hill: University of North Carolina Press, 1973.

———. *The Social Structure of Revolutionary America.* Princeton, N.J.: Princeton University Press, 1965.

———. *The Upper House in Revolutionary America, 1763–1788.* Madison: University of Wisconsin Press, 1967.

Nevins, Allan. *The American States During and After the Revolution, 1775–1789.* New York: Augustus M. Kelley, 1969.

Ostrom, Vincent. *The Political Theory of a Compound Republic.* Blacksburg: Center for the Study of Public Choice, Virginia Polytechnic Institute and State University, 1971.

Palmer, R. R. *The Age of Democratic Revolution: A Political History of Europe and America, 1760–1800.* Princeton, N.J.: Princeton University Press, 1959.

Pole, J. R. *Political Representation in England and the Origins of the American Republic.* Berkeley: University of California Press, 1971.

Robbins, Caroline. *The Eighteenth Century Commonwealthman.* Cambridge, Mass.: Harvard University Press, 1959.

Stourzh, Gerald. *Alexander Hamilton and the Idea of Republican Government*. Palo Alto, Calif.: Stanford University Press, 1970.

Vile, M. J. C. *Constitutionalism and the Separation of Powers*. Oxford, England: Clarendon Press, 1967.

Williamson, Chilton. *American Suffrage from Property to Democracy, 1760–1860*. Princeton, N.J.: Princeton University Press, 1968.

Wood, Gordon S. *The Creation of the American Republic, 1776–1787*. Chapel Hill: University of North Carolina Press, 1969.

Useful Works on Various Topics

BOOKS

Andrews, Charles M. *The Colonial Period of American History*. New Haven, Conn.: Yale University Press, 1936.

Beard, Charles A. *An Economic Interpretation of the Constitution of the United States*. New York: Macmillan, 1913.

Benson, Lee. *Turner and Beard: American Historical Writing Reconsidered*. Chicago: Free Press, 1960.

Billington, R. A., ed. *The Reinterpretation of Early American History*. San Marino, Calif.: Huntington Library, 1966.

Brown, Robert E. *Charles Beard and the Constitution: A Critical Analysis of "An Economic Interpretation of the Constitution."* Princeton, N.J.: Princeton University Press, 1956.

Clarke, Mary P. *Parliamentary Privilege in the American Colonies*. New Haven, Conn.: Yale University Press, 1943.

Dauer, Manning J. *The Adams Federalists*. Baltimore: Johns Hopkins University Press, 1968.

Davis, William T. *History of the Judiciary of Massachusetts*. New York: Da Capo Press, 1974.

Dietze, Gottfried. *The Federalist*. Baltimore: Johns Hopkins University Press, 1960.

Eidelberg, Paul. *The Philosophy of the American Constitution*. New York: Free Press, 1968.

Ellis, Richard. *The Jeffersonian Crisis: Courts and Politics in the Young Republic*. New York: Oxford University Press, 1971.

Frakes, George E. *Laboratory for Liberty: The South Carolina Legislative Committee System, 1719–1776*. Lexington: University of Kentucky Press, 1970.

Griffith, Lucille. *The Virginia House of Burgesses, 1750–1774*. Northport, Ala.: Colonial Press, 1963.

Guttridge, G. H. *English Whiggism and the American Revolution*. Berkeley: University of California Press, 1966.

Harding, Samuel B. *The Contest Over the Ratification of the Federal Constitution in the State of Massachusetts.* New York: n.p., 1896.

Haskins, George Lee. *Law and Authority in Early Massachusetts: A Study in Tradition and Design.* New York: Macmillan, 1960.

Hoerder, Dirk. *Crowd Action in Revolutionary Massachusetts, 1765–1780.* New York: Academic Press, 1977.

Hofstadter, Richard. *America at 1750.* New York: Alfred A. Knopf, 1971.

Kammen, Michael. *People of Paradox.* New York: Vintage Books, 1973.

Kellogg, Louise Phelps. *The American Colonial Charter.* New York: Da Capo Press, 1971.

Kenyon, Cecilia. *The Anti-Federalists.* New York: Bobbs-Merrill, 1966.

Konvitz, M. R., and C. Rossiter, eds. *Aspects of Liberty.* Ithaca, N. Y.: Cornell University Press, 1958.

Kurtz, Stephen G., ed. *The Federalists: Creators and Critics of the Union, 1780–1801.* New York: John Wiley and Sons, 1972.

Levy, Leonard W. *Freedom of Speech and Press in Early American History.* New York: Harper and Row, 1963.

Libby, Orin Grant. *The Geographical Distribution of the Vote of the Thirteen States on the Federal Constitution, 1787–8.* Madison: University of Wisconsin Press, 1894.

Lovejoy, David S. *Rhode Island Politics and the American Revolution.* Providence, R.I.: Freeman, 1958.

Mason, Alpheus. T., and Gerald Garvey, eds. *American Constitutional History: Essays by Edward S. Corwin.* New York: Harper and Row, 1964.

McDonald, Forrest. *We the People: The Economic Origins of the Constitution.* Chicago: University of Chicago Press, 1958.

McLaughlin, Andrew C. *Foundations of American Constitutionalism.* New York: New York University Press, 1932.

McWilliams, Wilson Carey. *Ideas of Fraternity in America.* Berkeley: University of California Press, 1973.

Merritt, Richard L. *Symbols of American Community, 1735–1775.* New Haven, Conn.: Yale University Press, 1966.

Morgan, Edmund S. *Puritan Political Ideas.* Indianapolis: Bobbs-Merrill, 1965.

Oberholtzer, Ellis Paxson. *The Referendum in America.* New York: Charles Scribner's Sons, 1912.

Olson, Alison Gilbert. *Anglo-American Politics, 1660–1775.* New York: Oxford University Press, 1973.

Pitkin, Hanna Fenichel. *The Concept of Representation.* Berkeley: University of California Press, 1972.

Pole, J. R. *The Seventeenth Century Sources of Legislative Power.* Charlottesville: University Press of Virginia, 1967.

Roche, John P., ed. *Origins of American Political Thought.* New York: Harper and Row, 1967.

Ward, Harry M. *Statism in Plymouth Colony.* Port Washington, N.Y.: Kennikat Press, 1973.

Williams, E. Neville. *The 18th Century Constitution, 1688–1815.* Cambridge, England: Cambridge University Press, 1971.

Zemsky, Robert. *Merchants, Farmers and River Gods: An Essay on Eighteenth Century American Politics.* Boston: Gambit Press, 1971.

ARTICLES

Adams, W. Paul. "Republicanism in Political Rhetoric Before 1776." *Political Science Quarterly,* LXXXV (September, 1970), 397–421.

Dutcher, George M. "The Rise of Republican Government in the United States." *Political Science Quarterly,* LV (1940), 199–216.

Katz, Stanley N. "The Politics of Law in Colonial America: Controversies over Chancery Courts and Equity Law in the 18th Century." *Perspectives in American History,* V (1971), 257–84.

Kenyon, Cecilia M. "Men of Little Faith: The Anti-Federalists on the Nature of Representative Government." *William and Mary Quarterly,* 3rd Series, XII (1955), 3–43.

Kirby, John B. "Early American Politics—The Search for Ideology: An Historiographical Analysis and Critique of the Concept of Deference." *Journal of Politics,* XXXII (November, 1970), 808–38.

Meader, Lewis H. "The Council of Censors." *Pennsylvania Magazine of History and Biography,* XXII (1898), 265–300.

Morgan, Edmund S. "The Political Establishment of the United States, 1784." *William and Mary Quarterly,* 3rd Series, XXIII (1966), 286–308.

Murrin, John C. "The Myth of Colonial Democracy and Royal Decline in 18th Century America: A Review Essay." *Cithara,* V (1965), 53–69.

Pargellis, S. M. "The Procedures of the Virginia House of Burgesses." *William and Mary Quarterly,* 2nd Series, VII (1927), 73–86.

Shoemaker, Robert W. "'Democracy' and 'Republic' as Understood in Late Eighteenth-Century America." *American Speech,* XIV (May, 1960), 83–95.

Surrency, Erwin C. "The Courts in the American Colonies." *American Journal of Legal History,* XI (1967), 253–76, 347–76.

Index